The Planets Within

The Planets Within

The Astrological Psychology
of Marsilio Ficino

Thomas Moore

Lindisfarne Press

STUDIES
IN IMAGINATION

A series edited in collaboration with
The Institute for the Study of Imagination

———————————

The Planets Within, Thomas Moore
Facing the World with Soul, Robert Sardello
Archetypal Imagination, Noel Cobb
Book of the Heart, Andrés Rodríguez

Lindisfarne Press edition 1990
© 1982 Associated University Presses, Inc.
Introduction © 1989 Noel Cobb

This edition of *The Planets Within* is a revised edition of the one first published
by Bucknell University Press in the series "Studies in Jungian Thought."

Published with the permission of Associated University Presses, Inc., by
Lindisfarne Press
RR 4, Box 94–A1
Hudson, N.Y. 12534

ISBN 0-940262-28-2

10 9 8 7 6 5 4

Printed in the United States of America

Know that you are another world in miniature and have in you Sol and Luna and even the stars.
—Origen, *Homiliae in Leviticum*, 5, 2

The dance along the artery
The circulation of the lymph
Are figured in the drift of stars.
—T. S. Eliot, "Burnt Norton"

We have an entire sky within us, our fiery strength and heavenly origin: Luna which symbolizes the continuous motion of soul and body, Mars speed and Saturn slowness, the Sun God, Jupiter law, Mercury reason, and Venus humanity.
—Marsilio Ficino, letter to Lorenzo
the Magnificent

For Pat — Luna and Venus in conjunction

Contents

Foreword

HARPING ON AN OLD TUNE?
Thomas Moore and the Imagination of Marsilio Ficino

Exactly five hundred years ago this year, in 1489, one of the great minds of the Renaissance, Marsilio Ficino, sat down to compose his astonishing treatise of archetypal imagination in everyday life: *De Vita Coelitus Comparanda*, "How Life Should Be Arranged According to the Heavens." The brilliant comet of Ficino's genius showered sparks of inspiration all through the fertile skies of late *quattrocento* psyche, leaving countless seed-fantasies to sprout into rare Neo-Platonic blooms in succeeding generations, but disappearing out of common view as the flames of the inquisition rose up to snarl at any sign of pagan enthusiasm. Now, half a millennium later, it mysteriously returns, swinging on a long-forgotten arc into collective awareness once again. Thomas Moore has performed a great service to Ficino's thought and to contemporary schools of soul-making by writing this loving and appreciative introduction to the master's "natural magic" which is "really a school of imagination" (Moore).

This is an important book! And, of the many reasons that it is important, I would like to name four. *First*, it shows a way whereby the world may be ensouled, whereby soul is given body and is also nourished by spirit. As James Hillman[1] has pointed out, there is no doubt that Ficino was the formulator of the central idea of the *quattrocento* rebirth: that soul is "all things together . . . the center of the universe, the middle term of all things." Further, this book, like Ficino's, celebrates and unfolds the rich complexities of soul, a sorely needed corrective in our time, not only to the "shrinking" aims of analysis, but to the vague spirituality of New Age psychologies.

Second, by following Ficino's own elegant modulations through the modes, Moore opens a door into Ficino's world, the imaginal world of the Florentine Renaissance. The author enables us to join hands with Ficino and thereby to accompany him on his journeys in pursuit of images of the phenomenal world to their archetypal origins, a method he called *Orphica comparatio*, archetypally identifying the mythic personage behind Plotinus' idea of *epistrophe*. With this, we are at the heart of that great pageant of imagination which we call the "Renaissance." And, what is more, the re-emergence of the pagan gods in the *quattrocento* takes on an entirely new, and urgent, relevance. Not only is a vision given us of our cultural roots in ancient Greece, but a vision is given of our origins in the archetypal world, *mundus archetypalis*.

At a time when the ruling structure of consciousness seems utterly ignorant of the archetypal forces informing the literal realities of our lives, this book is a God-send. Perhaps now what appears at first glance to be an inexplicably extravagant claim by a renowned authority on Renaissance Italy, Eugenio Garin, will begin to make sense — that "after Ficino there is no writing, no thought, in which a direct or indirect trace of his activity may not be found."[2]

The *third*, then, of the reasons why this book is important is that it gives astrology at last the kind of home it deserves: a palace designed by Leonardo, decorated by Botticelli, furnished by Lorenzo and filled with the living music of Ficino's lyre.

Astrology has too long been homeless, feeling ill-at-ease among the cheap oracles of the fortune-teller's tent or languishing in Theosophy's baroque tea-rooms; sickened by the stale hamburgers of the newspaper columns or enslaved by the mechanical melodramas of the faceless astro-computer companies. Placing soul, instead of prediction, in the center of his astrology, Ficino, as Moore elucidates, creates a perspective which gives attention to the planets as rays of divinity, rather than as objects of divination. A perspective which is both an imaginal placing and a dimension of experience. "In Ficinian imagination the psyche is pictured as a round of planets, all simultaneously contributing to the music of the soul" (p189). The task is neither one of outwitting the stars, nor of simply suffering their "accidental" interventions. Not atonement, but attunement. Know thyself, becomes: "know the stars!" Astrology as a way of living one's life in accord with the heavens.

By differentiating the specific qualities of the particular planetary rays, Ficino founds an archetypal phenomenology. All the world is infused with soul, each particular thing displaying archetypal radiance, its own unique face: pomegranate, grape, starfish, python, raincloud, rose, emerald, oaktree, waterfall, zebra, orchid, earthquake, papaya, dolphin and giraffe. Whatever it may be, each thing has an archetypal home: Saturn, Mars,

Jupiter, Venus, Mercury, Sol or Luna. Further, I am encouraged to discover the medicinal heat of solar ginger as well as the acrid, burning passions of solar sulphur. Amber, honey, cinnamon, gold and saffron—all teach me other secrets of solar nature. I can also learn to recognize Sol's dazzling and desiccating power in the ultra-rational abstractions of scientific prose. Or, I can meet its dark underside in the form of the swift jaws of the crocodile of spiritual fanaticism. Or, I can witness its nobility in the lion that "roars at the enraging desert" (Wallace Stevens).

The Ficino-Moore revisioning of astrology makes it supremely psychological, reclaiming the Zodiac as a theatre of soul, a Memory Theatre-in-the-Round, an alchemical vessel for the planetary workings of the imagination and a container for the sufferings of psyche—psychological not just in the introverted, introspective sense. Psyche, as World Soul, according to Ficino, and following Plato, is scattered throughout everything; everything manifests soul's interiority and depth. The planets mirror their metaphors within. They are also persons with characters, physiognomies, styles of speech and action, who form complex relationships among themselves. Psychology thus finds a cosmology for soul.[3] The Gods are embodied, astronomically, in the planets, but psychologically in myths and in the phenomenological texture of the sensible world. Ficino's psychology is one which would imagine the divinity within each thing, the God in each event.

The *fourth* reason why this book is important is because it deflates the explanatory compulsions of psychological theory and directs our attention to our lived world, calling into play the aesthetic, that is, the sensing, imagining heart. Nearly one hundred years of psychoanalysis does not seem to have awakened this heart; in fact, psychoanalysis seems to have colluded with the collective tendency to an-aesthetize this sensitivity, this openness to the actual qualities of the environment we inhabit. Psychotherapy needs to relocate the patient within the psyche, not assume that the psyche is stuffed inside the patient. We are *in* psyche, not psyche in us, as C. G. Jung so often pointed out.

Ficino's ideas of accommodation, arrangement, imitation, devotion, tempering and tuning are all based on the recognition of the qualities and characteristics of the archetypal modes. For Ficino, human temperament, *musica humana*, was the "proper arrangement of one's life so that all concrete experiences resonate, like overtones, the fundamental octave of possibilities represented by the planet-tones. Psychotherapy would be musical then insofar as one would temper and tune the planetary tonal centers so that each would hum within the surface events of life."

It is a delight to observe the subtle alchemy with which Moore transforms Ficino's astro-musicology into a musical psycho-therapy relevant to our own time. With Moore, our understanding of Ficino's contemporary significance for *practice* resonates even deeper into soul than the brilliant pioneering work of the previous generation. This is *our* Ficino!

The last chapter of this book, "The Well-Tempered Life," is a beautifully crafted hymn to the essentially aesthetic nature of Ficinian psychology. Returning to the ancient idea of harmony (based on well-tuned intervals, whether consonant or dissonant) as imputed traditionally to Pythagoras, Moore evokes, I feel, the archetypal presence of Orpheus within the "Ficinian" practice of archetypal psychology and psychotherapy.[5] For, "Ficino was writing, not philosophy as has been supposed, but an archetypal psychology."[6] This psychology, like the Orphic hymns to the many Gods, is polytonal, polytheistic. Psychological sensibility is achieved through being attuned to the multiple powers of the psyche, the planets, and their overtones in the material world. And, in "polytheistic psychology there can be no final point of view, no one reason for anything, no ending in therapy, no goal achieved. Though it is most difficult for a *senex* ego to accept such continuous variations, an imaginal ego finds in it variety both in logic and beauty" (p207).

This superb re-presentation of Ficinian astrological psychology ends with Angelo de Gubernatis' fitting image of the deep blue firmament shining with a thousand brilliant eyes: a cosmic peacock in all the splendor of its eye-bespangled feathers. *Cauda pavonis* as the perennial *primavera* of every renaissance, a rainbow reminder of our inherent multiplicity and our celestial roots.

In my library this volume takes its rightful place beside those other classics of archetypal psychology after Jung: James Hillman's *Revisioning Psychology*; David Miller's *The New Polytheism*; Patricia Berry's *Echo's Subtle Body* and Mary Watkins' *Waking Dreams*.

Noel Cobb
London. January 14, 1989.

Preface

"What is the stars?" asks a Sean O'Casey character, finding the edge of the cosmos farthest removed from him to be the heart of his own mystery. With the fifteenth-century Florentine Marsilio Ficino, we might ask the same question of essence about the planets, knowing that our real concern is not the physical constitution of those heavenly bodies but the puzzles of our own subjective experience. Yet the two, planet and person, play a dialectical drama, a reflecting dance in which one cannot exist without the other. So, to use the word *within* in the title of this book is simply a way of distinguishing it from studies in physics. The planets of Renaissance astrology and of this modern formulation of psychology are not "within" as if they were merely symbols for personality traits: Mars for anger, Venus for sex. They are "out there" because it is out there in things and in relationships that we find our souls. Nor are the planets within as though we contained them, as though they were a subcategory of our own subjectivity. They contain us as well; for we find our own consciousness and will immersed in patterns of thought and feeling, known by the names of planets, that we neither have conjured up nor have the power to dismiss. "What is the stars" but a constant invitation to expand the borders of imagination, to depersonalize subjective experience, to become attuned to a World Soul (*Anima Mundi*) "within" which the planets whirl.

If the first problem confronting the reader of this book is to place the planets, the second is to deal with the illusions of historiography. Since Ficino, the subject of this study, published his relevant writings exactly five hundred years ago, it will be tempting to slide into a fantasy of history while reading about his ideas. Indeed, when I first began to read Ficino in a quiet corner of the library at Syracuse University, I thought of him as an intriguing heirloom, like an antique piece of furniture whose shape and material are immediately appealing but whose function remains a question. But now in my mind Ficino has been unpinned from the corkboard of history. It is not necessary to be stuck in that habit of thought which turns people of the past into tabs to be inserted into the slots of our systematized historical curiosity. It is possible to realize how thin the ether of historical time is, and what a splendid conductor of thought and imagination, allowing Ficinos to speak directly to our modern, everyday concerns. This book does not aim at positioning Ficino historically; it treats him as a living psychologist with something to say about the modern psyche.

In a number of ways the book tries to be true to Ficino's own style. For example, though he was an influential, widely published intellectual, he was not an academician, except in the Platonic sense. This book, too, is not as academic in style as it could be; rather, as Ficino says of his own writing, it is a laboratory full of experiments and remedies. Also, as Ficino's major task was to transmit a neglected tradition with translation and commentary, this in turn is an interpretive revival of Ficino himself. Finally, since theoretical and practical attention to soul was central in Ficino's work, he may be seen above all as a psychologist; and in spite of sections of the book that look like history, art criticism, and zoology, it is throughout a psychological study of human experience.

Although I found Ficino by accident, that is to say by Mercury, I did not understand his language or get this commentary into print without the help of many imaginative persons. The Hermetic guide who pointed out the right roads and made subtle suggestions was David Miller. Other guides at Syracuse University were Stanley Hopper, Huston Smith, James Wiggins, and Richard Pearson. I am also grateful to Donald Vorreyer and Alan Donovan for moral support and help in obtaining a modest grant from Glassboro State College. I am especially indebted to James Hillman, whose writing was the Mercurial wand that opened a way into Ficino and into psychology itself, and whose friendship and support have guided this book into print. I wish also to acknowledge Lonnie Kliever, John Loudon, and the editors at Bucknell University Press for appreciating the value of this idiosyncratic approach to history and psychology.

The manuscript was completed before the appearance of Charles Boer's translation of Ficino's *De Vita*; therefore, except where otherwise noted, the translations are mine. But I enthusiastically recommend the Boer translation for its accuracy and style and for its helpful glossary.

It takes a certain Hermetic madness to see the soul of the planets, and so it is to my mad-hatted friends that I owe the greatest debt.

Introduction: The Recovery of Soul

The night sky has always been a source of wonder. Its dark, black space hovers over us as a constant reminder of the mysteries that impregnate nature, while its brilliant ornaments, the stars and planets, especially the sun and moon, nourish a deep curiosity about other forms of life. Some nights the sky teems with stars, while at other times the darkness is unmitigated. Low-lying clouds may cast a misty barrier between us and that deep darkness; but when we can see the sky, and if we have studied its patterns, it turns up at night like a familiar face. We can either recognize this sky by its patterns, or conversely, knowing its habits we can find ourselves and establish our own position.

If all this is true of the sky we behold with our eyes at night, it is also true of a dark universe we can see within ourselves with an inner eye. In that other universe we find ourselves in the midst of an inner darkness where are contained all memories of the past and fantasies for the future. Like the night sky, that deep inner space is full of mysteries; yet its darkness and distances too are spotted with patterns, lights, and recognizable figures. It can become familiar, like a face, and from it we can find our position. It would seem that we stand between two infinitely vast universes: the cosmos of the outer world still chary of revealing its many secrets, and the microcosm of the inner world of the psyche, equally possessive of its mysteries.

These notions, of course, are by no means original, since people for millennia have been looking into the night sky as into a mirror. Identifying the lights and moving patterns felt within as planets and stars, they have fashioned an astrological portrait of the psyche. Only with the arrival of the science of astronomy, with its technology and mathematics, did the sky truly begin to recede from our most intimate grasp. Finally, when through the omniscient eye of television we could all see the dust of Luna, the imprint of a human foot, wellheeled of course, and later a golf club teeing off on the body of what once was a daimon, a god, a celestial governor or archon, then deeply felt ties with the planets were severed. Now they are the object of scientific fascination, which is not without its own sense of wonder and adventure, but they have lost the power to mirror the deep self, to stand as elegant metaphors for the vast space and regular movements we feel deep inside. In our day the night sky has a different kind of fascination, a more literal concern. We wonder about traversing those distances and worry about the creatures we are bound to meet out there when we go traveling. We hesitate to guess the implications, with respect to our own cosmological, physical, and even moral beliefs, of other worlds and especially other peoples.

But if this transformation of awareness from astrological to astronomical consciousness has hardened somewhat our thrill at the night sky, it has done more extensive damage to that space we familiarly call inner. Those patterns and shiftings formerly identified as movements of gods and daimons affecting our souls now become instincts, drives, unconscious tendencies, conditioned reflexes, learned behaviors, and cathected complexes. While we have certainly gained something in the move away from superstition and ignorance, we have also suffered a loss. Whereas once the vast cosmos aptly mirrored the depth and vast extent of human consciousness, now many of our "shrinks"—an appropriate term perhaps—reductively tell us that our souls are really only the complex dynamics of electrical currents and synapses. Subjective experience, they say, is an epiphenomenon of that marvelous computer, the human brain. The brilliant planets have been exchanged for electrical sparks. Or, maybe the soul is the unraveling of childhood experiences, the nuclear family exploding in a mushroom cloud of symptoms and problems. Instead of recognizing, as did intelligent people in ages past, that there are movements within that are bigger than ourselves, superhuman, self-willed, and irresistible, we take it all on ourselves. Where before a person might acknowledge the onslaught of Venus or Saturn and in some humility try to deal with the overpowering situation, today we search for a pill to still the inconveniencing jab of a mood or "mental problem." Or, we become inflated. Where before Mercury or a Muse might inspire one with a new idea or a novel creation, today we speak of an individual's genius as if it were as much a component of his individual identity as the color of his hair. We have stuffed the microcosm of the psyche into a test tube and corked it with ego and scientific rationalism.

I am not going to suggest a return to the old ways of antiquity. We now have new information about the cosmos, and some new insight into the nature of the cosmos within. But, having felt the increasing sterility and soullessness of the purely objective scientific view of the world, can we not return to antiquity with new eyes? Can we not avoid superstition and literalism and yet recover what has been lost of antique sensibility? Is not a cosmos peopled—not the precise word—with daimons and deities more fit for humans than a world objective and lifeless? It is curious that an age we call the Renaissance, an era praised for its humanism, was also a time of the rebirth of the classical deities. Gods and humans go together. Take away the gods and dehumanization sets in.

All this is to say that the macrocosm may be allowed some interplay with the microcosm, and that entails a high estimation of human imagination; for it is only in imagination that the gods and their starry sky can be reborn without anachronistic literalism.

The purely physicalist view of the universe that has come to captivate consciousness is evident in spontaneous reactions of ridicule toward groups that today profess belief in an earth-centered cosmos. From one point of view such convictions seem to border the psychotic, so out of touch are they with the modern perspective. But from another point of view these non-Copernicans hold onto a valuable realization: that for most human purposes the ground on which we stand is the center of the universe. Human being is at the center of its own consciousness, where a centripetal imagination makes human contact with an otherwise cold, objective world.

Multiple perspectives are required if one is to affirm at the same time a geocentric sensibility and a Copernican cosmology, and it may take the same kind of flexible viewpoint to give a place in psychology to astrological symbolism. But this would not be a radically new vision; for, in the psychology of medieval and Renaissance man, the psyche was understood to be a microcosmic reflection of the universe. Many of those beautiful paintings of the gods and their mythologies that grace Renaissance villas and churches originally served an astro-psychological purpose. Every period has its spokesmen for the psyche. Even the Enlightenment era, that time when men stole the light of the planets and turned it literally on their microscopes and figuratively on their reasoning, had its challenge in William Blake: "Tyger, tyger, burning bright in the forests of the night." He brought the living light back to its dark abode. Sensitive to imagination and to the psyche, Blake knew that in order to see the stars there has to be darkness; indeed, the darker the better. Our psychology, too, needs light and darkness if it is to encompass the full range of man's days and nights on earth.

The Psychology of Antiquity

One hears an occasional complaint that the twentieth century is mad in its cult of youth. Aging is an embarrassment, something to cover up with powders and face lifts. But there is an extraordinarily subtle and insidious intellectual youthful myopia that touches upon the problem of this book. Exhilarated by the creations and progress of science and technology, we cultural young adults tend to think that there is nothing not new under the sun. Even students of psychology exhibit this shortsighted thinking, typical of the adolescent who thinks he is the first to step out on the earth, the first to do this and feel that. These students of psychology are apparently taken in by the modern instruments and jargon, the hardness of research and the certitude offered by numerical values. To be sure, the fifty-minute hour, the fifty-dollar session, the cocktail-party vocabulary of complexes and neuroses, the mounds of statistics and algebraic formulae, the orderly and systematic desensitizing vice-exterminating procedures of behaviour modification, to say nothing of lobotomies and shock therapies—these are the proud achievements of our century. But all of this does not mean that psychology as such is an infant.

Perhaps the reason a college psychology major would boast that he had traced the history of psychology all the way back to the nineteenth century has to do with a common modern bias. In our world science equals knowledge. A statement is true when it is scientific. When it has been cataloged, quantified, repeated, programmed, and published, then a theory or hypothesis is considered true. Other kinds of learning, such as the Liberal Arts, enjoy the blessings of Eternal Truth, but that kind is not very reliable. However, once one is willing to look beyond the positivistic, scientific method for knowledge, then one finds psychology not beginning in the nineteenth century, but only wearing down—momentarily.

Indeed, there is a wealth of psychological insight and creative thought to be found in our very unscientific heritage of religion, myth, philosophy, art, and literature. In archaic sources these areas are not sorted out in a way that would please our pigeonholing minds, but nonetheless the information is there. In fact, the true complexity of psychological reality is reflected precisely in those ill-sorted sources.

This book centers on one of the most soul-centered—psychological—movements of the prescientific age, in Renaissance Italy, where a group of varied and talented individuals clustered during the fifteenth century. Their explorations of the inner world, their maps and ingenious methods for surveying the inner life were not applauded as were those of their contemporaries, daring Columbuses who wandered into far-off, unknown regions. But these people may have found inner islands, land masses, and channels which would give us today a better sense of where we are, where we have come from, and the right routes to take toward fertile places and unexplored territories.

These psychological navigators, the "Florentine Platonists," were a band of poets, philosophers, artists, and theologians who were captivated by the spirit of Plato. Their quixotic leader, Marsilio Ficino, guided them in their Platonic studies, but his interests were broad and far-reaching. In everything, from philosophy to medicine, he taught them to see all things in the light of soul. Today, in our language, we could say quite accurately that Ficino held and taught that a psychological attitude ought to pervade all our researches and ideas.[1] Ficino not only influenced artists, poets, and philosophers with his ideas, he also developed what we today would call a practice of psychotherapy. As we shall see in some detail, he taught his clients and followers to imagine deeply and constantly. In fact, it is clear that Ficino considered a person to be in good psychological condition to the extent that he or she enjoyed a well-nourished and practiced imagination. Serious attention to images and knowledge about their subtle characteristics form the basis for a Ficinian psychotherapy.

What I propose to do in this book is to step back in time, to those strange days of the Florentine Academy, and particularly to some quite unusual esoteric writings of Ficino. This is what a Freudian analyst might call a "regression in service of the ego." It is hoped that this retreat will broaden and deepen our knowledge about psychology and serve as a refresher course for our cramped psychological attitude. But this step backwards in history is not taken without some problems. For one thing, Ficino used an entirely different language for the inner life. His terms were less abstract and less mechanical than ours tend to be. Rather than referring to love and anger as if these were simple circulatory movements of the psyche, like squirts of plasma or adrenaline, he alludes to the realms and powers of Venus, Mars, and other planetary deities. He sees the source of our troubles and successes not in instincts and conditioned responses but in deeper factors represented by the gods and goddesses.

How are we to take these references to the gods of Greece and Rome? Or, how are we to interpret his quaint and occasionally downright insane remedies? He advises a person lacking in the spirit of Jupiter, for example, to add peppermint to his diet. Is this legend, folklore, precocious pharmacology, or pure metaphor? Where does Ficino the psychologist end and the physician begin, or the theologian, or the magus, or the astrologer? How are we to distinguish between concerns of psychology and those of religion—that strange matter of the gods?

Two tactics would clearly be ineffective. We could understand Ficino literally, eat peppermint and do the other unusual things he advises—worship the gods, undertake the serious practice of astrology, and so forth. Or, we could translate his theories and suggestions for therapy into the language and practice with which we are familiar today. When he mentions Mars, we could substitute anger, and so on. But neither of these approaches will do; for there is more to Ficino's bizarre remedies than psychology as we know it, and it is not all superstition. Literalism will lead us only into occult quackery, and translation into some modern system, making of Ficino a Skinner, a Freud, or a Jung, would be to reduce and rationalize what is basically a transrational appraisal of the life of the psyche. To make Ficino's psychology into a brand of psychoanalysis would amount to cutting off his footing in the world of imagination, placing him on a modern-day Procrustean bed of scientific rationalism.

A Modern Reading of Ficinian Psychology

It may be difficult but it is not impossible to carry Ficino's insight forward into the twentieth century. Our first guide is Ficino's own fundamental tool—imagination. Ficino's psychology is expressed in images rather than logical, linear statements. So we may treat these images as we would others, as for example the images we find in literature, art, poetry, and even dreams. Strange as they are, Ficino's images are not entirely foreign to our history or to our art. The classical deities to whom he refers constantly appear in art, drama, and literature throughout the centuries. Their characteristics, the varied hollows of nature these gods rule, the deep centers of the psyche they personify—all of these have been depicted by poets and artists. Even the quaint medicines, the gems and animals Ficino associates with the various deities, and therefore with various tendencies of the psyche, have been sorted out and elaborated in lapidaries and bestiaries of the Middle Ages and Renaissance. The trouble is that we do not usually read these kinds of books psychologically. As we do with art, we view them as curiosities or as entertainment or as objects of scholarship. But these images—the precious stones and the real and imaginary beasts—are like the figures of our dreams. They are fashioned by the psyche and therefore reveal something of their maker. Like dream images, they require a sensitive, modest imaginative play so that their significance may emerge.

Besides our own imaginations freely playing (seriously nonetheless) with Ficino's imagery, we fortunately have guides: C. G. Jung and James Hillman. These specialists in matters psychological and symbolic will not be claimed as authorities so much as exemplars. Their writings show us how to dive deep into images without strangling them, without giving them a Midas touch transforming them into our favorite golden theories.

When I first read Jung, and especially later than when I read his more orthodox followers, I vehemently rejected the tack of finding "Jungian" concepts like "anima" and "shadow" in literature and art. It seemed softly and elegantly reductionistic. But as I read Jung carefully and more extensively, I discovered in him a true concern for the integrity of images. Jung bends the glow of an image toward personal experiences, feelings, and thoughts, but unlike many psychologists who deal in images he does not reduce the image to the personal level. Mars is ever more than human anger, Venus infinitely greater than human love. He knew that to interpret images is simply to search for other images that are similar, expecting to find in the similarities deeper understanding and insight. In his own hands, his favored terms—shadow, anima, wise old man, Great Mother—are mere helpful tools, metaphors for seeing through and into traditional words and pictures handed down to us through the centuries. In the face of any mysterious image, we may either stand mute and unaffected, we may slice and beat the image in order to make it fit our familiar patterns of thought, or we may delicately compare, search, and probe with an artist's eye, teasing some significance away. One of Jung's great contributions to art, and to religion in particular, is to demonstrate that images of tradition need not remain as lifeless, opaque hunks of matter. With imagination we can vivify them, rendering them more transparent by comparing them and restating them in the metaphors congenial to our modern perspective.

If in Jung there is the suggestion that psychology has to do with more than the personal life, that it is more than the ordinary person usually imagines it to be, then in Hillman's work this suggestion is repeated, amplified, and underscored. Hillman lays stress on soul and wants to bring psyche back into psychology. He has gone his own way, yet, like Jung, Hillman directs our attention to depth. For Hillman an image is bottomless, and the way to let its significance seep into our skin is to dive into it. Hillman also accents the pathological currents in psychological experience, veering away from normative ideals too tight, too optimistic, too one-sided as reflections of the way psychological life proceeds. He also opts for a polytheistic rather than a monotheistic view of the world. There are many legitimate perspectives on experience, he suggests, and a single one becomes dominant only to the detriment of the psyche.

Hillman's concern for soul and his polytheistic position place him shoulder to shoulder with Ficino. In fact, as I have read the two of them I have had an eerie feeling that a mysterious dialogue was taking place across the reach of centuries. I have also conceived of this book as a kind of dialogue, a constant movement between the laconic remarks of Ficino and suggestions for giving those remarks a life and context for our day. This book is not intended as a running commentary on Ficino's text, nor is it an historical or philosophical analysis. It is rather an effort to explore and unveil significance in selected images found in Ficino's work. It is meant to be a kind of depth psychology—an exploration of imagery with a clear psychological attitude behind it. I do not intend to stop at a comparison of Ficino's words with other historical concepts or curiosities. I am asking what his strange philosophy and remedies have to say about the psyche today.

The Planets

To study Ficino seriously is to put oneself in rather extra-ordinary company. Although Ficino's writings are not well known—only a few have been translated into English—historically he influenced a number of significant artists and philosophers. We can trace a direct line from his Neoplatonic fancies to the paintings of Botticelli, for example. He also influenced

Giordano Bruno, that exceptional philosopher who theorized about multiple worlds and extraterrestrial civilizations, studied Egyptian religion piously, and found himself imprisoned, tortured, and executed by an Inquisitorial church. Bruno was an avid student of Ficino's esoteric writings. Another outstanding philosopher familiar with Ficino's writings was Robert Fludd. Fludd, like Ficino, planted his speculations in the imagery of music, and in other ways he tried to map the interplay of body, soul, and spirit. Like Ficino, Fludd was known as a magician, astrologer, philosophical musician, and physician.

Now, following Hillman's lead, I am suggesting that we allow the extraordinary Ficino to influence our perspective on psychology. Specifically, I am interested in the same text which charmed Fludd and Bruno, a three-volume work entitled *Libri de Vita Tres—Three Books about Life*. These three books are about life and health, physical and psychological. They are full of suggestions for healthy living and warnings against certain inadvisable practices. The third volume is especially interesting for its natural magic, astrology, and musical symbolism. It is this volume, *De Vita Coelitus Comparanda—How Life Should be Arranged according to the Heavens*—that serves as the primary source and stimulus for this book. Since the title is long, and since "heavens" in Ficino's writings refers primarily to the planets, I will refer to the work simply as *The Planets*.

The title itself adumbrates some of Ficino's insights into psychology, insights developed chiefly through arcane images in the work itself. For example, the word *arrange* suggests both multiplicity in the psyche—you have to have many parts in order to make an arrangement—and a musical notion about psychological health, a notion Ficino develops quite ingeniously in *The Planets*. Furthermore, the planets bear the names of gods and goddesses. These, advises Ficino, can be arranged for the good health of the person. A healthy life is a musical life—a strange suggestion that demands a good explanation.

But a good explanation does not explain everything away. It does not define, in the literal sense of setting limits; rather, it extends the limits and deepens one's familiarity with the material. Our job is to keep imagining, drawing closer to the elusive core of the image. Ficino's text is not unlike a dream which calls for familiarity and increasing intimacy if the atmosphere and aura of its secret are to be sensed.

Ficino's little book affords us an opportunity to take a fresh look at the planets, not the planets of the night sky, but rather the planets within. His philosophy of soul and his practical instructions for healthy living send us off into deep exploration of those dark spaces of the psyche and the occasional lights. Before examining each of the planets we will look closely at some of Ficino's basic assumptions, review the building blocks, the vision out of which he creates an astrological view of psychological life. We may see then, through his eyes, that astrology is not only a superstition, not only a faddish delight. It is also a way of imagining our inner world, complete with our flights of visionary intuition and our painful pathologies.

PART I
Poetica Animae:
A Poetic of the Soul

I have noticed how easily an image of someone mourning moves many people to pity. And just as the image of a lovable person is moving and has an effect on one's eyes, imagination, spirit, and humor, so the heavenly visage is no less vital and effective. Does not the gentle and happy face of a prince uplift everyone in a city? Does not a mean and sad face terrify? What about the face of the heavens? Do you think it is possible to resist the lords of all things earthly?

—Ficino, *The Planets*, chapter 17

To the extent that the ruling heavens favor your beginnings and further life, you will pursue the promise of your birth; especially if Plato is correct and antiquity with him, in saying that when anyone is born they are given a certain daimon, a life-guardian—destined by one's very own star.

—Ficino, *The Planets*, chapter 23

1
Marsilio Ficino: Physician of the soul

As our view of Western history becomes more sophisticated and complex and as we aquire new information and apply more subtle theories of history itself to the facts, broad and simplistic categories of time give way to smaller and overlapping periods and eras. We can find patterns of rise and fall, decay and rebirth, in almost any selected segment of time. "Renaissance" seems to be an eternal pattern happening always at some level. Nevertheless, that remarkable era we know as the Italian Renaissance still stands out as an extraordinary moment in our collective past. An inexhaustible curiosity and spirit of exploration led to world-shaping discovery and invention, and at the same time a revivified imagination produced unequaled art, architecture, music, and literature. In all of this we see a rebirth of Greek and Roman classics, or, to put it more precisely in the words of the distinguished Renaissance scholar Paul O. Kristeller, this was a time of the "rebirth of the arts guided by antiquity."[1]

The guidance of antiquity, however, extended beyond the realms of art and literature. We find a return of the classical gods and goddesses not only on painters' canvases and in sculptors' stone, but also in shadier places, in books concerning magic and occult mysteries. Antique philosophy, a delight to many a Renaissance thinker, provided not only the groundwork for philosophical and theological design and argument, but also a source for speculation about such things as alchemy, astrology, magic, and occult medicine. Indeed, historians like Panofsky, Wind, and Seznec assure us that even in the highly visible and widely proclaimed works of artists deeper mysteries are hidden.

Marsilio Ficino was the admiring inheritor of both streams of knowledge—the humanistic and the occult. Today, on those rare occasions when his name does appear in books and essays, Ficino is recognized chiefly for his translations of Plato and the Neoplatonic philosophers and for the influence of his Platonic thought in art and literature. But he had that darker side, too. Though he was certainly a scholar and lofty-minded philosopher, he was also obviously concerned with practical matters of living. In this exceptional but telling work of his we are about to explore, Ficino reveals his attention to practical techniques for making his speculative views on the soul connect with daily living. Indeed, he was a philosopher, but he was also concerned to spell out a practical yet psychological way of life. Along with his philosophical ideas he fabricated a remarkable amalgam of music, magic, medicine, astrology, art, and ritual—all directed toward a release from materialistic shortsightedness and the establishment of a soul-focused life-style.

Florence and the Medicis

Ficino saw himself as a physician of two sorts. In the preface to his books on health he refers to his double birth. As the god Bacchus had two mothers, he writes, he himself had two fathers. His physical father commended him to Galen, physician of the body; and his other father, Cosimo de' Medici, from whom he had been reborn, dedicated him to Plato, physician of the soul. Ficino's soul-father, Cosimo de' Medici, was perhaps the most influential and productive member of that outstanding family, in spite of the fact that his grandson, Lorenzo, was called "the Magnificent." The Medicis were merchants and bankers in a society that was self-consciously cosmopolitan and internationally significant. The republic of Florence meandered along its twisting historical path governed by various councils and other bodies. In or out of office the Medicis were, of course, influential, if not always to their advantage, as in Cosimo's costly ill-fated support of Pope John XXIII. Cosimo had a passion for giving all sorts of ideas concrete form; so he gave financial backing for architectural projects and he supported artists like Donatello, Fra Filippo Lippi, and Fra Angelico. His son, Piero, provided shelter and patronage for Botticelli.

Besides his generous concern for the papacy, art, and architecture, Cosimo had his less rational side as well. His friend, Vespasiano da Bisticci, the bookseller, records for us another curious interest, one we shall see developed in Ficino. Vespasiano writes: "Astrologers found him well-versed in their science, for he had a certain faith in astrology, and employed it to guide him on certain private occasions."[2] Here we encounter a deeper, more complex notion of "Renaissance man" than the popular notion of a person who can paint, play music, write poetry, and design weapons. In their speculations and probing discussions the men of the Renaissance were blending concerns of reason and unreason, of philosophy and magic; more importantly, they were aware of the substantive connections between the arts and between the arts and religion. On the model of Cosimo and Ficino, we might say that a Renaissance person as a type is someone who, by virtue of a sensitivity to image, sees an interrelatedness among all things.

Although Cosimo's largesse as an art patron and his assiduous care in building libraries play significant roles in the full story of Ficinian cult of imagination, his most practical gift was one of time and space. He provided Ficino with a villa outside Florence, at Careggi, where the scholar could do his work of translating and composing free of cares and interruptions. That is not to say that the villa was a quiet place of never-ending study. There gathered around Ficino artists, philosophers, and poets who were inspired by his intellectual and psychological leadership. They were so taken by Ficino's revivification of Plato that they modeled their association on the Platonic Academy, and each year on November 7 they would festively reenact the *Symposium*. Marsilio, the dwarfish, humpbacked, notoriously ugly "physician of the soul" translated and taught, but he also cared for the psychological life of his friends. We have a hint of this care in a letter from Cosimo to Ficino. Ficino was a musical therapist, having developed a highly sophisticated theory and practice of music in the service of psychology. For his patients he would carefully select music tuned to the needs of their soul and play it on his lyre. In his letter Cosimo invites Ficino to visit him: "Do come then, and do not forget to bring with you the Orphean lyre."[3]

Ficino himself tells us that Cosimo conceived the idea of an Academy when Florence was host to a portion of a great council of Eastern and Western churchmen. The council had begun in Ferrara but ran into trouble; so Cosimo persuaded his friend, Pope Eugenius IV, to transfer the meetings to Florence, a move that took place in 1439. The council brought prestige and commerce to Florence, but more importantly it provided a connection with the East. Cosimo's library of rare manuscripts grew quickly, and through the presence of scholars unusually well versed in Greek and Eastern thought his own mind was fertilized. Particularly influential was Giorgius Gemistus Plethon (1360–1452), a philosopher who had been born in Constantinople and had spent many years in Mistra, in the region of ancient Sparta. He was not only

acquainted with Greek philosophy in its own language, he was
also a student of Zoroastrianism and Chaldaic astrology. The light
of reason and the darkness of the occult often traveled close
together in those fertile times.

Ficino was only six years old at the time of Plethon's visit—he
was born in 1433—when Cosimo de' Medici became intrigued with
the notion of an ancient wisdom contained in the works of Plato
and the later "Platonists," actually the Neoplatonists. His
enthusiasm and curiosity were more deeply aroused decades later,
two years before the founding of the Academy, when a monk
from Macedonia visited Florence. The monk brought with him an
incomplete copy of the *Corpus Hermeticum*, containing fourteen
of the fifteen treatises. Cosimo had Ficino interrupt his translations
of Plato in order to make accessible as quickly as possible this
exciting esoteric compilation. Once again, Plato and occult studies
run into each other, and this time the darker partner takes first
place.

Under Cosimo's enlightened patronage, unfailing intuitive
judgment, and clever political moves the Florentine intellectual
community thrived. In this atmosphere the followers of Plato
could pursue their cultivation of "*virtù*," the individual's total
development of himself beyond all limits and the shaping of his life
into a work of art.[4] Ficino frequently exhorted his friends and
followers to live the best life possible. "*Optimo*" and "*optissime*"
continually qualify the phrase "*modus vivendi*" in his books and
even in his private correspondence. His expansive view of the
possibilities for human life appears again and again in his writings,
as when in his major work, *Theologia Platonica*, he writes: man
"spans the heavens and the earth; he plumbs the depths of
Tartarus; nor are the heavens too high for him, nor is the center of
the earth too deep."[5]

At Cosimo's death in 1464 he was proclaimed *Pater Patriae*,
father of the country, and for Ficino he had truly served as a
spiritual father. Cosimo's son, Piero, called *Il Gottoso*—"The
Gouty"— took over leadership of the family, but he died five
years later leaving his son, Cosimo's grandson Lorenzo the
Magnificent, in charge. Ficino named Lorenzo *Figlio del Sole*, "Son
of the Sun", for, though his style and interests were different from
his grandfather's, nevertheless, the Florentines flourished with
renewed vitality under his enthusiastic patronage and stimulation.
Lorenzo was tutored by Ficino, Landino, and other exceptional
intellectuals, and not surprisingly he became an intelligent and
perceptive patron. He nurtured young artists like Botticelli,

Michelangelo, and Leonardo da Vinci, transferring to their sensitive minds the Platonic and Hermetic thought of his teacher, Marsilio.

These few historical remarks about Ficino leave us with an image of a most unusual person living in a remarkable time and place. It is both a historical portrait and a fantasy of a city, an academy, and individuals working diligently but with great excitement in the midst of fundamental ambiguities and paradoxes. They were attempting to care simultaneously for intellect and body, philosophy and religion, and they knew, following Ficino's fundamental insight, that such a deeply pluralistic effort would be possible provided concern for soul were central. In effect, this means that psychology was at the core of their wide-ranging endeavors. Today, since the scope of psychology has been so truncated, to place psychology as it is usually theorized and practiced at the centre of study and work, would be reductive. But Ficino found soul to be the proper mediating factor in all his studies—in philosophy and theology, in medicine and psychotherapy, and in his religious devotion. His major philosophical work, *The Platonic Theology*, constitutes his attempt to reconcile the interests of philosophy, psychology, and theology at the speculative level; while his more pragmatic efforts to do the same appear in the work we are about to study. Even as a priest, it is recorded, he performed exorcism, a way for caring for the soul through religious ritual.[6]

The populace of Ficino's Florence must have had a vital psychological sense as well, for it was customary for them to celebrate publicly the completion of a painting or fresco. Also, we find in Medici architecutre an uncommon complexity blended with purity of form—a style remarkable for its liveliness and depth of impact. Florence itself excels among cities for its embodiment of soul-values, evident in the total environment. Finally, where there is psychological awareness, there is attention to death. Incessant wars and threats, poisonings and intrigues, disease and epidemics made death visible and familiar. Death, of course, was given due attention in poetry and in art, and in mimed rituals the triumph of death could always be assured an attentive audience in the streets of Florence.[7] It was a time and place where images were taken seriously, where art and religion blended lofty theological argument with deeply felt and keenly respected superstition.

In the next chapter we will take a close look at the nature of the psyche, and we shall see that the soul is always in a mediating position between spirit above and matter or body below. Looking at the historical setting in which Ficino's psychology developed, we can see the upward movement tending toward theological and philosophical speculation. Existing English translations of Ficino, as well as commentaries on his work, dwell upon this upward region of his thought. However, to some extent this emphasis on the spiritual misrepresents Ficino's own writing, since even in his speculative works he makes connections constantly with the psychological realm. There is also the danger of taking the ideas too literally, of getting lost in arguments concerning the purity of religious tradition and the existence of God. Historically, the climate around Ficino also favored an oblique movement toward superstition and magic. Here too, we have to avoid literalism. As long as there is a connection with psyche, a sustaining metaphorical attitude, then the dark side of magic can be understood as the expression of psyche as well.

Related to the problem of keeping reason and the nonrational alive in our consideration of Ficino's psychology is the enigma of interrelated internal and external worlds. Ficino's real contribution to art and perhaps to psychology have to do with this problem. For Ficino the external world is the way to the internal realm of the soul. When Neoplatonism is interpreted too rigidly, one gets the idea that there is no place for the body or the material dimension. Ficino's Neoplatonism lies unconcealed in all of his writing, yet he does not advise a retreat from the body. He does insist upon acknowledgment of the centrality of soul, and therefore any exclusive concern for the body would be a crucial mistake. But as long as soul is at the center, involvement with matter is a means for psychological deepening. Therefore, the very tangible productions of art, and even the pleasure one derives from art, are means for nourishing the soul. So too are magic and astrology. For those with a mind to psychological reality, these occult arts serve to draw the psyche into areas not otherwise accessible. They ritualize and map psychological worlds which are impossibly irrelevant and misguiding to the scientific mind but significant for the soul.

The Hermetic Influence

Before examining more deeply Ficino's idea of the soul, it might be useful to consider briefly the Hermetic works which so impressed him as he was writing *The Planets*.

As important as the texts themselves was the atttitude of Renaissance Platonists toward them. Cosimo, Ficino, and their circle believed that these highly symbolic writings were the work of Hermes Trismegistus. Hermes, they thought, was an extremely ancient writer, the earliest in a line going from Hermes himself, sometimes considered a contemporary of Moses, through Orpheus and Pythagoras, among others, to Plato.[8] In fact, these writings probably date only from the second and third centuries of our era. But, like people in any historical period, the Florentine group was deeply impressed by the reputed antiquity of the mysterious texts, a quality that only intensified their aura of mystery.

Ficino was convinced that Hermes was the first to make a move out of matter and truly engage in theological wonder. Ficino writes: "Mercurius Trismegistus [Mercurius is the Roman form of Hermes] was the first philosopher to raise himself above physics and mathematics to the contemplation of the divine.... Therefore, he was considered the original founder of theology."[9] For Ficino, then, there was something primordial about the words he read in the Hermetic texts. Even for us these writings carry a mythological tone, and their antiquity, if only fictional, has an impact on the reader even today. In spite of all our modern sophistication, there is no need for us to be unduly concerned about Ficino's mistaken dating for the Hermetic material. In his imagination as in ours, Hermes may stand as a mythic figure, the personification of a foundational source of wisdom, not unlike Moses in the Judeo-Christian tradition.

In *The Planets*, therefore, we encounter an imagination inflamed and incited by archetypal imagery. As the scholar of Renaissance magic and esoterism Frances Yates observes, Hermetic knowledge was not intended for leisurely speculation. On the contrary, it was honored as *gnosis*, a saving kind of knowledge, an apprehension of mysteries which run deep in nature and in the person, a transforming knowledge which can only be acquired through learning that is far beyond intellect alone. As Ficino implies throughout *The Planets*, one can develop a psychological attitude—that is, understand the processes of the soul—only through constant, daily, if not hourly, attention.

Ficino was influenced by other authors interested in psychology but less arcane, such as Thomas Aquinas and Augustine. It is also quite likely that he had read Nicholas of Cusa, another imaginative thinker a generation removed, who placed high value on symbolic sources and what he called "enigmatic metaphors."[10] But the most obvious source for *The Planets* is the Hermetic collection, as well as a later Arabic compendium of the twelfth century known as *Picatrix*. A brief overview of these last sources will prepare us for Ficino's own psychological theories and the symbolic language he uses in presenting his psychology.

The first book of the Hermetic opus contains a story with familiar Gnostic themes.[11] Pimander, the divine Mind, appears to Hermes and describes the origin of nature. God brought forth a demiurage, he relates, a god of fire and breath, who fashioned Seven Governors "who envelop with their circles the sensible world." All of the lower world depends upon the Seven Governors. Then the Father God created a Man in his own image, a Man so beautiful that God fell in love with him. He allowed the Man to enter the sphere of the demiurge and there to behold the Seven Governors. They too fell in love with him and gave him part in their rule. Finally, the Man broke through the circles of the Governors to know the power of God himself.

Gifted with all of this power and knowledge, the Man revealed to Nature below the beautiful form of God, and Nature loved him, having seen his beautiful features reflected in the water and his shadow on the earth. The Man, too saw a form like his own reflected in the water and wished to be united with it—a wish immediately accomplished. Nature and Man were united in love. Thus, mankind has a double nature: mortal in his body, immortal in the essential Man. His mortal nature is under the dominion of the planets, but his immortal nature is not.

Yates comments on this Hermetic story of Creation and Fall, noting the intimate relationship between man and the star-daimons or Seven Governors. This is a central idea in *The Planets*—mankind is in touch with the planetary daimons. The relationship between the "natural" or material part of the person and that other part which is eternal and self-aware is essentially erotic. For Ficino, all movement of the soul comes from eros. It is also important to notice that the essential man is not under the dominion of the planets. Keeping this in mind will help when we come across statements of Ficino against astrology, confusing in view of his frequent recourse to astrological phenomena.

This first Hermetic book also implies, when read psychologically, that there is more to the person than ego. Natural man, or the person living unconsciously, is moved to experience all kinds of behavior according to patterns common to all humans. We all love, hate, desire, strive, fail, wish, and wonder. But the essential man, some non-ego part of the person, is initiated into the secrets of the Governors, those sometimes tyrannical rulers of the spheres of life, whose influence seems impossible to break. We are not

entirely, that is, compelled, on the analogy of astrological compulsion, to remain at the mercy of these Governors. We can vivify
the essential Man in us all and thereby transcend what seems
"natural." The life of the soul, in fact, may seem unnatural, the
famous "opus contra naturam," a working against what seems to
be our nature. When people say, "that's human nature," there may
be neglect of soul; because what seems natural may be only the
atmosphere of the *archon*, the Governor of that sphere of life lived
and felt unconsciously. A psychological attitude goes against what
appears to be only natural, peeking through that limited realm,
gaining a perspective on the planetary spheres where they are
revealed to be circles of glass. One may love, hate, and wonder
but know that one is doing so, seeing oneself from beyond the
Seven Governors.

Another of the Hermetic books, *The Mind to Hermes*, contains
two additional ideas central to Ficino's thought. Everything is full
of soul, it teaches. In Ficino's writing, too, soul is ever at the
center, which is to say that it is thoroughly psychological. In our
day we have difficulty imagining that persons, to say nothing of
nature and material things, have soul. Yet Ficino is only echoing a
truly ancient notion, going back at least to Heraclitus and Thales,
that the world is full of soul. Historians and anthropologists
commonly treat animism as a backward mentality; yet animistic
religion, found close at home in American Indian traditions,
recognizes soul (*anima*) in everything that exists. In a very genuine
sense, once an individual acquires a consistent psychological
attitude, all things, every object and every action, take on
significance to the soul. Writing a letter may be an expression of,
or a caring for, the soul. Something as simple and mundane as a
can of beer finds its place in the structure of the soul. Ficino's
astrology and certainly his medicine make no sense unless this
soul-centeredness is perceived.

A second point in this book of the Hermetic texts follows from
the first. All beings are in movement. The presence of soul implies
movement—not simply the ability to walk and run as Aristotle
suggests, but an internal movement, a wandering and shifting of
the soul itself. As the experience of life deepens and becomes
focused in a wide variety of events engendering anything from
joyful ecstasy to depressing pain, soul itself seems to move. From
highs to lows, in depth and in superficiality, vanishing into thin air
or close to home, psychological vicissitudes can be felt as
movements of soul. Soul even seems to travel through the body
making its path traceable in a pounding heart, tingling nerves, or

throbbing headache. We move through decision and action, and we are moved by passion and emotion.

The planets are in motion, and if they do reflect our interior lives, if we do indeed have planets within, then these are in rhythmic motion. They form literally millions of patterns, which an astrological chart can depict with only the crudest precision, and with almost no sense of the unending motion. Perhaps this is why Ficino was particularly fond of mechanical replicas of the heavens—they could move and show the mobile patterns of the planets and stars.

Still another Hermetic text, _The Asclepius_, expresses ideas we will find at the core of Ficino's theory of magic. It is breath or _spiritus_, this book asserts, that keeps life in all things. Or, as Yates puts it, air is the instrument or organ of all the gods. In Ficino's theory _spiritus_ is the means of magical effect between planetary daimons and the physical world or the life of the individual. The method by which this _spiritus_ is conveyed from planets to the individual is described in _The Asclepius_ as a matter of image-making. Any image, perhaps a statue, that represents characteristics of a particular planetary deity may collect, hold, and bestow the power of that deity on the person using that image. Images have deep, archetypal power. We may take this part of the theory somewhat literally and consider the value to soul of images and art, or we may look more psychologically and examine imagination itself, its power to connect the ego to the larger movements of the psyche.

Other Hermetic texts describe correspondences between planets and animals, plants, talismans, and medicines. They also suggest the possibility of drawing power from one planet in order to offset the troublesome dominating influence of another. Finally, the _Picatrix_ provides detailed descriptions of talismans, amulets, and other objects useful in natural magic. Again, all of these unusual notions appear in _The Planets_.

A Poetic of the Soul

Ficino's work is sometimes called "poetic theology," a phrase offered by his star pupil, Pico della Mirandola. But his writing is also a poetic psychology, a psychopoetics. His insights are expressed imagistically rather than discursively. His psychology is also poetic in that its purpose is to nourish and educate imagination, the vital instrument by which the natural is rendered psychological, and soul is allowed a place in life. Why wear an amulet signifying the speed of Mercury except to keep that quality of the soul in mind? For Ficino the gods themselves are facets of the soul requiring attention. Consciousness is not all rationality and strong-willed ego-states; it also embraces "softer" functions like memory, recognition, acknowledgement, reverence, respect, and awareness.

Let us proceed then to study more closely the images of Ficinian psychopoetics, avoiding literalism of either the intellectual or superstitutious kinds, in search of a psychology relevant to twentieth-century life. If we find talk of talismans, archaic or otherwise, inaccessible, we may translate them into modern forms—perhaps a cherished photograph, painting, piece of jewelry, or clothing. The point is not to get stuck in archaic details. We have to approach Ficino's psychology of imagination with imagination if the substance of his vision is to come through. This attitude may jar one's historical and philosophical sensibilities, but if done carefully it should enhance rather than detract from these other legitimate approaches to the same materials.

The study of psychology remains elusive if it is not entered into psychologically. Ficino's writings are permeated with attention to soul, which is not surprising since he himself wished to be known as a "physician of the soul." But it is possible to look without seeing. Writings such as those we are about to examine often fall flat under the historian's nose and the philosopher's scalpel, and yet psychology by nature has a dimension of depth. We have to bring a psychological attitude to Ficino's words if we are to have any chance of perceiving his psychological insights. Therefore, we must unabashedly work with his images, relate his archaic and abstruse statements to modern life, and even occasionally treat his consciously conceived words as if they were the products of dream.

2

A World with Soul

Not in the entire living world is there to be found anything so deformed as that which does not have the gift of soul.

—*The Planets*, chapter 1

Soul is an elusive word. For many, soul is an invisible but finite essence, made of some spiritual substance, that keeps the body together and functioning in life and flies off to another dimension at death. In relation to the body, it is like a genie in a bottle. We read legendary stories of people selling their souls to the devil, and taking these tales at a rather literal level we might imagine the soul as a piece of merchandise. In Sunday school or elsewhere we may have been taught that the soul can be blackened, soiled, and spotted and that it can be laundered, made pure and white again. This soul is often the chief concern of religious practice, and even today Christian psychologists want to distinguish this metaphysically substantial soul from the merely psychological psyche.[1]

The soul Ficino places at the center of his professional and personal life is not this creature of folk religion. For him soul is a quality of existence, and the human soul is precisely that which makes one a human. Soul is a quality rather than a quantity. For that reason it is better to speak of soul rather than *a* soul. When we say that a person has soul, we usually mean that he shows evidence of internal movement. The vegetative soul of Aristotelian tradition is said to give the body movement, but the human soul in the Platonic tradition gives the *person* movement. People who clearly have soul show a certain depth, vitality, individuality, familiarity with pain and death, and good humor. Even objects can have soul, or so our colloquial speech has it. Books have soul when they are not excessively technical, abstract, and dry. Music has soul. Food has soul, and not only the food of a single culture.

40

The character of our soul is even written on our faces and
sculptured into our bodies.

Soul is also depth, a metaphor we use to point to a certain
intensity of experience. Having soul, we feel a reverberation and
resonance carrying through *beneath* the surface of everyday
experience. With soul, events are not merely two-dimensional;
they carry an invisible but clearly felt dimension of depth. These
resonances do not appear as meaning and explanation, nor even as
understanding—that would be height, the work of intellect. Soul
cannot be fabricated by evaluating experience, trying to figure it
out, or through intense introspection. The significance of soul is
clearly downward, away from the head, closer to the stomach
where the outside world is absorbed, internalized, and broken
down; toward the intestines where in an extensive labyrinthine
journey the introjected world becomes partly self, partly waste;
down toward the lower orifices where what is not made into self is
eliminated; down near the organs of sex where the pleasure,
relational, and sensation fluids are focused.

The depth of soul can also be seen in cosmic imagery. In Greek
mythology the natural world accessible to our senses is mirrored
by an underworld where there is no flesh or bone but only
phantasms or immaterial visages.[2] Here again are labyrinthine
passages leading to numerous chambers where strange happenings
reflect the world above. For the Greeks, depth was associated with
death. Demeter, the mother who gives the world its beauty and
fruitfulness, is inseparable from her daughter Persephone, who is
dragged into the underworld, to become the queen of death, the
personification of depth.[3] Soul, then, involves a dying to the
natural world, and indeed imagination is not unlike digestive
transformation. To live with soul requires a willingness to descend
into the depths of events, to let their literalness and our own literal
reactions die in favor of another perspective, to see the world as if
from below. Like Orpheus, we can sing of our exploits, having
become acquainted with the underworld through a descent.

A peculiar story of descent often told and interpreted is the
journey of the hero who traces the night journey of the sun from
West to East in the waters of the ocean, in the belly of a great fish.
Here the tomb seems much more like the womb and is experienced
as a state of confusion, uncertainty, darkness, regression,
immersion, and anxiety about future activity to follow the passive
containment of the fish. I once knew a young man who said he had
never heard of this story of the big fish, not even the biblical
account of Jonah and the whale. At the time, he was experiencing

a tenuous, brushing touch with the social world. He seemed on the verge of abandoning all attempts to deal with the pressures of the external world, especially the world of his family and the beatings and humiliations his father and brothers gave him regularly. He told me one day that he had had a strange dream. He had been swallowed by a large fish and was held in its stomach for a long while until he was able to cut his way out, whereupon he found himself on a beach in a strange country. This man's suffering urged him downward toward the waters below, toward the chaos that precedes creation,[4] the regressive return to a state prior to one's origins, far away from the natural world and deep in the geography of soul. Ficino's fantasy of Hermes, the *first* theologian, seems to have had a similar effect upon him. By starting over, in fantasy, he could create new syntheses and feel that he was always in touch with powerful, efficacious ideas.

Although pathology and suffering reveal soul starkly and piercingly,[5] it is also felt in the more ordinary resonance of daily events. For example, when one *gives attention* (one meaning of religion) to clear products of depth—to dreams, fantasies, wishes, moods, slips of tongue, and other nonrational expressions, or, of course, even to decisions, plans, explanations, and strivings—then, even in waking life, in the very heat of daily business, one can sense the reverberations. It is as if life on the surface had a resonating chamber, a musical underworld, like the hollow bowl of a lute or the tube under a chime. Then there is depth, felt subjectively and recognized by others. Depth of soul becomes a quality of character and personality.

But soul is more than a quality of human character. When an individual with imagination encounters the world, then the things around him have soul. What we usually call "external reality" is seen to have depth and transparency. Nothing is only what it appears to be. The human imagination is always at work, though often below the threshold of awareness, making metaphors of everything. Sometimes this play of imagination takes a rather simplistic form and borders on superstition. When I lived in Ireland I was impressed by this kind of imagination. A mountain in Tipperary has a ragged gouge in its ridge, and to the local people this is the "Devil's Bit," a sign that the devil had taken a bite out of the mountain and had spit a huge rock onto a low-lying plain. I was once walking down a narrow country road in Ulster when I noticed a circle of trees out in a field. I started to walk toward the ring of trees when an old man came up to me and advised that I stay away from this place where the fairies danced.

These examples are the stuff of legends and superstitions, and there is no doubt that these are not necessary for a soulful world. But this not so subtle work of imagination makes the point that phenomena easily explained scientifically and reductively by empirically minded persons can just as well have a more fantastic character, and through legendary fantasy even so obvious a natural form as a mountain ridge can bring alive human feelings and fears.

When Ernst Cassirer defines man as a "symbol-making animal," and when Norman O. Brown ends *Love's Body* with the laconic remark that "all is poetry," it is easy to give quick but superficial intellectual assent. But the implications of these insights are quite extensive. They imply that all day long, day after day, everything we do, see, and touch has more than a pragmatic significance. At the very moment that we make use of any object or talk to any person, they are being transformed into memory as metaphors. The friend I talk to at lunch appears at night in a dream, now not the friend but an image of an attitude or spirit within me.[6] In imagination, perception is never one-dimensional or at one level. Events always have deeper significance. Therefore, in our encounter with the world there can be no absolute separation between our imagination and the people and objects we meet existing in their own reality. Indeed, the layers of significance and the skeins of memory and fantasy at work in every activity build the depth I am calling soul. As James Hillman has written: "Phenomena come alive and carry soul through our imaginative fantasies about them. When we have no fantasy about the world, then it is objective, dead.... [Fantasy] is a way of being in the world and giving back soul to the world."[7]

Let us be clear about this word *fantasy*. Fantasy consists of the images and stories we have within us as we go about our daily affairs. For example, a teacher in a classroom may have the fantasy of being a father to the young people in front of him. Or, as sometimes appears to be the case, the teacher may enjoy the fantasy that he is a little dictator, or an orator, or an actor. The fantasy is the image, conscious or unconscious, lying beneath the behavior or permeating the action; and it is the fantasy that truly tells the expectations one has or explains the satisfactions or frustrations one feels in the performance of an action. Perceiving the fantasies at work in our lives we can draw closer to the depth and to the soul-dimension.

In the introductory chapters of *The Planets*, Ficino establishes a theoretical base for his astral magic and medicine, and there he suggests that all things have soul. Not only is there a human soul, he points out, there is also a soul of the world, vivifying the body of the world. He adds a warning: "Every body easily grasped by your senses, as if it were suited to your senses, is crass; for it falls far short of the divine soul" (Chap. 3). In other words, simply to grasp the things of the world at the level of sensation is to overlook their soul-dimension. Of course, it is possible to encounter the world body, material things, as if it did not have soul. It takes soul to perceive soul. It is fairly easy, for instance, to fell a redwood in order to build a house—a material action for a material end. But it takes fantasy and imagination to see the sacredness of the redwood, to appreciate its age, its vulnerability in a society hungry for building materials, and its natural beauty. When we allow fantasies to flow, the sacredness of common things again becomes evident. There is indeed a relationship between soul and religion, between psychology and religious awareness; for without soulful fantasy all is profane and secular, a world reduced to serve as fodder for our pragmatic intentions. With soul comes an intense sense of value, an ordering of desires, and a respect for common things because they have such impact upon the human spirit.

Soul as Mediator

If there were only these two in the world—intellect and body—but there were no soul, then the intellect would not be drawn to the body (for it is entirely immobile and is not supplied with a principle of movement, although it is far distant from the body), nor would the body be drawn to the intellect since it is just as incapable and ineffective in moving by itself and is far removed from the intellect. But if soul is interposed, conforming to both, there may be an easy attraction from one to the other. (Chap. 1)

It is common for people in general, and even psychology students, to understand "psychology" as the study of the mind. But neither in etymology nor in the history of philosophy and psychology can psyche be identified with mind. Ficino makes the distinction between the two clear at the outset of his book. Not only are they distinct, he says, but they may be quite distant from each other, though some connection between the two is essential. The intellect, for example, requires the soul in order to keep it in touch with body. Soul is "adapted" to both mind and body, like Janus—a favorite image used often by Ficino—soul faces both the world of intellect and the realm of matter.

If there were no soul, but only mind and body, says Ficino, there would be no connection between them. For example, without soul ideas would remain ideas with no connection to the human world. We all know people who are very clever working with words and ideas, who can trace the history of philosophy and compare whole systems of thought, but whose reasoning seems incomplete. There is no body in their thinking, no grounding. I do not mean that thought has to be related consciously to the practical world, but thinking can take place in an upper region that is far removed from what we know to be human. With soul, the severest speculation can have body and depth. It can be significant on some level other than the purely intellectual.

On the other hand, it is notoriously easy to live at the level of the body and be cut off from ideas. We can respond automatically to immediate or somewhat removed physical needs and set aside the requirements of mind and spirit. If the isolated mind is excessively conscious and rational, the severed body is characterized by unconsciousness. We can be very active caring for the body, exercising remarkable practical intelligence, without benefit of ideas or thoughts about what we are doing, what is behind our actions, or what our true values really are.

We do not have to look far to find a world without soul. It is all around us. On one hand we find gross materialism in economics, politics, values, and life-style. On the other we see vast educational systems for people of all ages and a large segment of the population involved in religious institutions. Yet the two spheres seem separate, joined only when one serves the limited purposes of the other. In universities the liberal arts, studies in explicit expressions of soul, are being squeezed out by swelling schools of business and technology. Young people go to college mainly for their bodies—to get a good job and enjoy the creature comforts (by which we mean body) accessible only through vocational training. A few individuals commit themselves to intellectual learning, most with the intention of teaching others like themselves.

It is clear that what is missing in all of this is the third mediating factor, soul. Even liberal studies—the arts and humanities—have the soul intellectualized out of them, so that a Shakespeare sonnet may be dissected in the work of historicism, linguistic criticism, or soulless symbol-analysis. One would think, or hope, that at least in our schools of higher learning attention might be given to the soul, but that is not the case. A student on a college campus is bifurcated into a mind crammed with information in a classroom and a body frantically served by the social life of the campus. An indication that a similar split has occurred in religious life is the tendency for psychology-minded clergymen to establish groups for sensitivity training and sensory awareness. In religion the spirit has reigned high and supreme and readily falls into its opposite—plain physical expressions of emotion. There is nothing wrong with either spiritual experience or sensory awareness, but when they are so far separated from each other, without benefit of the mediating consciousness of soul, then individuals and societies feel alienated and split. *Schizophrenia*, the psychopathological term characterizing this generation, has many meanings in popular conversation; one of them is the sense of being split, torn apart, cut off from something, God knows what, that would make sense of our confusion and strenuous activity. That something is soul, the connecting link between mind and body.

Soul, however, is not simply a linking factor, a way of bringing mind and body together. It unites spirit and matter in its own way. In adapting itself to both, in its Janus character, soul draws unique qualities from mind and from body, creating its own "style." Instead of abstract thought and unconscious actions, soul expresses itself in images, dreams, and stories. These have significance something like the intelligence of mind, and they have body similar to physical reality, but they are uniquely different. A dream is experienced much like waking life, yet it is clearly less substantial. It is as if the metaphorical layers of waking life had been stripped of their foundations in actuality and experienced in themselves. Stories sound like narratives of actual events, yet they may have no relation to any historical event at all. Dreams and stories have significance, but it is not clear and orderly.

Feelings, too, are part of soul, but feelings can be disconnected from fantasy, and then they seem to be nothing but body. It is easy enough in group therapy, for example, to stimulate intense emotion, and some feel that the upshot of such emotion is therapeutic. But "letting the feelings hang out" is not in itself a soulful activity; it may be achieved without insight, without relationship to the content of the emotion, and without a connection with ideas. It is noteworthy that many psychologists who advocate "emotional catharsis" also betray characteristic anti-intellectualism.

Yet emotion is an important factor in the life of the soul. As the word itself suggests, emotion moves: as Jung taught, emotion creates value and moves us to action, while it also can be identified as the movement of the soul itself.[8] Indeed, emotion and fantasy are like two sides of a coin. At times we may feel an emotion without having any idea what it is all about, while at other times we may have fantasies without feeling. Usually the two go together, as in memory or expectation when images of the past or the future bring with them emotions that are pleasant or very unpleasant. In any case, emotion with fantasy draws us into deep reflection and therefore toward soul. The arts can either move us so that we feel manipulated into fear, relief, or sympathy, or in a way that leads us deeper into reflection, providing us with further fantasy for our emotion. In a sense, emotion is like behavoir—one has to grasp the fantasy behind it in order to grasp it in its wholeness. Emotion stands out as a signal of the soul, but to perceive the nature of that signal one has to reflect upon the fantasies contained in it.

Soul also appears, of course, in relationships where we dramatize our fantasies. It seems that soul cannot escape the entanglements, the highs and lows of human intimacy, without betraying its very nature. Soul appears too in physical symptoms of disease and in body language and physical mannerism. The body can be seen as the expression of soul, since it is like sculptor's clay. The human body reveals subtle shifts in minute forms, telling the movements of the soul. A quiet woman once sat in a therapy group frequently stroking her throat softly with her fingers. One day the group took an imaginary journey into the body, and afterward she told how she tried to imagine herself in her stomach, but she couldn't get past her throat. She found herself there, trapped in that narrow passage which was filled with obstructions—broken glass, furniture, metal, and other sharp materials. She couldn't stay there long, even in fantasy, because her throat began to hurt. Discussing this fantasy later she talked about memories and wishes associated with her family, focused especially in an overwhelming sorrow that seemed stuck in her throat. She expressed the hope that some day she would be able to look at those sharp pieces one by one, cry them out of her throat, and finally open the passage to the rest of her body.

Psychology is the study of everything from the point of view of the psyche. That is its etymological meaning, and that is the traditional meaning espoused by Ficino and by his predecessors and followers. To see a sore throat simply as a physical manifestation is to look at the world, as Ficino says, as if it were suited only to our senses. We can also look from the viewpoint of soul—psychologically. Perhaps the trouble we have developing an effective discipline of psychology, to say nothing of nurturing a genuine psychological consciousness, is that soul is so simple and obvious. We are not yet attuned to the language of soul; we are not comfortable thinking metaphorically. We like to take the direct path saying that things are what they are, not realizing that things are not only what they are. We overlook the wealth of images all around us by seeing only physical containers of those images. In spite of exceedingly complex technology, we miss the obvious signs of soul: a physical complaint, an animal in a dream, a witch in a fairy tale, a god in mythology, a tear in laughter and sadness, the lead weight of a depression. There are the signs of soul waiting to be seen for what they are.

Mediation of the Spirit

The whole world is alive, and we may drink in its spirit. But this spirit is properly absorbed through the person's own spirit, either naturally attuned to the world spirit, or even better, rendered more suitable by art, that is, by becoming as celestial as possible. (Chap. 4)

With these words Ficino introduces another puzzling factor involved in the relationship between person and world—spirit. If soul is a difficult word to use, spirit is more so. We speak of spirit as a ghost, as the effusive quality of a confident football team, as a fluid flowing at a cocktail party, as the spirit (*Zeitgeist*) of an historical epoch, as that which moves us to action—"the spirit moved me." More important and more confusing, in the Platonic tradition and therefore in Ficino's writing, we equate spirit with the highest region of the threefold cosmos: body, soul, and spirit. But this spiritual realm is something different from the spirit Ficino alludes to in the passage quoted.

In Ficino's writing spirit is an element essential to all psychological life. It is the factor which accounts for the activity of soul in the material world. Without spirit you cannot have soul. Just as soul is the link between mind and body, spirit is the medium between soul and the world. As D. P. Walker, the distinguished Renaissance historian, has noted, Ficino's basic notion of spirit is that of the early physicians who conceived of it as a subtle substance in the blood. He writes, quoting Ficino directly:

Spirit by the physicians is defined as a certain vapor of the blood, pure, subtle, hot and lucid. And, formed from the subtler blood by the heat of the heart, it flies to the brain, and there the soul assiduously employs it for the exercise of both the interior and exterior senses. Thus, the blood serves the spirit, the spirit the senses, and finally the senses reason.[9]

Spirit is like a subtle, invisible vapor, therefore not unlike the spirit bubbling out of a glass of champagne or bubbling over in a football team. It can't be seen, but it can readily be felt. In *The Planets* Ficino tries to find a place for it:

It is a very subtle body, almost not a body, indeed it is almost soul. Or, it is almost not soul, as it were, a body. In its power it is less of an earth nature and more like water, or air, or most of all the fire of the stars. (Chap.3)

Spirit can be perceived by the senses, but it is not something physical. For that reason, it is not taken too seriously in the modern world. We consign all those interested in distinguishing spirit to the circles of esoteric religion. Yet for Ficino spirit is an ordinary phenomenon essential to all life. If one were to assign to it one of the basic constitutive elements of physical and psychological existence, it would definitely not be earth, more like water or air, but most like fire, the fire that constitutes the stars.

It is curious that Jung mentions in his autobiography his attempts to understand spirit when he was young. "Spirit, of course, meant for me something ineffable, but at bottom I did not regard it as essentially different from very rarified air."[10] We may get the idea that spirit is like air from common language as well. We say that a person has an "air" of authority, and we talk about the atmosphere of a place or surrounding an event. This is very much in the "spirit" of spirit.

Spirit can be felt as an emanation, a subtle "substance" that emerges from bodies and situations. A walk deep into the woods conveys a spirit different from the kind generated by a walk down the main street of a large city. A horror film has a spirit quite different from a Peter Sellers comedy. A flower emanates a spirit different from that of an automobile engine.

This may all seem obvious and unimportant; yet Ficino builds his entire psychotherapeutic system on this notion of spirit. He believed that soul needs spirit, in all its variety, in order to thrive; therefore, psychological care and exercise involved for him thoughtful exposure to various types of spirit. In order to do this, of course, one would have to be able to discern the varieties of spirit, and then make a conscious effort to expose oneself to the right kinds. Although there are innumerable kinds of spirit, they may be ordered around the fundamental characters of the planets. As Ficino expresses it, the planets issue forth "rays" of spirit peculiar to each of them, and these rays are absorbed by objects in the world, either natural objects or man-made artifacts. Every single thing with which we come in contact, then, exposes us to one or another planetary influence. We absorb and take on the spirit of that planet, as we go about ordinary living, perhaps unconscious of the varieties of spirit.

Ficino refers to spirit as the food of the soul; through spirit, soul is continuously being created and nourished. As he says, this all may happen naturally (unconsciously), or by art, that is, by conscious intention. This is not to say that we can simply fashion our psychological life at will; the process is more indirect than that, but we can develop an awareness of soul, a psychological attitude, by which we can cooperate and indirectly influence the character of our psychological life. We can nourish the soul and live psychotherapeutically by having our psychological life reflect the heavens. That is what Ficino means by becoming as celestial as possible. We can have depth and variety, movement and form, in our inner world. We can have planets within, with all of their benefits of spirit, like the planets of the outer cosmos.

We arrive here at the crux of Ficinian astrological psychology. This is no superstitious playing with birth charts and sun signs, though even these have a place in Ficino's practice. More importantly, through an astrological consciousness we may recognize the polycentric nature of the psyche and become aware of the impact of even minor objects and events on the spiritual life of the soul. The planets, signs, houses, and aspects of technical astrology are only a means for imagining the multiple facets of the psyche. Applying Ficino's insights to modern life, these technical aspects may or may not be used. One may turn to art, to dreams, to alchemy, to religion, or to psychology itself for paradigms of the soul and the imaginative discernment of spirits. The essential point is to make connections bween everyday experience and the deeper life of the soul.

In order to make these connections, it is necessary to cultivate that neglected but essential faculty—imagination. Imagination allows of a vision that penetrates the surface of things and grasps those factors that have significance for the psyche. In imagination events appear not only in their particularity or at the level of idea and concept; they are also seen to contain certain images of importance to the soul. Ficino recognized the importance of what we call imagination, but in his theory of knowledge he uses different terms to describe this faculty.

Idolum: The Idol of Perception

We have to sort out some confusing terms Ficino employs in placing imagination in context. He does speak of *imaginatio*, but that Latin word does not mean the same as the English imagination. *Imaginatio* in Ficino's scheme is more like the Aristotelian *sensus communis*, the faculty of perception that unites all the disparate sense impressions into one. Ficino's word for imagination is *idolum*, a term used by Plotinus. In the writings of the Church Fathers *idolum* has the pejorative meaning of "idol" and is related to our world *idolatry*. The Greek root is *eidos*, Plato's "idea," which literally means an image or likeness, or an image reflected in water or in a mirror (OED, "idol"). It is essential to keep this notion of image in mind which examining Ficino's idea of imagination.

Ficino divides the functions of the soul in the following manner:

Mens	Mind
Ratio	Reason
Idolum	Fantasy Sense Perception Nutritive Power

Mens is the highest part of the soul, given to Saturnian contemplation. Reason, in the middle, gives soul its human aspect; in spite of all the nonrational factors of soul we will investigate, rational consciousness is still the hallmark of humanity. Consciousness and self-awareness make connections between the realm of ideas and the sphere of physical experience; so Ficino claims that Reason can move between Mind and Body. Lowest in the hierarchy, *idolum* nevertheless is given the power to animate the body; for, in the end, it is the image that stimulates a physical response. Indeed, Ficino calls *idolum* itself the image of the rational soul, a reflection of our conscious reasoning powers, which can entertain and make judgments, says Ficino, about images, even if they are not embedded in concrete objects. Fantasy, an aspect of *idolum*, holds a kind of conception called "intention", which can be stored in the memory. Ficino observes that "the fantasy is full of the individual forms of things."[11] Imagination—*idolum* and fantasy—therefore has its own reasons and logic; it contains the seeds of experience which are planted in external experience and impressions.

If we remember the "idol" in Ficino's *idolum* and the "image" in imagination we will have the important kernel of this epistemology: images play a central role in our contact with the world, and the idea that when we encounter something outside ourselves we are passive or receptive is contested by Ficino. In every event we bring a storehouse of images which are activated by external objects. The outside world works on our memory, and memory colors the manner in which we perceive the world; it contains the seeds, the seminal fantasies by which we enter a fully human experience. It would be a mistake, then, to think that we as subjects encounter a dead world as object; rather, there is a mutually efficacious dialogue between memory and fact. The seeds of imagination transform a measurable event into a subjective experience, which results in a certain cultivation of the world but also in a nourishing or depriving impact on psyche.

As if to accent the fact that imagination is a world unto itself, that it is different from the dimension of ego and objects, Ficino retains the ancient idea of an astral or ethereal body. The soul has its own vehicle more subtle than the crass physical body. Round in its natural shape, it takes human shape in the individual, and finally it returns to its source, round. Once again the imagery of circles and roundness suggest that imagination is somehow trans-human, its seeds not restricted to human experience and certainly not to the life of the individual. It has its own body not dependent upon the life of the human body.

Most psychologies reduce imagery to personalistic dimensions, suggesting for example, that the work of an artist may be traced directly to his childhood experience or to a later trauma. Such a reductive view is alluring because it seems to make sense that in our "impressionable years," as the cliché goes, we gather the seeds for later life. But Ficino's consistent and puzzling references to a circular soul-movement or the roundness of the ethereal body remind us that the life of soul is not entirely dependent upon personal experience; it is not all contained within our skin. We not only have "collective memories," we also experience certain patterns that shape all of life. When we crave for dependence like a child, find ourselves using language of childhood and having thoughts of mother and home, or maybe even dream of children, we may see here not simply the return of a concrete memory, but the presence of a deep, recurring pattern, *imaged* well as childlikeness, but not necessarily related to the personal experience of childhood. Such a pattern might be found in everyone, in animals, and even in other parts of nature. The fantasy of child in this case has an existence removed from personal experience.

The soul is not simply an epiphenomenon of the body; it has its own laws and habits, and the images we behold in fantasy reflect this life of soul, not human life as it is embodied. Ficino says as much in rather obscure imagery: "As the light of the moon in a cloud produces paleness out of itself, so the soul produces in the celestial body the *idolum*, as a comet produces its tail."[12] Images in our mind's eye radiate like moonbeams or a comet's tail from the activity of the soul. To glimpse the images is to catch sight of the soul, whose movements are connected to but distinct from the experiences of the ego. We might say that as our deeds reveal the character of ego, imagination and its images tell the nature of the soul.

Therefore, the soul in Ficino's thought has three vehicles: body, spirit, and imagination (*idolum*).[13] Each of these carries the movements of the soul, in each we can find the soul's activities. There is psychological significance, therefore, in the spirit we feel and sense in ordinary life, in the human body and the material world, and in the products and processes of imagination. These are vehicles of the psyche, although we tend to overlook this fact. It is easy enough to reduce imagination to aesthetics, body and matter to "objective reality," and spirit to occasionally interesting but essentially esoteric beliefs.

Since imagination is such an important faculty of the soul, Ficino keeps it in mind even in his "natural magic," which consists chiefly in drawing down the spiritual rays of the planets through image-making. An image associated with one of the planets, say a solar amulet, has the power, says Ficino, to transmit to the individual using it the spiritual power of that planet. We will discuss this further on; here notice the role of imagination. By *keeping in mind* the characters of the various planets, knowing especially the spheres of life they "rule," and the images associated with them, we may organize life imaginatively. We may see deeper fantasies permeating experience and therefore glimpse the life of the soul more directly. Basically, what Ficino proposes as a technique of psychotherapy is an astrological art of memory.[14]

We have seen that imagination and memory are inseparable, that images in memory play an active role in perception and in the apprehension of significance and meaning. For Ficino memory has at least two functions: first, the individual is educated to employ practical means for remembering fundamental images. Amulets, charms, paintings, poems, ceremonies—all of these serve to remind the individual about basic structures of life. Secondly, memory may be less personal and more collective. By recalling the nature of the gods and goddesses, for example, we keep in mind those profound spheres of significance. On one hand, memory is an imagistic mnemonic device, on the other it is a means of making connections between discrete events and larger patterns. As Frances Yates has explained in her study of the Renaissance art of memory, this art may have begun as a mnemonic technique useful in oratory, but it became something much more profound. Perhaps it would be helpful to recall the nature of this art as we study Ficino's astrology, which may be seen not as a simplistic naive belief in planetary influence, but as a technique of enlivening imagination and memory. The signs and planets of astrology provide a means for ordering experience and inner movement, just as any system of imagery might help us see through surface events to their fantasies. In Ficino's own words: "the soul, when stimulated by images of bodies, brings to light forms that are lurking in the recesses of the mind."[15]

It is not surprising, then, that Ficino would have had a remarkable influence upon the art of his time. Although he was not known himself as an immediate admirer or sponsor of art works, his ideas placed art at the center of life rather than at the periphery. In his philosophy art would not appear as entertainment or aestheticism; it was a means for nourishing the soul, an art of memory. In the spirit of "art for art's sake" we may validly criticize those forms of art still practiced today where art serves as propaganda or for ideological expression, but we may also place art outside the concerns of true quality in life. Following Ficino's premises, we may say that art serves a significant psychological purpose: it literally feeds the soul, keeps its archetypal memory supplied, and ultimately serves to order life at the psychological level.

Of course, if we approach art or other symbol systems with a superficial eye, with an eye "suited to the senses," then what we will see has no relation to soul. It takes soul to perceive the psychological. After advising his clients how to make the proper images, Ficino adds an important warning: "Do not merely look, but reflect in the soul" (Chap. 19).

Self-recognition

While imagination is the *sine qua non* of psychological living, a second step consists in imaginative awareness of oneself. We are not all alike, and at different times in personal history one factor or another may be predominant. In Ficino's regimen for healthy living, a person has to know who and what he is so as to know what particular things to avoid and what to pursue. In *The Planets* he writes:

> Whoever discovers his own genius through the means we have stated will thus find his own natural work, and at the same time he will find his own star and daimon. Following these beginnings he will do well and live happily. Otherwise, he will experience misfortune and feel the enmity of heaven. (Chap. 23)

Notice that he is not suggesting that we ought to begin with our own ego-desires and tendencies or the direction indicated by personal history. Self-knowledge begins with discovery of one's own "star" and "daimon." The soul's work (*opus*) does not take off from an ego self-concept but from a recognition of an inner spirit, guide, or daimon. Psychological movement is a response, not an initiative.

Heraclitus, the original depth psychologist, had professed: "Man's character is his daimon." This is not to say that "daimon" is simply a fanciful, imaginative name for character.[16] Rather, one's character is determined, at least in part, by some non-ego factor in the self. It is impossible to define the nature of this daimon—one might investigate the claims of Plato's Socrates, Plutarch, Goethe, Rilke, Yeats, and many others who have claimed their relationship to an inner vital fantasy. But one can recognize an inner as well as an outer necessity, felt not only as fate but also as in some sense a personal force. This daimon is often associated with the persons who visit us in dreams—personifications of psychological reality irreducible to impersonal concepts or definitions. For Plutarch the daimon is like a star floating above earth, connected to the soul.[17] The daimon resides in the head, the locus for the later Roman version of daimon—genius.[18]

If daimon is related to demon, it could be that the daimon, like Satan, is an adversary to the ego. When the daimon seems to bless the life of ego, he appears as an angel; when he takes the role of adversary, he is the devil. In either case, Ficino advises us to discover the peculiar nature of our daimon. Daimon in ancient

Greece was sometimes called god, but the daimon was a nameless god. Therefore, the daimon may be our own, perhaps like the guardian angel of Christian lore. The daimon is a guiding spirit, whether friend or adversary, who calls for a response. To know oneself, it is not sufficient to know one's personal history and character; one must also be able to recognize this daimonic factor.

One's own daimon may be sensed, like that of Socrates, as an inner voice, or it may be less definite: an urge, a longing, a deep wish, a persistent fear, a recurring dream theme or image, perhaps a daimon of accident or trickery like Kerenyi's Hermes who caused him to find abandoned books, take the incorrect but fortunate road, train, and so on.

The daimon need not be nameless; indeed, one's daimon, in Ficino's analysis, might be represented as one of the planetary archons, and here is where astrology assists imagination. If a horoscope is not seen as a literal guide to behavior or a supernatural portrait of the personality, then it may be taken as a symbol system heuristically drawing us into reflection upon identity and fate. In this latter case, the natal chart brings forward certain planets for particular attention: by zodiacal position, rulership, or aspect. Today when people ask about each other's sun sign, could there not be a sense that one indeed does have a daimon, that there is an inner necessity to which one is responsible? A significant psychological advantage to the birth chart is the ritual sense of establishing one's uniqueness in a cosmic setting. Going to the trouble of finding latitudes and exact times, getting in touch with relatives, checking with histories of daylight saving time and war time—all of these activities have psychological impact, refining a sense of uniqueness that is not simply egoistic, although it could obviously be shaped that way. But once again we run into that parallel and paradox of the macrocosm and microcosm. When a person places his birth in relation to the planets out there, could be not also be establishing a connection with the planets within and with that vast universe of the interior life?

Clearly, the astrological system is not an essential or necessary way for discovering one's genius, but it serves as a good model or metaphor. One might accomplish the same goal by paying close attention to the figures appearing in dreams and to the nonrational components of everyday life. The daimon may betray his appearance in fascinations and projections, or possibly in fears.

To discover one's daimon and genius is also to find one's weakness, the vulnerable spot of the soul; for a generally recognized characteristic of a god or daimon is jealousy. Although a god may represent the vital center of a definite sphere of life, like Venus and her sensuality, the god may also wrap its arms around the devotee and keep him from other possibilities, other deities. This is what Ficino knew to be sickness, true sickness of the soul: to be under the domination of one planetary daimon, caught in the embrace of a single jealous deity.

In Euripides' *Bacchae*, Pentheus, the conservative, controlling, repressive king, is offered a release from his deadening character through Dionysos, the god who loosens and dismembers. But Pentheus swings from his former kingly, domineering role toward identification with Dionysos. He is finally and completely undone in his new allegiance to an attractive but terrifying deity. And in Peter Shaffer's ritualistic drama *Equus*, the young man, Alan Strang, has been freed from the domination of his parents by the god Equus, only to be engulfed by that same deity whose jealousy will not allow a passing sexual liaison between Alan and a sympathetic stable girl. The gods are jealous, each ready to assume a monotheistic hold on the individual.

Therefore, one's daimon might appear in one's weakness and vulnerability, at the tender place of fear and concern. But of course that is the gift of woundedness: to discover one's genius, one has to be receptive and attentive to one's vulnerabilities and in them find ultimate strength. Obviously, this psychology is very different from those which advocate ego-strength. A truly strong ego is an imaginative one that does not have to be occupied with defending itself but can search out its genius, make contact and cooperate with the multiple possibilities the daimons represent and provide.

Constellation

In Ficino's psychology illness comes in the form of monotheism,[19] life dominated by one god, imagination fixed in a single kind of consciousness. Such a domination could appear as an inclination toward depression (Saturn), a constant preoccupation with relationship and sexuality (Venus), or an abiding and interfering temper or aggressiveness (Mars). Ficino's advice is twofold: find a way to offset the tendency by inviting an opposite kind of spirit; and, at the same time, experience the powerful daimon to the hilt. For Ficino himself, the daimon that plagued him was Saturn, as prominent in his horoscope as in life.[20]

Ficino followed his own advice, taking practical precautions against increased Saturnian spirit, while at the same time entering deeply into Saturn's heaviness.

The first tactic may sound like compensation, ego-manipulation and defensiveness. But Ficino's intention is to maintain variety of spirit without getting rid of the dominant one. The quality of soul created by multiplicity is the important element: avoiding single-mindedness with its static and rigid character. In his books on health Ficino frequently advises people to watch out for the dangers of Saturn, suggesting, for example, a turn to Jupiter to assuage the desiccating assaults of Saturn. He particularly advised scholars, whose work is largely Saturnian, to find concrete ways of drawing other kinds of spirit into their lives. He alludes to the practice of Pythagoreans, who engaged in this kind of psychological effort: "The Pythagoreans, who feared the tyranny of Saturn because of their zealous study of philosophy, dressed in white clothes and daily used songs that were Jovial and Phoebean."[21]

Another factor that distinguishes constellation from compensation is the indirect nature of the former. Compensation is an ego activity, an attempt to find harmony and balance. Constellation is a more imaginative act aimed at making a cosmos of variety and multiplicity in one's psychological environment. As anybody who has ever been depressed knows, you cannot simply "put on a happy face" and feel free of Saturn, and certainly you cannot gain the benefits of depression that way. The purpose of constellation is to provide other spiritual nourishment; to constellate is to make a "starry sky" of one's consciousness. It requires a psychological awareness in the sense of knowing the many facets of the soul, recognizing in everyday objects and activities their characteristic spirits, then providing oneself psychologically with a cornucopia of possibilities. It all demands imagination and attention to a level of the ordinary that is psychological rather than pragmatic. As a result, to the psychologically attuned, individual activities and things having little or no practical worth might become quite important. A trip to the zoo, an hour in the garden, even a moist Venusian movie might well serve the soul, even though it may interfere with pressing practical concerns.

Cultivation

While constellation refers to an inner patterning, the provision of various kinds of spirit for the vitality of psychological life, it implies a corresponding "cultivation" of the environment. Ficino's therapeutic advice constitutes an "ecology of the soul," the creation of an environment designed for the soul, an arrangement of external life to correspond to the soul's requirements. An outstanding factor in Ficino's system is his awareness of the psychological values inherent in the material world. Matter is spiritual to him insofar as various material objects are capable of providing as many different kinds of spirit, and that variety nourishes the soul. For example, concerning spirit he writes:

> Every spirit, since it is naturally rather fiery, and light and volatile like air, is also like light, and therefore similar to colors and vocal airs and odors and movements of the soul. For that reason spirit can be moved quickly and formed through these things. (Chap. 11)

These phrases sound like sympathetic magic, treating like with like. But there is something more than magic at work here, or at least a very natural kind of magic.

Since spirit is so subtle, he seems to be saying, like fire, light, air, odor, song, then those things in the environment that have such subtle properties and significance are important sources of spirit.

From the way we design our cities to the choice of the clothes we wear, we are creating an environment with a particular kind of spirit. Clothes, for example, not only reflect something of the nature of the soul, they also nourish it with a particular kind of spirit. When our cities are planned for optimum functioning and cost efficiency but with little regard for soul qualities, then psyche suffers. In architecture nonfunctional space and impractical niches and vaults may well serve the soul and therefore, at least at the psychological level, be of true "functional" importance. Decoration is also significant to the soul—the columns and statuary of medieval cathedrals, and the colors and shapes imprinting such idiosyncratic character on the buildings of that highly spiritual architect and city builder, Paolo Soleri.

In contrast, a few years ago I toured the headquarters of a major financial institution located in a suburb outside Chicago. The place seemed designed with great effort to exclude spiritual multiplicity. Outside and inside were white—walls, ceilings, corridors. By order of the president of the company, I was told, there was not one painting, sculpture, photograph, or plant to be seen. It was a place with one whitewashed spirit, built and un-ornamented for the computers and automated, programmed workers. There was no soul because there was no color, no curves, nothing to disturb the single spirit of sterility.

The soul feeds on images because images are the source of spirit. The varieties of spirit are as many as the varieties of images, though images can be grouped thematically as can the kinds of spirit. Certain images and certain spiritual characters seem especially important for the life of the soul. In one of the later chapters of *The Planets*, Ficino describes quite carefully the most important image a person ought to have close at hand, preferably in his home. This is an image of the universe, perhaps an astrological portrait of the zodiac or horoscope. Ficino tells when to begin work on such an image and which colors to use. Finally, he notes that a person blessed with such an image will go out into the world aware of the presence of the planetary daimons behind everyday events. He concludes this description with a remarkable comment: "The makers of images may see these things."

Makers of images can see through the otherwise opaque shell of the sensible world. But who are the image-makers? Artists and architects, musicians and sculptors? Yes, these are the image-makers important for the soul of a society, artisans whose spiritual significance was once recognized so that they were associated with churches and pastors of the soul. But insofar as each one of us has the capacity to imagine and to entertain fantasies, we too are image-makers. We can also ornament our bodies and our homes and cities in a way that nourishes soul. It is sometimes said that we make the universe into a cosmos when we give it order. But *cosmos* also means "ornament," and it is also by ornamenting our inner and outer lives that we make a cosmos, a domain for psychological living. Insofar as we neglect imagination and images in our environment, to that extent we suffer neglect of soul and expose ourselves to psychological trouble.

What Ficino describes, then, is a circle of spirit. Our concern for soul and spirit reaches into the material world where we make our images, and these images in turn nourish the spirit that made them. Ernst Cassirer, the noted historian of Renaissance philosophy, noticed this circle. He first quotes Ficino:

"It is also characteristic of our soul that it is concerned not only for its own body but for the bodies of all earthly things and for the earth itself, to cultivate them and further them."

Then Cassirer comments:

This cultivation, this "culture" of the sensible world constitutes

a basic moment and a basic task of the spirit. . . . The spirit
descends to the sensible and corporeal through love, and love
raises it again out of this realm.[22]

Even in our ubiquitous spirit of functionalism and pragmatism,
and in our concern for profit and commerce, the culture we build
is also a house of images, the visage and efficacious channel of
spirit. The question is, is this spirit we produce or evoke, consciously or unconsciously, vital food for the soul or a bland, mal-
nourishing diet? Does it mirror and affect the soul in a supporting
way, or is it an image and source of sickness?

I asked a group of university students to take a close look at
their campus and its buildings, inside and outside, and report on
what they found. Which deity did they suspect was presiding over
the consciousness of the architects and designers? Recall Ficino's
dictum that the god is a facet of the soul. They went out and saw
Greek and Georgian buildings, indicating devotion to an idealized
past. They saw an administration conceived along a rigid pyramid
form. They saw many compartments: colleges, schools, divisions,
departments. They saw classrooms—colorless, pictureless, desks
uncomfortable, hard, arranged in rows; they saw teachers
standing at the heads of classrooms dispensing information, testing
and grading. They saw much analysis at a distance, little concrete
involvement in matters discussed. They saw buildings of stone and
a campus divided by cement into geometrical forms. All these
clues pointed to one god, Saturn.

When a whole society or a subsociety like the university
establishment is dominated by a single structure of consciousness,
in this case Saturn, the cold, heavy, distant deity, then all of this
outward form seems natural, the only way it can be done. But
consider a college campus informed by the spirit of Venus or
Aphrodite. I am not saying it would be better for learning, but it
would definitely be different. There would be no dry lectures or
dry books coming from this moist goddess. Growth in new ideas,
new forms, new styles would be prominent. Relationship, sensuality, concern for beauty and comfort, gracefulness, care for the
body and for emotions—these would be both the benefits and the
problems of this kind of dominance.

Thus we learn from a Neoplatonist of the fifteenth century the
importance of a material world perceived and shaped for the good
of the soul. His suggestions for psychotherapy are broad and
embracing, including a reintegration of an aesthetic sense into the
main concerns of human life. Furthermore, his astrological

imagery offers a unique way of developing a religious sensibility, a way of imagining the gods deeply immanent in every facet and turn of experience. Thales, the early Ionian philosopher, had proclaimed: "The whole world is full of gods." Ficino's psychology echoes this claim and centers even the gods around the needs and characteristics of soul. He presents a curious psychological theology and a theological psychology.

The English words *health* and *wealth* come from the same root. For Ficino, psychological health is being achieved when the soul is enjoying the wealth of spirit offered by the many gods. The soul is wealthy when it reflects in its innermost structure the night sky with its slow, steady, variegated, rhythmic dance of planets. Individual and social culture has a psychological dimension; it is an ecology of soul. We will now turn our attention to processes in that ecology—the dynamic of eliciting and maintaining psychological life through procedures of psychological alchemy.

3

"Dissolve and Congeal":
Psychological Alchemy

In one of his last writings C. G. Jung related a recurring dream he had had years before.[1] In this series of dreams he was always discovering a part of his house he had never seen. Frequently it was an annex or a wing, old and unfamiliar, containing a laboratory and antique furniture. In one of the last of these dreams he found an old library with books full of symbolic pictures. About the time of this dream he bought an old text from a book dealer, a volume dealing with early Byzantine alchemy. The pictures in this sixteenth century book reminded Jung of the illustrations he had seen in his dream, and so, excited by this correspondence, he began to study alchemy in ernest. Several books of his own followed upon this unusual discovery—*Psychology and Alchemy, The Psychology of the Transference, Mysterium Coniunctionis,* and others—in which he offered a key for opening some of the mysteries of this ancient ritualistic, mythical, and visionary art.

In spite of Jung's efforts to suggest a way toward understanding this strange practice, alchemy remains dense and difficult. Some still see it as a mere rudimentary form of chemistry, the work of adventurous but primitive minds ignorant of the laws of chemistry and forced to express in archaic symbolic pictures and phrases their insights into the workings of metals and minerals. But Jung saw in alchemy a principle evident in many sectors of human life, in astrology as well as in human relationships: faced with the unknown, human imagination gets busy, finding in the dark surface of the mysterious, reflections of its own enigmas. So it is that one's soul can be moved to paranoid fear or fascinated interest at the sight of a stranger in a passing automobile, and the dim night sky can give rise to fantasies of flying saucers or a zodiac of animals and planetary deities. So too for minds uncontaminated by the knowledge of atoms and protons, the colors, smells, tastes, and visible transformations of chemicals heated and fermented stir the imagination. The imagery of alchemy is, in Jung's view, a portrait of the soul doing the imagining.

63

If we accept Jung's hypothesis—and there is plenty of evidence in the alchemical writings themselves to support it—then we may turn to alchemical literature for psychological insight. This was Jung's purpose in translating and puzzling over difficult passages for years, and he claims that for many alchemists themselves the spiritual or psychological values were most important:

> For many alchemists the allegorical aspect undoubtedly occupied the foreground to such an extent that they were firmly convinced that their sole concern was with chemical substances. But there were always a few for whom laboratory work was primarily a matter of symbols and their psychic effect. As the texts show, they were quite conscious of this, to the point of condemning the naive gold-makers as liars, frauds, and dupes.[2]

It is a general psychological fact that work of the soul can take place, even with such extensive system and tradition, with or without self-awareness.

Alchemy is not, however, simply another, albeit unusual, source for knowledge about the psyche; it has its own unique perspectives and problems, and it illuminates a specific dimension of psychological life. Many symbolic systems speak about the soul, but they do not all deal with the same issues.

Although in *The Planets* Ficino refers to alchemy rarely, the nature of his concerns, especially relationships between body, soul, and intellect, connects closely with the aims of alchemy. One of the major objectives of the alchemists was to overcome the illusion that the entire world is nothing but a complicated mixture of solid matter. They wished to achieve a steady consciousness of the distinction between mind, soul, and body. As one alchemist, Michael Meier, put it: masters of this art want to change the square into the triangle; which is to say, their work aims at transforming the four elements of material nature—earth, air, fire, and water—into the three elements of human existence.[3] From the alchemical point of view, psychological life begins with the separation, not the mere distinguishing, of body, soul, and spirit.

Two Faces of the Soul

Unlike that which is concerned either with things divine or with things of this life, soul is moved by an affection for both. (Chap. 1)

Often when psychologically attuned writers point out that we live in a world where soul is largely missing, they imply more than mere absence. Soul may not only be missing, it may be lost or stuck somewhere. In many traditions throughout the world it is believed that the soul can wander and get lost; it can take a vacation (*vacatio*) from the body and never come back. Or the soul can become too much embedded in a world of dense materialism. Soul, a quality of existence, can disappear then in the ethereal heights of spirit or in the gripping, blinding, overwhelming attractions of the body and its world. Jung was quite impressed by traditional societies who feared loss of soul, while he recognized the same danger in modern industrial life. Thus he entitled one of his popular books *Modern Man in Search of a Soul*. Ficino noticed that the soul's affection for the body is like the love of a mother for her child or like the pull of gravity on a stone tossed into the air.[4] Both Ficino and Jung speak of an "affection" of the soul for body and for spirit. "Since the soul animates the body," Jung observed, "just as the soul is animated by the spirit, she tends to favor the body and everything bodily, sensuous, and emotional. . . . She must be called back by the counsel of the spirit from her lostness in matter and in the world."[5] Here Jung is commenting on the views of a sixteenth-century alchemist, Gerard Dorn.

One of the tasks of alchemy, therefore, is consistent with a prime concern of Ficino in his work on health: keep soul in the middle. Do not let it disappear in mind or in body. When soul is lost in either of these extremes, gone too are the benefits it brings to experience. When soul is absent, gone are internal values, a sense of significance, and a sense of self. Physical and intellectual labor proceed without vitality, enthusiasm, feeling, and a sense of inherent purpose. Without soul, relationship and connectedness with people suffers. Nations, cities, families, and marriages retain the appearance of cohesiveness, but without soul genuine involvement is missing. Of course, on the other hand gone too are the problems soul brings: emotional entanglements, hurt feelings, depressions and suspicious exhilarations, pain and longing. Without soul we walk through the busy, crowded areas of daily living like "the dangling man" or like "the stranger" who sees it all as if it were happening behind the glass panels of a museum. Physically present, even analytically active in mind, psychologically he is cut off, distant, uninvolved, unmoved.

In Ficinian psychology, as we have seen, spirit is the subtle substance connecting soul with the inner and outer cosmos. In the presence of soul, spiritual substance is picked up, amplified, and received. An example is music. Music can be received as an intellectual achievement, or it may be received at the sensory level—the more decibels the better. Or, finally, the spiritual evanescence of a piece of music can be caught with the antennae of soul, in which case the decibels and intellectual cleverness may fit into a pattern that makes sense of it all. People with soul betray the coming and going of spirit. A person with soul has presence and is free of ego rigidity and protectiveness; he is not problem-free, but he can give soul room to play in pain or pleasure. It is interesting to compare spiritual masters who are lost in the ethereal regions with those for whom spiritual discipline has been a nourishment of soul. Intellectuals need not seem isolated in the cold corridors of their ivory towers either. With soul the house of intellect breathes with vitality and communicability.

Soul can get lost in psychotherapy as well. Those weekly trips to the analyst ought to be founded on a true care for the psyche, but too frequently such "psychological attention" amounts to nothing more than mind-play—the fun of figuring out why life is so difficult. Soulless, intellectual therapy can go on forever because two people will never run out of reasons for problematic behavior and feelings. But the client, if not the professional, should know that all the reasons in the world make no difference. Nothing happens. Worse, psychotherapy of this kind, concerned more with intellectual insight and the application of that insight to life (no mediating soul) might well cure a person right out of the very movements of soul that promise psychological existence.

We have already discussed the way in which soul can be neglected and forfeited in psychotherapy that is primarily sensational—in every sense of the world. The outpouring of feelings is attractive to soul because the soul has an affection for the body. It may be satisfying, but that is not to say that it is genuinely psychological.

All of this confusion stems from an alchemical problem: keeping soul separated from body and spirit (mind). To keep them mindful of the issue, the alchemists had an interesting motto: *"Solve et Coagula."* Dissolve and congeal! It is an alchemical concern both to rescue soul from flight into spirit, and to draw soul out of the confines of materialism. Alchemy moves in two directions: it spiritualizes what is otherwise dense and literal, and it concretizes that which is excessively intellectual or spiritual. It speaks to both affections of the soul. Another alchemist, Arnold de Villa Nova, underscores this dual perspective and purpose, though he stresses, as did Ficino, the special importance of dissolving physical and literal encrustations of the soul:

> Unless the bodies become incorporeal, and the spirits corporeal, no progress will be made. The true beginning then of our work is the solution of our body, because bodies, when dissolved become spiritual in their nature, and are yet at the same time more fixed than the spirit, though they are dissolved with it. For the solution of the body means the coagulation of the spirit and vice versa; each gives up something of its own nature; they meet each other half way, and thus become one inseparable substance, like water mixed with water.[6]

This passage is worth closer study, since it expresses precisely the middle region of psychological reality. Alchemical work begins, Villa Nova says, with the solution of our body. Body in this context can mean many things: attention exclusively to physical and materialistic concerns, a tendency toward literalism in our understanding of events, or excessive involvement with ego defenses and projects. As Freud pointed out, ego is an extension of the body, an unnecessarily limited sense of identity based on a body fantasy. The first task toward a psychological attitude, toward the recovery of soul, is to dissolve these extreme literalisms.

Arnold assures us that when these materialistic concerns are dissolved and become more spiritual, they will not lose all body. Alchemical *solutio* does not have to involve Heraclitean enantiodromia—a rush into an opposite problematic. In *solutio* each gives up some of its nature. Spirit takes on body, body assumes some spirit. Lofty ideas lose their abstraction and distance and appear psychologically as fantasies, wishes, wonderings. Actions and projects take a rest in *solutio* and out of them pour the same psychological issues.

In the language of elements, airy ideas and earthy projects melt into watery fantasies. In the middle psychological realm spirit and matter meet "like water mixed with water." The alchemists knew the connection between their *solutio* and the waters of baptism. They knew that the water of the psyche not only dissolves, it also forms a uterine matrix out of which something new is born. The alchemical *solutio* involves an ending and a beginning, it is in fact a process of initiation into a different level of understanding and an unfamiliar dimension of experience.

According to the alchemists *solutio* breaks the bodily substance down into its parts, even to its atoms.[7] Psychologically this amounts to a breakdown of literal experience and understanding into fantasies and images. When our attitude toward our own experience turns from earthly literalism and fixity to a more watery awareness of unconscious movements of the soul, then behavior seems less solid and substantial. The difference between reality and dream shrinks. The surface membrane of life gives way to depth, another dimension. It becomes apparent that our actions are all movements in a psychodrama, in many psychodramas— worlds designed by imagination, the sets through which we walk peopled by characters authored at least in part by our fantasies, in part by the imaginations of others, in part by something quite mysterious. It is a truism in our Freud-tinted age to note that we often marry our fathers and mothers. Jung deepend this aware-ness, suggesting that we also strike out in anger against the collec-tive shadow we refuse to claim as part of our human inheritance. He also picked up on Freud's observation by noting that we try to unite with our alienated souls by marrying alluring likenesses and projections. All our actions, in fact, involve us in deep mysterious themes and plots. The alchemical process of drawing soul out of matter aims at showing us the fantasies that are congealed in our actions and in our thoughts. Dissolved, they rise to the surface, to the screen on which we behold our dreams and reveries, and there we can see the characters and motifs which animate—ensoul—our lives. Alchemists looked at the chemical reactions in their retorts and saw mystical marriages, dragons and peacocks, and scenes from the Biblical book of Genesis. With a more penetrating insight, we too can behold in the retort of our reflectiveness the characters, human, superhuman and subhuman, the mythical themes and stories, and the religious devotedness and ritual which form the elements of experienced reality.

This very process of reflection establishes the mid-region of soul. For in imaginative reverie and wonder, dry ideas about our-selves and our world are moistened with a relatedness to our own inner life, and habits of behavior lose their hardness, becoming more moist and fluid. In psychological reflection mind and body have a place to meet. The square of unconscious life becomes the triangle of psychological awareness.

But what are the advantages of this "triangulating of the square"? First, the psychological attitude gets one off the carousel of self-improvement and compulsive activism. Most people turn to psychology in order to change. They want life to be different, but this goal is rarely achieved, if ever. If a determined person consults a psychoanalyst for inner reconstruction, he should know that the classical Freudian position holds that human beings fortunate enough to be civilized are ipso facto neurotic. All available techniques aim at making him less neurotic. If he consults a behaviorist he may find that a symptom like overeating or smoking may be rooted out, but what is left is a hole, an empty spot where once there played an enacted fantasy. If he goes to a humanistic psychologist and directs his efforts toward personal growth, he may find that growth can be suffocating, that however positive he thinks and lovingly he relates, pain is still an inescapable part of experience. On the other hand, the psychological attitude provided by alchemy "only" offers a deepening of experience. One becomes less caught up in and attracted to the surface of events and begins to see through to the deeper layers. Alchemists were patient workers; an alchemy of the soul demands patience and subtlety in appreciation. Sensational cures mean nothing. But there is in the alchemical process freedom from the binding intellectual knots, the psychological moralism, and the feverish activity of the ego associated with "square" living.

Solutio, again like baptism, also involves a cleansing, a purification, a washing away of debris, allowing a clearer perception of essentials. In *The Planets*, Ficino typically relates purification to the psychological process of becoming celestial: "A person becomes celestial when he is purged of impurities, completely cleansed of those things which are in him but are different from the heavens" (Chap. 4). What could be in a person and different from the image reflected in the planets and stars? For one thing, there could be so much debris in one's life, unsorted and unreflected, that no movement of the soul can be felt. The planets are in constant motion, as are the spheres of psychological existence represented by the planets. "In solution," the movements taking place deep within can be felt and recognized; that is, when fantasies are allowed to flow and the psychological dimension is given some attention, one senses a kind of purgation, a removal of blockage.

But purification can take place by "putting things in order," not just by removal of obstructions. The commonly held interpretation of Aristotelian "catharsis" sees it as a flushing out of emotions. According to this interpretation, drama is effective because by participating vicariously in the action on stage we experience emotions—pity and terror—which have been blocked within ourselves. But more recent readings of Aristotle explain catharsis as participation in drama by which we gain the playwright's perspective on the life-situation presented, and with that fresh viewpoint feelings and fantasies involved are "cleared up."[8] Returning to Ficino's leitmotif of the sky, we may say that catharsis takes place when the many details of psychological experience are given points of focus and related to patterns, like the designs of the zodiac. It is not a matter of putting one's life in order in some egoistic, rational, controlling manner; rather, it is an imaginative comparison of one's experience with images and patterns. Why read a novel unless the story provides a fresh viewpoint on actual experience? Once again we find a profound connection between psychological vitality and imagination.

Sublimation/Condensation

In popular imagination the alchemist is a seeker of gold, not unlike prospectors of the Old West, ever hoping to extract that precious substance from base metals. While apparently there were those "puffers" who minted coins and sought wealth and fame from the laboratory work, some of them at least were after an inner gold, the golden self, the inner person who endures and sparkles with spirituality. They sought to distill from the chaos of materialistic life a precious element.

The various phases of the alchemical process were variable, shrouded in mysterious symbolic language, and connected to other esoteric systems such as the Kabbalah and Gnosticism. I do not intend to give any kind of systematic interpretation of alchemical processes, but simply to highlight a few procedures which relate closely with Ficino's psychology. Besides "solution," which, as we have seen, is part of Ficino's process of constellating the psyche, there is also the process of sublimation, a phase Ficino would associate with movement away from literalism toward the spiritual.

As the alchemist set about his task of translating the secrets of his tradition into laboratory procedures, he would heat various mixtures and notice their odors, often pungent and rancid, as well as changes in color and shape, and the cloudy mists and beads of moisture that would condense in the retort. He watched as a twofold process unfolded: a vaporizing of what was solid and moist, and a condemnsation of that which was misty and airy. *Solve et coagula.* Psychologically, flighty ideas and spiritual schemes need concretization (condensation), while excessively literal matters require vaporization (sublimation).

Sublimation aims at a result similar to the goal of *solutio*: the extraction of fantasies and feelings which lie congealed in literal actions and beliefs. But this is not the kind of sublimation Freud developed in psychoanalysis. For him sublimation is a raising of sexual impulses to a higher level where the sexual instinct acquires a new object, one more important to society. In alchemy sublimation does not lead to a new object; quite the opposite, by allowing congealed fantasies to loosen and rise into awareness, one discovers the essence already present in literal events. There is no escape from worldly experience, but the soul-values inherent in the physical world come into consciousness. As Heraclitus taught: "Soul is vaporized from what is moist." Soul begins in the moist, solid earth, the realm of ordinary experience. Without this embodied world there could be no soul. Ficino especially develops this idea in his commentary on Plato's *Symposium*—love of the highest things is nourished by love of the physical world. A psychological attitude does not come about through escape from the tangles and problems, or the joys and pleasures, of ordinary life. Like the clouds, psyche remains close to earth but not embedded in it. It has the moisture of mist, feeling and passion leading not simply to action but toward deep reflection.

Heating, cooking, boiling, and baking are alchemical procedures—literally and figuratively. Dense, solid experience can be cooked with thought and reflection until its subtle elements, trapped within, escape. Under the heat of passion, knotty problems in life rise into consciousness in the forms of images and moods. As a person "stews over" predicaments and plans, life may become less productive but its soul-value deepens. In therapy, or in any psychologically moving situation, what has been stagnant and heavy begins to bubble. Dormant memories of the past rise to the surface, and feelings formerly kept covered and quiet break through. On the "hot seat" of confrontation with formerly neglected issues, memories and feelings begin to loosen and move about. What has been allowed to settle as sediment, causing heaviness and immobility, under the heat of alchemical attention becomes unsettled and unsettling.

At various times in psychological life it seems appropriate to boil, bake, roast, fry, or just keep warm. Sometimes a fantasy needs incubation—warmth and containment. The alchemical vessel was seen as both womb and tomb, a place for birth and a place for decay, but always a place for containment. In us the retort is the vessel of memory and imagination, holding events and fantasies where they can be subjected to the heat of passion and feeling or to the simmering of thought and reflection. In this retort, events of life decay, losing their literal form, but they also ferment, acquiring taste, bite, and body. A good cook of the psyche knows the best combinations of temperature and time, when to let things simmer and when to bring them to a boil.

Anyone, however, who knows anything about alchemy knows that it was not meat and potatoes the alchemists were stewing in their ovens and test tubes. Their combinations were more like the mixtures children sometimes concoct, mixing together anything they can find. Alchemy begins with a mess, with garbage and waste, the alchemical *massa confusa*, the bloody mess which is the raw material, the *prima materia* of the golden self.

Ego does not help much in this matter, since it prefers neatness. To ego cleanliness is next to godliness. Ego spends a good deal of its time and energy trying to make life neat and cleaning up the mess we inevitably get ourselves into. But alchemy, a thoroughly non-ego work, suggests that the way to soul is through the mess, not around it or in spite of it. And, according to many alchemists, if you don't have a mess to begin with, you had better work hard to get one. You may need a phase of *putrefactio*, a word that doesn't need translation or explication. In recent years people have described psychotherapy as "getting your shit together"—a rather alchemical notion. And you can't get it together if you don't have it in the first place.

All of this, of course, is unbelievably uncouth to ego—down-right unhealthy and noisome. But even some counselors and therapists are now beginning to see that people who really need therapy are not those whose life is a mess but those who have been avoiding and covering up the mess. Jung claimed that the mess was necessary for the discipline of psychology itself:

> No wonder that unearthing the psyche is like undertaking a full-scale drainage operation. Only a great idealist like Freud could devote a lifetime to such unclean work. It was not he who caused the bad smell, but all of us—we who think ourselves so clean and decent from sheer ignorance and the grossest self-deception. Thus our psychology, the acquaintance with our own souls, begins in every respect from the most repulsive end, that is to say, with all those things which we do not wish to see.[9]

Sublimation is in no way a turning away from things repulsive and shadowy; on the contrary, sublimation begins with acknowledgment of this lower part of humanity. There, says Jung, acquaintance with our soul begins. Sublimation and vaporization of the fantasies active in our messy lives are essential, continuing processes in the maintenance of the psychological perspective. In the minds of many, apparently, the goal of psychotherapy is to clean up the mess once and for all, but in a therapy influenced by alchemy, as is the Ficinian approach, psyche's garbage will always be present, available for incubation and cooking—the ever-present raw material for the creation of soul.

Quintessence: The Elixir of Life

You may ask why, if elements and living things generate beings similar to their spirit, stones and minerals do not. They stand midway between elements and living beings. The spirit in them is held by a more crass material. When it is properly separated and kept separate, it has the power to produce seeds similar to itself, when applied to certain materials of its own kind. Natural philosophers carefully separate this spirit from gold by a certain sublimation in fire and apply it to metals to make gold. This spirit properly drawn and separated from gold or something else the Arabians call an elixir. (Chap. 3)

From the depths of the heights, we may now leave the malodorous phase of *putrefactio* and move on to the elixir of immortality. For alchemy is not all putrid and foul; it strives for the highest possibilities. As Ficino says, the elixir is a spirit extracted from gold or some other precious substance through a process of sublimation. Once extracted, it can be applied to others things, thereby propagating itself. The elixir was also known as a panacea and source of eternal youth. The elixir, therefore, is the secret of secrets, the key to all psychological creativity. In the first chapter of *The Planets*, Ficino says more about the elixir, although there he calls it the "quintessence"—that element of spirit transcending the four elements of the natural world:

Remember, as the power of our soul is always applied to the members through spirit, so the power of the World Soul is diffused in all things through the quintessence, which flourishes everywhere as spirit within the World Body. It is contained in those things which have the most spirit. We could absorb this quintessence more if we knew how to separate it, pure, from other elements. Or, we could absorb it more through more frequent use of things rich in it—things exceptionally pure like choice wine and vinegar, balsam and gold, precious stones, myrobalan; things which smell sweet and glitter, especially things with a subtle essence, things warm, moist, and clear; not only wine, but also the whitest sugar, or especially gold or the fragrance of cinnamon and roses.

The secret of the elixir is actually quite simple: surround yourself with things and immerse yourself in activities that have the most obvious spiritual significance. Remember that for Ficino spirit is a subtle substance that emanates from ordinary things, and in fact the materials he lists are all quite solid in themselves, but they all also give off a subtle fragrance or brilliance. He is not suggesting, therefore, a quest for spiritual development outside ordinary life, on a mountain top or in a monastery. What is essential is to have the proper perspective on life itself. In a letter to his friend, Antonio Hyvano, Ficino complains that the soul is daily sold to the earthly body, and "the only person truly alive is the one who lives most remote from this false life, at least in attitude."[10] The immortality granted by this elixir of spirit is not unending physical life or life after death, but life outside life itself, the life of the soul that transcends personal biography and the limits of ordinary time.

We may look at vinegar, wine, and precious stones either as concrete methods, like amulets and charms, for keeping imagination alive to the spiritual dimension of things, or we may see them as metaphors for all those objects and activities in life that have clear spiritual import. On the surface at least, reading a book would be a more spiritual activity than brushing your teeth. Ficino's prescription advises filling life with clear spiritual activities, then bringing that spiritual awareness to more dense activities. The spiritual attitude gained from art, reading, serious conversation, ritual, celebration, camaraderie, athletics and other "spirited" activities is itself the elixir than can transform all of life, making everything food for soul. The elixir is elusive because it is not a substance but a perspective. It is a panacea in that this perspective can transform everything, and it contains the secret of perceiving the immortal dimension behind all mortal events. The elixir is of the realm of the soul, not a material thing.

Discussion of the elixir brings up an issue important to certain psychologies today, especially those not caught up in the empirical and experimental fantasy—the problem of the relationship between religion and psychology. More and more psychologists are taking an interest in religious practice because it is evident that spiritual masters have insight into human behavior and feeling. The trouble is that the craving for spirit, valid and necessary in itself, threatens a reversal of the old problem of materialism. Soul can get lost in those high regions of pure spirit. Meditation and other spiritual disciplines may offer the spirit the soul requires, but they may also lead us astray psychologically. Ficino's attitude, while strongly spiritual, overcomes that tendency. He advises a search for spirit contained *in* the concrete world, not outside of it. His is not a *flight* psychology, alluring to many since spiritual flight can draw us up and away from the problems of the soul. In his description of the elixir he makes it plain that spirit can be found in daily living, and through the elixir all of life can be transformed into a source of spiritual and psychological nourishment. This is only a more immediate reflection of his intellectual effort to reconcile the soul of Platonism with the spirit of Christianity.

It is evident, then, that certain alchemical principles play a significant role in Ficino's theory and therapeutics of the soul. These principles keep soul separate from, though connected to, intellect and body, that is, intellectualism and materialism. The alchemical perspective affirms the value of the most ordinary affairs of life as prime matter for psychological realization. It also demonstrates from another viewpoint the immanent nature of the spiritual, and the dynamics involved between spiritual and psychological realities. It helps maintain psychological consciousness, a middle arena, a hollow space for reflection and incubation, a chamber of resonance and, like the alchemist's retort, a theater of images.

This sketch of alchemy also prepares us for a very curious and fascinating piece of imaginative work in Ficino's psychology: his psychological interpretation of the four elements. Here we find a further spiritualization of matter and another resource for the creation and increase of soul.

4

The Elements of Psyche

You know well that the gross body is nourished by the
four gross elements. Know then that the spiritual body
is nourished by its own kind of four subtle elements:
wine corresponds to earth; the aroma of wine takes the
place of water; songs and musical melodies are air; and
light stands for the element fire. Spirit is especially
nourished by these four.
                                    —*The Planets*, chapter 24

We have seen how the alchemists tried to transform their consciousness so that the world, formerly appearing as solid stuff
accessible to the senses, might be seen as a mixture of body, soul,
and spirit. To apprehend the World Soul, *"Anima Mundi,"* is in
essence to see with a psychological eye. To use James Hillman's
phrase, one "sees through" the literal facade of thoughts and
actions, conscious of the fantasies embodied in them. It ought to
be clear by now, however, that seeing through the otherwise
opaque surface of things is not a simple intellectual investigation.
Psychological perception is different from sheer mental insight in
that imagery and emotion play significant roles. Ambiguity and
paradox, multiple meanings and unfinished reflections are proper
to this kind of awareness. Psyche is basically quite simple and
evident, as obvious as a dream, yet its language is sufficiently
different from rational thought that it can be extremely difficult to
cross the narrow chasm that separates the psychological from the
intellectual.

Ficino clarifies the peculiar nature of psychological reality with
an imaginative twist of imagery. He takes the four elements of
nature classically identified as earth, air, fire, and water; and he
translates these into the world of psyche, substituting for each of
the four an element more suited to the subtle nature of psyche.
These new elements are themselves images which set a scale for
psychological matters, marking out a range for psyche somewhere

between gross material objects and abstract thought. Ficino leads us to imagine an intermediate world which has its own kind of body, but which is clearly more spiritual than the physical realm.

Jungian psychologists are familiar with a psychological interpretation of the natural elements. They customarily transfer the traditional terms to a psychological level. A person's psychological makeup might be mapped accoring to the elements: one might be dominant, another lacking. Astrologers evaluate personality according to these elements as well, of course, since each sign of the zodiac is imagined to have an elemental character: Aries/fire, Taurus/earth, Gemini/air, Cancer/water, and so on. Psychologically then, an individual might reveal an oversupply of the element air—perhaps someone extremely intellectual, full of ideas, lofty schemes, plans, and wishes without body and substance. Or, quite the opposite, a person may seem extraordinarily earthy— immovable, fixed, conservative, practical, and maybe dense. These elements have no ultimate, metaphysical significance, but as a complex image they serve the imagination in its exploration of psychological patterns. Understanding the imagery of these elements also helps clarify sometimes the underlying imagery in dreams. When water appears in a dream, for example, it might help to see it as one of the basic elements constituting the psychic world of the dreamer.[1]

Ficino's approach is similar in that he uses the idea of applying the four elements to psyche, but he changes the imagery.

Elements of Nature	Elements of the Soul	
Earth	Wine	Bacchus
Water	Aroma of Wine	
Air	Music	Apollo
Fire	Light	

Ficino's choice of these new elements of the psyche is consistent with other imagery we have seen him use. Each of these is at once solid and substantial in some way, yet it also emanates an invisible quality. Wine is certainly a substance, but its effect is felt in the soul as well as in the body. The aroma of wine is subtle but unmistakably perceptible. Music pours out of an instrument and light is clearly visible, yet both are intangible. These are metaphors for the psychological dimension—the world of the psychological is as real and perceptible as the aroma of wine, but it is just as subtle.

Ficino presents his four elements not merely as building blocks of a psychological or spiritual world but also as nutriments for the psyche. Just as we have to take in and digest the physical world in order to survive, these spiritual elements have to become food for the soul in order for it to thrive. Again, this seems to be a fundamental, almost naive notion, yet it is a widespread fact that personal and social values simply overlook these subtle needs. An outstanding example is education: parents are concerned and vocal these days about the training their children are getting in reading, spelling, and arithmetic; and the government is quite concerned about school lunch programs. But what about the psyche of the child? Attention is given to social adjustment, when problems appear, but at this point it seems a futuristic fantasy to imagine an educational system staffed with experts on the processes of the soul and structured to care for the profound psychological needs of children. In this area people we call primitive are far advanced, providing their children with important and efficacious rites of passage. Ficino's language and his whole approach to psychotherapy may appear quaint and irrelevant; but beneath his curious imagery lie important insights that do in fact speak to modern social and personal crises.

Wine

The word Ficino uses for the process of absorbing spirit from the world around us is *haurire*—"to drink." As we go about our business in the daily routines of life, we might, if properly attuned or "accommodated," drink in some food for the soul. We have seen that one of the best ways of doing this is to surround ourselves with fertile sources of spirit. One of the obstacles standing in the way of spirit, frustrating our "thirst" for spiritual vitality, is the resistance of ego.

In its most fluid and minimal conception, ego is simply the power of agency an individual enjoys. A person has a desire and acts it out. Fritz Perls, the founder of Gestalt therapy, defined ego as the point of contact between subject and object, a point existing in time only momentarily. But clearly ego is much more than a function. The sense of "I" involves as well an extremely sensitive awareness of individuality. Perhaps the Freudians are correct, who identify the ego as a fantasy projection of the physical body. "I" am obviously contained within one skin; my body makes me distinct and separate from other "its" and other "I's." The fantasy of ego as we commonly know it seems to be motivated to bolster that sense of uniqueness, if not superiority. What Freud called "narcissism," a tendency to bend attention and energy back upon ego, appears to be such a common cause of distress that one is tempted to label the twentieth-century sense of identity as the narcissistic ego. In love, war, and politics, in the midst of involving international or personal projects, a whisper is almost audible: "How am I doing? Am I accepted?"

The narrow role of ego is further strengthened by personal history. "I" includes all accomplishments and failures of the past. We see in the history of the ego causes of present problems, and we are concerned about the future development of this ego. Indeed, there seems to be something essentially conservative about ego as we know it. It is fairly easy to imagine that habits and manners of an early period remain the same in the ego's old age. In a sense, ego seems to age much faster than the physical body, so that a ten-year-old may sound like an old man. Identifying with personal experience of the past, an individual readily freezes his possibilities, limits his potentiality to what is "tried and true." Rather than multiply the directions for personal biography, frequently ego, narcissistic and defended, maintains a straight and narrow path. It is no wonder that ego and soul seem to be at odds.

Because ego is so often narcissistic and defensive, when phenomena from the outside world or from the larger self make an appearance, ego may experience these as violation and threat. Ego resists movements of the soul. Repression is not motivated simply by moral sensitivity—the ego fears change because change is death to an immobile sense of "I." In relation to ego, change is not really transformation but simply flexibility. If one is moved in soul toward anger, but the ego-pattern does not admit of this emotion, conflict arises, and of course ego can win out, at least temporarily. If one is moved toward grief, but the ego is structured only for strength and a "stiff upper lip," then that spirit is kept from the life of the psyche. Eventually, it seems that these lost spirits make their imprints unconsciously—in disease, compulsions, posture, facial expression, obsessions, and dreams.

This ego we are discussing, all too commonly, is not only narcissistic, it also appears as an avator of the *senex*, a pattern of consciousness we will discuss in the chapter on Saturn. Basically, *senex* is a fantasy of kingship, of senile rule over a warring kingdom. As an attitude of soul, *senex* is cold, distant, conservative, and rigid. Among scholars, for instance, the *senex* attitude betrays itself in language: they advocate "rigorous scholarship," "rigorous logic," "rigorous self-control," and even "rigorous exercise." Yet, inextricably tied to all this *senex* rigor is "rigor mortis," the hardness of death so characteristic of an ego so influenced.

"Rigor mortis" brings us to the first nutritive element of spirit in Ficino's scheme: wine. It takes little research to gain entry into this image, especially since Ficino himself gives us an important clue for interpreting the elements. He divides them according to two gods he calls brothers: Bacchus and Apollo. The first two elements, of course, are those of Bacchus or the Greek Dionysos, the god of wine, among other things. Dionysos is the dying and rising god, a reflection of the Egyptian Osiris, worshiped as god of the Underworld, the god whose chief characteristic, found in his own myth and in the lives of his followers, is dismemberment.

Dionysos is the god of being-torn-apart; or, put in another way, to be torn apart is to experience the god Dionysos. Dionysos is the grape crushed and fermented to resurrect as wine, and wine is the god taken into the body, affecting the soul. Profound paradox can be found in the nature of most deities, but in Dionysos paradox is of the essence. In Dionysos death and life are practically indistinguishable. To experience the Dionysian affirmation of life, proclaimed and championed by Nietzsche, one has to be torn apart. Touched by a Dionysian spirit, ego feels the stupor of drunkenness and the pain of dismemberment, but these are only phases in the process of the reestablishment of life. The tight hold of ego loosens, with Dionysian wine-spirit—stiff joints are oiled, the brittle paste that holds together the unified personality dissolves, revealing an inner multitude of possibilities along with their very "unrigorous" virtues: ambiguity, paradox, contradiction, amorality, ambivalence, and uncertainty.

Wine, therefore, as an image, is the answer to the hard defensiveness of the narcissistic ego. It parallels the earth element in nature, for in the natural world substance, cohesiveness, and stability form a true foundation. But in the psychic realm, one's base has to be fluid like wine, and it has to support, not stability and security, but multiplicity and movement.

By introducing the element wine under the patronage of Dionysos, Ficino makes it clear that Bacchic insanity and illogic are fundamental to the psyche. But the character of Dionysian consciousness is intricate and vast, requiring volumes of exposition. One can find the modern role of Dionysos elaborated

in numerous outstanding authors: Nietzsche, of course, Norman
O. Brown, Carl Kerenyi, Walter Otto, and James Hillman, to
name a few.[2] The Dionysian modality described in these authors
serves as an antidote to that excessively masculine—particularly
Apollonian and Saturnian—attitude that so petrifies ego. To say
"yes" to life without avoiding life's death and pain creates a
drunken, androgynous, sensual, polymodal response.

The dismemberment motif in Dionysian consciousness demands
much more exploration, but let us leave that for other contexts and
look more closely at Ficino's image.

Wine, corresponding to the element earth, is the psyche's body
and represents things physical and sensual—body experienced
psychologically. Both wine and its god have long been associated
with sensuality, being close in touch with physical existence.
Dionysian physicality, though experienced in soul, is an attribute
of the real body, not some visual projection of the body. Isadora
Duncan freely admitted the role of the Dionysian in her life, but
she felt this God as a continuing threat to her sanity; Dionysos is a
stirring of the soul and body, an eruption of life from its vibrant
source, a simultaneous brush with the terrors and ecstasies of life
and death.

Body is truly a fundamental source for psyche's imagery; it is
only our bias for the visual that leads us to expect psychological
imagery to appear as pictures. A fully experienced image is a
synaesthetic impression, to use a term favored by art educators
today. That is to say, an image is a total sensation: seen, heard,
felt, smelled, and intuited. The sound of a familiar voice in a
strange crowd creates an image of itself. Emotion electrifies the
touch of a lover's hand creating an image irreducible to physical
factors. Having a late winter cold with all the attendant feelings
and remedies and memories creates a complex image in which we
participate with body and soul.

If a person wishes to overlook certain psychological factors at
work in his life, he may have to become desensitized to his body,
for the body is a psychological resonator. Conversely, as one
becomes more sensitive to the body, subtle expressions may
increase awareness of the soul. The sensory awareness techniques
of humanistic psychology, if not confined to the physical realm
alone, can serve as exercises for increase psychological perception,
but sensory awareness ought to direct us more fully to the image,
not to crass sensation. An alert body is not only good for mental
activity, it is a body ready for imaging.

Still another characteristic of wine, so simple that it is easily overlooked, is its capacity to bring pleasure. Pleasure is for Ficino a remarkable and important capacity of the soul, for it leads the soul out of constant activity. Pleasure brings a halt to ego-projects and acts as a bridge between activity and contemplation. Ficino identified these as the three fundamental forms of living: activity, pleasure, and contemplation; and, although the last he considered the highest form of life, pleasure came a close second. The motto of the Florentines at the Academy read: *"Laetus in praesens"*— "Joy in the present." We find this phrase as a salutation in Ficino's correspondence, and it was inscribed on the walls at Careggi. Pleasure, like a glass of wine after hard work, stops the world, preparing an individual to be more receptive to the subtle nuances of his environment, luring him into reverie and reflection.

Bacchic in nature, pleasure intervenes in our plans and efforts. Pleasure is time-out. Pleasure teases us to discover who we are instead of who we are trying to become. *Laetus in Praesens.* Pleasure brings the present to the foreground. As a delay and detour of our past and future ego perspectives and plans, it creates some havoc and minor disturbance—just enough for the opening spirit needs. In pleasure time slows down. Reflections in the pool of the soul come into focus. Pleasure in doing nothing allows for a more receptive posture toward the creativity of the soul.

Taking time out for pleasure differs, naturally, from the egomaniacal pursuit of entertainment. Originally entertainment meant "to keep hold of"—*intertenere*; so we speak of "entertaining" ideas or suggestions. Allied to pleasure, to be entertained is to be held passively in a fantasy—a football game or a light drama, for example. But the vessel of entertainment itself usually discourages the kind of movement vessels can prompt, processes like fermentation and incubation. Pleasure does not strive toward goals and accomplishments, quite the contrary; yet pleasure is an inducement further into some fantasy. Entertainment, on the other hand, in the popular sense at least, is a way of avoiding soul. This is not to say that the many forms of entertainment that play such an influential role in modern life do not in themselves have soul; rather, one's attitude toward entertainment can be soulless. In fact, sentiments surrounding the search for entertainment often seem to express the soul's affection for the body and its potential for unconsciousness. Pleasure lies deeper. It cracks open the soul, while entertainment keeps it soothingly shut.

Wine of the psyche, therefore, offers a pleasurable, sensual, inebriating dismemberment of the materialistic attitude, thus establishing a foundation for psychological participation in life.

All those things and activities which lead us out of literalism, reorient the logical mind, and bring a pause to active projects are made of the atoms of this wine element. At the root of the psychological perspective stands the ancient god of the vine, the deity who simultaneously embraces both life and death.

The Aroma of Wine

While discussing alchemy and Arnold de Villa Nova's image of "water mixed with water," we alluded to the fact that earth, interpreted as density and literalism, has to be broken up, dissolved in solution, if the fantasies congealed in literal activity are to be released into consciousness. Now Ficino's second element of the psyche parallels water, and it too represents the continuing Dionysian process of dissolution. The aroma of wine, clearly a more subtle image, stands in relation to wine itself as water to earth. Here Dionysian dismemberment through sensuality, pleasure, and drunken madness (the dissolution of reason) appears more complete, and consciousness has been rendered more psychological.

Onians informs us that in classical Rome it was believed that wine was the very sap of life; indeed, in the words of Petronius, *"Vita vinum est"*—Life is wine.[3] Onians also observes that wine was believed to go to the head, literally, where the genius or daimon resides. Therefore, wine was not only the source of physical longevity, it was also the nourishment of the soul. The Romans had a curious custom of smearing wine on the temples,[4] a practice Ficino recommends in *The Planets*. He also advises drinking wine twice a day and taking each day equal portions of wine and light, a mysterious prescription the meaning of which might be apparent when we have considered the Apollonian elements of the soul.

Onians explains the practice of dabbing wine on the temples as a way of getting the wine directly to the head where it is needed, but in view of Ficino's image of the aroma of wine, one might imagine that having wine *on* your head would keep that aroma with you and fully in consciousness. Although wine affects the soul and, as we say, does go to the head, nevertheless it is rather crass. The aroma of wine is more suited to the nature of soul itself—invisible, but perceptible and efficacious.

If the element wine is an image for those things which break up our literal perspectives, then the aroma of wine depicts those more subtle things which maintain the psychological attitude. The aroma might be those fantasies and memories which surround objects and actions, like a fragrance; keeping them in mind keeps us removed from the literal objects themselves. If we know, for example, that whenever we get a craving for buying things, the fantasy behind that is a search for vitality or a sense of power or novelty and freshness, then we may not have to literalize that wish in the way it is fantasized. It may be possible to stay on the psychological level and respond to the needs of the psyche more directly. These needs are more like fragrances, not as obvious and substantial as literal behavior. A dab of wine keeps the soul in mind.

Aromas and fragrances, as Cirlot reminds us, are both stimulants and symbols for memory, a faculty of the soul we keep running into.[5] Like the fragrance of flowers or of incense, an aroma reminds us of the recent presence of an object. The object is no longer present, but there is a trace left behind. In the human realm a fragrance is like an impression, a thought, or a brief memory. Even more literally, fragrant objects have a relationship with memory. It is well known that odors have an uncanny power to bring up memories of events long forgotten. The smell of a schoolroom can revive images from years past, or the scent of outdoors, of freshly cut grass or hay, or certain flowers, or even machines and gasoline—these aromatic traces bring forth memories of forgotten pleasure or buried traumas. The right combination of food cooking on the stove can speed us back to childhood experiences and feelings for parents, brothers, and sisters.

Opening the chest of personal memories is a mild Dionysian experience that peels off the boundaries of the present, letting in lost ways and hopes of being. Worlds of the past, even though they may be only present fantasies of the past, intrude upon a different present, revealing perhaps the narrowness of our thoughts in the present. Neglected values, unfinished situations, and forgotten ideals return to inebriate the soberness of the present. These stories and images of the past have an aroma, a spirit and tone, which can nourish the soul. They are fragrances of the psyche, a bouquet that comes from aging and slow fermentation. They are related to the cooking and fermenting of alchemical processes.

The soul is nourished by memories because they are the stuff of the psyche. They are events transformed from their literalness into fantasy and feeling. They continue to have the power to move the soul because, even in concrete events, it is the fantasy in which we participate that is moving to the psyche. Nor is it only the personal memory that gives fantasy to events; it is also the "memory" of the basic pattern behind the action that conditions one's psychological experience. If, in marrying a sweetheart, as they used to say, one is really trying to get hold of the sweetness of one's own heart and soul, then it is *that* fantasy that is so moving and overwhelming. These fantasies flow like currents through imagination and account for the vicissitudes of psychological experience. In other words, it is the fragrance of events that waft their way to the soul, not the concreteness of events. Psychological values imply a certain death to literal experience. As we have noticed, the world of psyche is an underworld to the world of surface meanings.

For the Greeks, psyche exists in the underworld, and in popular imagination the inhabitants of this underworld are ghosts. W. B. Yeats, writing with typical Irish sensitivity to the ghostly realm, connects ghosts with the fragrance of wine, echoing Ficino's image quite directly:

> A ghost may come;   110
> For it is a ghost's right,
> His element is so fine
> Being sharpened by his death,
> To drink from the wine-breath
> While our gross palates drink from the whole wine.[6]

There is the whole point: the element of psyche is so fine, sharpened by death, enjoying the breath of the wine while we in our unpsychologized bodies, to use an awkward phrase, prefer the whole wine. We prefer, typically, plain experience, or at most matters of cause and effect, while the ghost—psyche—is fed best in images and fantasies. Stretching a point and a pun, one might say that Ficino calls for the revival of a neglected sense, an olfactory awareness used to make "scents" out of this world.

Music

Dionysos and Apollo are brothers, Ficino says: they both serve the same goal we have been examining from many points of view—the creation of a psychological perspective. But, of course, they accomplish this feat in different ways, Dionysos through direct experience of the physical or fantasy world; Apollo, the Far-Shooter, through a more abstract, distant process.

The third elemental building block of psychological existence in Ficino's paradigm is music. Music has an important place in all of Ficino's writing as it had in his practice. Music is generally recognized as a spiritual phenomenon, though it is quite difficult to say why and how music could be so important for the soul. After surveying the planets in the next section of the book, we will take a close look at music as a factor in the health of the soul, especially as a means of tempering the soul, maintaining its polycentricity; so, for now, we will consider a few of Ficino's more general remarks on the subject.

> Since song and music come from the mind's thought, from the impulse of the imagination, and from the passion of the heart, and, together with the broken and shaped air, move the air-like spirit of the listener, the bond of soul and body, music easily moves imagination, affects the heart, and penetrates the innermost sanctuary of the mind.[7]

We saw earlier that in Ficinian psychology spirit is much like air, even an individual's spirit is airlike. Since music is also like air, and is carried on and through the air to the ear of the listener, it is only natural that music should have easy entry to the person's spirit. But more than that, says Ficino, music is also the product of mind, imagination, and feeling, and therefore it readily stimulates these same faculties in the listener. Music is well suited in a number of ways to the soul.

Philosophers, theologians, and music theorists of the Middle Ages and early Renaissance distinguished three kinds of music: *musica mundana, musica humana,* and *musica instrumentalis.* The first kind of music they believed to be created by the movements of the universe itself: the steady, slow rhythmic movements of the planets and stars, the coming and going of the seasons, and so on. *Musica humana* they imagined in a similar way, movements of the macrocosm reflected in the human soul. Theologians, especially those influenced by Augustine, identified as music patterns of virtues and other spiritual qualities within the human psyche. Last, and least of all, stood *musica instrumentalis,* what we know today as music, tunes and melodies played on instruments or sung.

The psychological element of music, with which we are concerned here, is clearly an example of *musica humana,* but to understand its meaning it will be necessary to refer to the music of sound. In one case, Ficino was interested in using the sounds of music in order to affect the soul. Music was another art of memory or imagination, a way of getting the soul in touch with various kinds of spirit. But in another sense music was, for Ficino, a quality of the soul itself, an elemental factor in its constitution, parallel to the air element in nature.

We might begin an examination of this element by inquiring into its specific nature—how does this art differ from others? What are some particular characteristics common to both the sounds of music and the soul?

One of the most striking powers of music is its capacity to produce a *multidimensional image.* Earlier we discussed the synaesthetic nature of some images, how they are constructed out of several sense impressions. The total impression produced by a piece of music has dimensions of space and time qualified by a specific spirit or atmosphere, a highly differentiated sense of movement, and accompanying emotion. It also has, of course, an intricate structure appealing to the intellect. The one thing music itself does not produce is a visual image, a factor which has both advantages and disadvantages.

The multidimensional image produced by music corresponds to the kind of fantasy at work in ordinary human situations. In any setting in which we find ourselves in a day's time, we respond psychologically not merely to a visual impression, but to the total environment as it strikes our imagination. Two people in the same setting can be expected to have different psychological reactions, because even though their physical environments are the same, they are contained within different images. Some settings, of course, make typical impressions on most people: a cathedral and a ball park may be expected to create unique psychological reactions in most people. Sitting in a doctor's office places the soul within a multidimensional image: the quiet, white uniforms, an air of efficiency and professionalism, a mysterious labyrinth of offices and examining rooms, shiny silver instruments associated with pain and opening the body, memories of past visits and problems, a stream of expectations—all of these go together to make the image which impacts upon the soul. Music has the unusual capacity to create such a multidimensional image and therefore differs from purely visual arts like painting and sculpture (allowing for touch in sculpture). Other arts, of course, like drama and dance, also create full images, so we will have to dig further to find the unique character of music.

What is special about music is that it can produce a rich image without visual content, and since visual impressions are closely related to language and can be quite specific, music is of its nature rather ambiguous. It is difficult, if not impossible, and likely undesirable to produce musically a specific, concrete meaning or referent. Occasionally composers will attempt to stimulate in the listener a visual impression through the use of a title or subtitle or mimicry in sound. Psychologists, too, use music as a means of priming visual impressions in people. But this programmatic and therapeutic use of music is just that: making music useful. This is not the inherent nature of musical expression.

Music leads the listener primarily to the contemplation of the qualities of time, creating at the same time, in the words of Susanne Langer, a secondary illusion of space.[8] Musical terms give us an idea of the qualities of experienced time that music creates and reflects: music has movements, episodes, motifs, counterpoints, scales and modes, melodies, harmonies, fugues, and fantasies. The emotions of its movement depend upon expositions, developments, reprises, tensions, climaxes, and cadences. On the whole, therefore, music abstracts from specific, individual content to portray the dynamic patterns of life and of the soul.

In music we can hear the dynamics of psychological movements and feel the emotions connected with them. Music, then, provides a kind of catharsis, as we discussed before, a way of helping imagination sort out and find order or pattern in experience. The terms used in music could fairly easily be applied to the soul, to the extent that music theory is itself a potential archetypal image-system for the psyche. Like music, life is built up of episodes and motifs, these are based on more universal scales and modes (patterns we will explore in a later chapter), counterpoints and harmonies fill life as do climaxes and cadences, and finally melodies correspond to our unique personal histories—what Jung would call a process of individuation built upon collective materials. It is difficult to say, then, which comes first: music of the soul or music in sound. In the latter we recognize the music of the former, or, in Ficino's own words: "Through the ears the soul perceives certain sweet harmonies and rhythms, and through these images it is exhorted and excited to consider the divine music with a more ardent and intimate sense of mind."[9]

Ficino places music among the Apollonian elements. According to the Homeric Hymn to Hermes, Apollo learned the art from the child Hermes. Therefore, music, even in Apollonian hands, is a kind of hermeneutic, a mode of interpreting life midway between blind experience and distant explanation. But music does abstract from the concrete content, the individual material of the soul, and is for that reason quite properly within the domain of Apollo, the

Far-Shooter. Apollonian consciousness, if not in the classic period at least in modern literature, is high in the sky, removed from the action so as to gain a broad perspective. It differs from the Dionysian in that it keeps a distance from the concrete. But the Apollonian art of music, though interpretive of the dynamic factors of experienced life, is not so abstract as to be noninvolving. Indeed, the image produced by music is remarkable precisely because of its singular capacity to hold the listener's attention within itself. The listener cannot stand back, as from a painting, and analyze. Music professors and students do that as a strategy in pedagogy, but even they, when they truly listen to music, must become absorbed by it. One is *in* the image, not outside of it.[10]

Not all music is Apollo's; indeed, there seems to be an archetypal contest between those who prefer Apollonian music to that of Dionysos or Pan or some other god or goddess. Apollo's music is by nature subtle and spiritual, but it is nevertheless exciting and moving and offers all the psychological advantages we have seen. Bach wrote a cantata on the theme of the contest between Apollo and Pan, showing in text and music the different character of these two, but finally Apollo wins the agon and the judge declares: "Phoebus, your melody was born of grace itself. And he who understands this art, will lose himself in it." Apollo's music interprets for our soul's ear the patterns of life as it moves in time, but it takes us into itself, allowing us to feel not only the various mixtures of tempo and movement, the tension and release, but also the feelings and deeply felt fantasies associated with those movements. Music in sound meets itself in the music of soul.

If the soul is nourished, as in the aroma of wine, with concrete visual fantasies of the patterns underlying surface experience, it is fed at a higher level with the spirit of its own music. To put it more plainly, we gain psychologically when we perceive the various patterns of the soul's life abstracted from content. When we sense fast and slow rhythms, tensions and cadences, and dissonance and consonance, we are nourished psychologically because our consciousness and our participation in these realities of our own inner life are deepened and differentiated. In order to sense this level of life we must get away from content, from specific life problems and even specific recurring themes so that we can appreciate the dynamic of life itself. For this reason the aural metaphor is more appropriate than the visual, and Apollonian abstraction, in the sense described, plays a significant psychological function.

In a letter to Francisco Musano, in 1473, Ficino tried to set his friend's mind at ease concerning his interest in music and the soul. He wrote:

> Do not be astonished, Francisco, if we mix medicine, the lyre, and the study of theology. You should recall, as the philosophers say, that body and spirit in us are joined to the soul. The body is cured with the remedies of medicine. But the spirit, which is airy, the bond of body and soul, tempers and heals the vapor of the blood with airs, odors, music and songs. Finally, the *animus*, as divine, is cared for by the mysteries of divine theology. Though nature is one, it is composed of soul, body, and spirit. The Egyptian priests had one occupation for drugs, faith, and mysteries. . . . . . *Laetus impraesens.*[11]

Psychotherapy in Ficino's system involves a sharpening of imagination, tuning the instrument of the soul so as to be receptive to the various kinds of spirit available in season. In his chapter of *The Planets* devoted to music, Ficino refers to the musical phenomenon we call "sympathetic vibration." If two strings are tuned to the same pitch and one is plucked, the other will sound as well. So it is, says Ficino, with the soul. When the imagination is tuned to the varieties of spirit, in the presence of that spirit the soul will be set in motion, animated by that particular spirit. A person whose imagination is tuned to pick up on those things especially good for the soul will in fact get them. Without imagination we remain stuck in a drab psychological state, deprived of the variety of spirit soul requires for vitality. In a strange sort of way, we need to be musicians of the soul, with taste and a good ear.

Light

Ficino was mightily impressed by the sky that arched over his life day and night; he saw everything that happened in relationship to that sky; we might say, in "light" of the sky. For it was the light of the heavens that to his mind accounted for human dignity. Through participation in that light we have knowledge of the things of our world and of ourselves, because light is knowledge. In his essay on light, *De Lumine*, he turns that phrase around and gives us a hint as to the nature of light. The light of reason, he writes, is the reason of light.[12] Light comes first, then our intelligence, because our powers of reasoning are only a participation in a higher intelligence.

If we take the phrase in its usual order, "the light of reason," we will be bound to end this discourse on the elements of spirit at the dubious pinnacle of human rationality, hardly an adequate conclusion to Dionysian mysteries and Apollonian musical hermeneutics. But this mistake is frequently made, in intellectual circles and among psychotherapists. In the light of reason, many think, we will be saved from our follies. But we ought to know from history, both cultural and personal, that "enlightenment" often paints only a partial picture. Our Western historical era of Enlightenment made, perhaps, some important advances in humanism, but it also gave us an image of man as clockwork, an image that still remains among enlightened technologists. Mystery and depth in human experience are expunged by that light that hangs above us like a glaring lamp used to intimidate criminals and extract confessions, or so the movies say. Enlightened technocrats would doubtless confine Ficino and his like in a special fenced hospital on account of his ravings. We also know the pinched vision of enlightened liberals who claim to know how to raise children rationally, cure neuroses rationally, and dispense with religious traditions rationally. The light of reason shines where it will, but its power seems severely constrained. Apropos here is the famous Sufi story of the man squatting in the circle of light cast by a street lamp looking for a lost key. "Did you lose your key here?" asks a passerby. "No, I lost it over there," the man replies, "but I can see better here by the light." This is the light of reason so many like to use to explore the mysteries of our world.

Ficino is recommending to us, then, not the light of reason but the reason of light, *ratio lucis* in his text. This is the crowning element of psyche and its prime spiritual nourishment. It is not the product of human ratiocination but rather the gift of the God Apollo, the sun God. His benefit to mankind is not simply technical understanding or even philosophical elucidation; on the contrary, the God offers us entry into an image of brilliance, a fantasy of light. Psychologically, in the light we achieve a new quality of understanding, an "in-sight," a view of the *"eidos"* of Plato, a vision of the interior of things. And the vision establishes a relationship between ourselves and our world whereby we perceive our place and sense the connection between human ego-mentality and far deeper sources of understanding. The quality of this kind of intelligence, far beyond rationality, appears in Ficino's descriptions of the light. The light of the heavens, he says, is an image of all the following: the fruitfulness of life, the perspicacity of our senses, the certitude of our intelligence, and the bountifulness of grace.[13] These are all qualities of intelligence, the way understanding is experienced. That is the gift and not the simple power of thought. Ficino includes grace, a word not much in vogue these days, but one which conveys our dependence upon the mysterious gifts of life. It implies a spirit of receptivity and humility, even in the face of intellectual accomplishment.

We have seen repeatedly how Ficino sets as an ideal a celestial pattern. In his essay on light he personifies that pattern to some extent. He speaks of *lumen*, this transrational intelligence so difficult to define, as *risus coeli*, the laughter of the sky. He imagines the sun as the eye of the heavens, an eye that conveys true spirit, as does the eye of the lover—an image Ficino uses in his commentary on the *Symposium*—or eyes on a smiling face. Obviously, then, the intelligence he is speaking of is spiritual, a hint intuitively grasped rather than a conclusion planted in a syllogism or a fact inductively discovered.

Consider the difference between a communication received from another person in words and the message conveyed through facial expression or even a twinkle in the eye. This latter is the analogy for the kind of spiritual insight Ficino would have us pick up in the world itself—an awareness of the twinkle in the eye of the cosmos, being clued in on its secrets, its underlying purposes and fantasies.

When Ficino speaks of the "reason of light" he is stating in other terms what we have seen all along: soul is central; even our thinking participates in psyche. Behind our thoughts, or better, permeating our reason itself, are the fantasies of the soul. The rational is contained within the psychological.[14] If the psychological derivation of our thoughts is not appreciated, then we tend to take ideas literally, and spirit becomes as much a quicksand for the soul as materialism. Ficino's image of light, pervading all levels of knowledge, works against such a literalistic perspective. We can see, in fact, how his imagery develops this with some detail.

In *De Lumine* he suggests several different paradigms showing hierarchies of knowledge, all interconnected. In the fifth chapter he distinguishes light in the following manner:

Light of God—goodness and truth
Light of Angels—intelligence
Light of the Heavens—the abundance of life
Light of fire—the propogation of the powers of the heavens

Here the image of light, taking different forms in the hierarchy, allows us to apply a process James Hillman has called "reversion" to our thoughts and behavior. By reverting back along this line we can find the deeper psychic containers for our ideas and behavior. The light produced by a simple, earthly fire reflects in a simple way the fire of the stars; our individual ideas and wishes can be traced back to larger movements of the soul, to multiple structures of consciousness and habits of thinking represented by the many planets "burning" in the night sky. Our present wish for a speedy sports car might take its place among other wishes contained in a larger movement toward youthfulness, which itself might be held in a deeper fantasy of freshness and beginnings. Ficino traces this beam of light all the way back to the sun, the sun god, or to the Christian God, where the differentiation of the fantasies ends and one simply encounters psychic life itself.

Another paradigm, in the thirteenth chapter of *De Lumine*, shows this mutual containment more clearly. "The spirit enjoys greatly its own clarity and that of the sun. *Animus* enjoys the clarity of the spirit and mind. But it appears that this light is the mind shining through the body, reflected as in glass, and so made visible."[15] Here we move from the sun, to the spirit, to the *animus*, to the body. We ought to be able to see the workings of one in another.

Finally, Ficino offers an even more elaborate hierarchy in nine stages, corresponding, he says, to the nine Muses of Apollo:

1. the sun
2. the firmament, bright because of its fineness, hidden to us.
3. the stars (visible)—white
4. the stars—red
5. the stars—mixed
6. simple, uncomposed sublunar things, translucent
7. translucent sublunar things composed of glass or crystal, translucent but holding less light
8. things composed but translucent, like carbuncle, or oily things that hold light
9. colors and colored images, which may in the extreme be white or black, or in the middle, green.

Earlier in this essay on light, Ficino had mentioned that the light of the sun contains all colors. Similarly, all nine of the phases listed contain light, but all in different proportions and in different degrees of perceptibility. Remember always, of course, as Ficino mentions several times in the essay, that light is intelligence, a kind of knowing. Therefore, he is saying that there are many levels of psychological perception, and, according to his theory of the elements, to perceive these is to nourish the soul. Our understanding of the many personal and cultural events of life may be more or less concrete, so that in one case we may see only as far as the motley colors of individual situations and at other times we may perceive deeper patterns shining through as in crystal.

It is quite clear, then, that in Ficinian psychotherapy the goal is to develop an Apollonian, lucid insight *into* the deep patterns at work in ordinary experience. The soul itself is fed by these deeper "lights," by our perception of soul-values lying deep within, just as the lights of the universe are deep in space. Ficino's image of light sustains his psychology of depth. Toward the end of *De Lumine* he mentions that the Pythagoreans found the vestal fire burning in the center of the world—another fire and another source of light.[16] In this psychology we are concerned not with turning the light of reason on the dark, unknown, and troubling phenomena that seem to invade life fairly regularly, but rather to discover within events and within ourselves the reasons or patterns or seeds, as Ficino sometimes calls them, of that inner light, that internal universe and vestal fire.

The Apollonian movement clearly directs us upward toward spiritual insight and the large patterns of human life—the musical movements of the soul and the light that pervades psychological experience. The Dionysian movement is closer to earth, deeply involved with the experienced world. Both perspectives are useful and significant; it is not enough simply to experience with imagination, nor is it sufficient to leave the experiential level and engage in psychological analysis. Like Apollo and Dionysos, these are brother perspectives. As Ficino says: "I do not know how, having arisen first from Apollo, we fall into Bacchus. Indeed, we go from light to heat, from ambrosia to nectar, from insight into truth to ardent love of truth. Phoebus and Bacchus are indeed brothers—individuals and companions" (*The Planets*, Chap. 24).

If we are to develop an archetypal psychology based on Ficino's view of the soul, we would have to attend to both the experiential and the analytical, understanding the latter as an exploration of images and fantasies at various degrees removed from concrete experience. All too often psychology chooses only one of the brothers, emphasizing either primal screams and hot seats or cool, intellectual analysis. Neither of these, of course, are the categories of Ficinian theory, since in both Dionysian and Apollonian activities psychological reality is the focus of concern. Experience for its own sake—crying, screaming, raging or caressing—and abstract introspection or theorizing both evade soul. Archetypal psychotherapy is, as its name implies, a caring for the images that permeate human experience. They may be perceived with immediacy or with distance, one in the heat of experience, the other when things have cooled down. Both approaches are useful, both shift our attention from mind and body to the soul.

5

Necessary Madness

Most current notions of psychological health are mere transfers from the medical fantasy of homeostasis and resistance to invading aliens. A psychologically healthy person is one who has built strong psychic muscles of ego-strength and willpower and a talent for avoiding pain and risks. Good mental health is equivalent to sound social and personal adjustment. We expect all normal people to "keep an even keel," even when the waters are choppy and the winds of spirit reach gale force.

The individual psychological lifeline may be graphed as a sine wave or a host of sine waves out of sync than as a straight line. Only a small portion of ordinary human experiences fit within the strict confines of the stable life; indeed, the most significant experiences seem to fall far above or far below the median line of normality and stability. The "peak experiences" Maslow studied and advocated may not be all that he touted them to be, but they seem important for the animation of life, for infusing needed nourishing spirit. But the "lows" and the "blues" may also serve the soul well, pushing us to extremes where fresh vision and altered perspective afford new spiritual discoveries.

According to a frequently told Gnostic tale, the soul, in the process of a person's birth, descends from beyond the planetary spheres, where it exists in bliss, quite free of materiality, and falls into the body. It is born into a deep sleep in the material world as in a great fluffy down bed. There the soul slumbers forgetful of its vital past. Only when occasional vague feelings of nostalgia and homesickness arise does the soul stir and move in the direction of its origins.

Ficino's Neoplatonic mind knew and appreciated this attitude toward existence. He warned about the soul's affection for the body and for things material. He observed that the soul "in embracing the body too much goes a long way from that purity in which it was born."[1] In other words, it is quite easy to live as if physical survival and fulfillment were the whole point. Yet, occasionally a feeling of longing will make itself felt—a very important yet often overlooked emotion, one which can draw the soul back towards its needs.[2] The feeling may seem as natural and as persistent as the instinct of the salmon returning to its spawning place, though the backward goal is often vague and undefined. People say, "I have a feeling of dissatisfaction, even though there is no reason for it." Or they will simply express a gnawing, disturbing longing. The feeling of nostalgia might even appear in memories of past episodes, of a Golden Age in the personal past. The past often serves as a metaphor for authenticity, whether it is the personal past or cultural history. We think back sometimes in order to feel deeply and to recover something which seems to be lost. A tone of melancholy sometimes colors cherished memories, a feeling tone Freud defined as a sense of loss.[3]

What is lost, its absence felt in these moments of nostalgia, is the soul itself, a state of being animated and spirited, filled with anima (soul) and spirit. The soul is asleep and needs to be wakened. But the soul's sleep is supported not only by materialism but also by a commitment to ideals of sanity and stability. It is not only the fluff of materialism that soothes the psychological unconscious, the steady, monotonous hum of the sane, adjusted life gives its support as well.

It follows, then, that the awakening of the soul may entail some kind of insanity and instability. In relation to what is commonly taken to be normal and sane, there are psychological potentialities that must appear at least mildly insane. Ficino does not deal with this way to soul in *The Planets* but he does consider it briefly in his commentary on the *Symposium*, and since the imagery he uses nicely complements the other aspects of psychological awakening we have examined, it might be useful to give some attention to this—the theory of divine madness.

Ficino's theory is built upon Plato's "four frenzies," an idea discussed and expounded throughout the Platonic tradition. But rather than compare various versions of the theory or summarize modern interpreters, keeping with the purpose here of extracting and explicating Ficino's quite practical psychology, we may focus on the imagery Ficino uses in the exposition of this theory. For the interesting point in this theory of "mania" is the suggestion that in order to transcend ego concerns and materialistic unconsciousness, we require inner figures associated with specific kinds of nonrational consciousness. These are: poet, priest, prophet, and lover.

Each of these figures personifies a mode of consciousness sufficiently different from ordinary ego-awareness as to seem mad. Yet, we need these figures constellated within our consciousness; they provide necessary madness. As I have said, this madness is not the same as psychosis, but we need a strong term to convey the nonrational nature of certain structures of consciousness required to maintain a psychological perspective. Ego is not coterminous with the soul. Some states of consciousness transcend ego-awareness, and for that reason they are beneficial to the soul. This is not an exciting new idea in this age of "altered states of consciousness," interest in meditation and fantasy, and the like. But here in Ficino's psychology we find a place and purpose for such extraordinary states of "mind," not simply for spiritual development in the usual sense, nor certainly for the sheer "entertainment" these states may bring. In Platonic madness the soul is free of body and ego and may be quite creative in that state. As Ficino says, "many poets compose in madness and afterwards do not know what they have said, as if God had used them as musical instruments."[4]

Let us look, then, at four kinds of non-ego states, paying particular attention to the spirit or atmosphere they provide for psychological life and to the personifications associated with them. These four represent four sources of spiritual/psychological nourishment, four states of consciousness to which ego must learn to respond, and four psychological activities necessary for awakening the soul.

Poetic Madness

The whole soul is filled with discord and dissonance; therefore, the first need is for poetic madness, which through musical tones arouses what is sleeping, through harmonic sweetness calms what is in turmoil, and finally through the blending of different things, quells dissonant discord and tempers the various parts of the soul.[5]

What is immediately clear from this passage is Ficino's concern for soul, not for poetic inspiration or good verse. His interest in poetic madness centers on the soul itself, the psychological effect of this transcendence of ego. Nor is he excited about the enjoyment of a transcendental state of consciousness. E. R. Dodds, that psychologically attuned classical scholar, noted in his essay "The Blessings of Madness" that Plato himself was not interested in poetic ecstasy in itself. Dodds rightly cautions against glorifying ecstasy and trance for their own sake.[6] Anyone can let his mind roam and come up with bizarre images; some people take pride in this ability, others are embarrassed by it. The poet is the one who deals with the images: gives them educated attention, tries to become familiar with them, finds ways of verbalizing them, deepens his own touch with life through them. These too are the concerns of the poet within.

Ficino describes poetic madness as a healthy response to a soul filled with discord and dissonance. We have to be clear about his meaning here, since later we will find him including dissonance in the makeup of a healthy soul. In this context, dissonance means faulty tuning, not a timely, invigorating departure from harmoniousness. We will see later that a well-tuned soul is one in which archetypal possibilities represented by the planetary deities are carefully distinguished and all represented. It is a soul having distinct, multiple parts, just like the tones of a tempered musical scale. If some "tones" are missing or not carefully distinguished from each other, the result is a fundamental dissonance, faulty tempering, an instrument out of tune. Poetic madness tempers the soul, especially by waking those parts that are dormant.

Imagination comes alive through the peculiar mania of the poet, who is one of the many persons who live in the psyche.[7] When we allow the poet in us to come to life, we get to work attending to images, holding them in our fantasy, contemplating them and enjoying them, being moved by them. By this very process the soul is awakened, a psychological attitude begins to take form. Images obviously are the fodder of the faculty of imagination; so as images arise and are attended to, imagination grows more fertile and active, giving one's psychology better economy and increased potentiality. The possibility of good temperament is increased.

In his self-professed masterpiece, *The Interpretation of Dreams*, Freud explained that only a portion of our fantasy life comes to consciousness, since a large part is repressed for moral reasons.[8] But such a personification of the soul as the poet may be repressed because of an undervaluation of that function. In other words, not only our fantasies themselves, but the very fantasy of caring for fantasies, our poetic potential, may be repressed. In his commentary on the *Symposium* Ficino notes that when the lower parts of the soul are hard at work, the higher functions may be almost asleep.[9] The inner poet, anesthetized for the benefit of lower psychological concerns, cannot bring energy to images, and as a result the soul loses its temperament and vitality. We become psychologically distressed (distempered) and inert.

Without access to fresh images we are compelled to relive continuously the personal past: its habits, values, and patterns. When we seek help in decision making, when we look for meaning, when we feel the nostalgia for depth, we look to past experience. The personal past can give the illusion of authenticity, especially when it is idealized or romanticized. Even Freud's focus on the family and on childhood, when taken literally, offers scant resource for ensoulling the present. In his scheme there is one myth (Oedipus), one love (a parent), one kind of energy (sexual), and one enemy (another parent). The ultimate repetition-compulsion appears in Freud's theory itself: the continuous attempt to resurrect "mom and dad."

The notion of a poesis of the psyche, however, suggests that the past is not the only cache of available images. Fantasy is an unending source of imagery, and the poet within can be more creative than to translate it all into the family story. He can get over the fascination with the past and find other ways to imagine, to pattern and interpret the wealth of images at his disposal.

As Ficino describes it, poetic madness has a certain destructive aspect: "The most powerful emotions of the soul even dissolve and disintegrate the body; this happens not only in the course of an affect but also during intense speculation."[10] Like alchemical *solutio*, alchemical atomizing, and the elemental fragmentation of wine, poetics dissolves the body, that is, the materialistic, egoistic attitude. New images given the soul in poetic reverie and work stand over against established images of the world and self, exploding them, dissolving them, more fully exposing their interiority. Through poetic madness the opaque, brittle shells of meaning we have built and protect egoistically shatter and become visible as images themselves. That is to say, they are seen through and perceived psychologically, from the perspective of soul. This is one way to read Norman O. Brown's ecstatic conclusion to *Love's Body*:

> The word within the word, the unheard melody, the spirit ditties of no tone. The spiritualization of the senses, a restoration of the unsullied sense-activity of man in paradise. Remain faithful to the earth; but the earth has no other refuge except to become invisible: *in us*.[11]

"In us" refers to our poetic imagination, utterly essential if our words and worlds are not to remain at the literal level.

To pragmatic consciousness this pervasive poetic, metaphoric attitude will seem bizarre, crazy. Attending to images can very well appear on the surface as madness, and empirical, pragmatic minds can become quite resourceful finding language to say so. Condescendingly we can watch "primitives" dance the images of their ancestors, knowingly and tolerantly we can watch an artist fall apart in a Bohemian life-style. But even such simple activities as telling dreams, drawing fantasies, even acting out a bit some pressing imagery—all of these can easily by regarded as suspicious behavior. Colleagues of mine used to become quite concerned when I would lead classes through a long, open-ended dramatization of someone's dream; yet these "techniques" are common to religious ritual from ancient to modern times, as in the famous dream ceremony described by the Oglala Sioux, Black Elk.[12]

Poetic madness is first in Ficino's paradigm because it is primary in the work of psyche. Psyche expresses itself in imagery, day and night. But imitating this definite psychological tendency may well appear as madness; for, unlike the works of ego, images are not linear and logical, they pile up on each other and defy reason. Poetic reasoning leads not to satisfying conclusions, but to unending sense of deepening. The poet typically appreciates and praises, whereas the rationalist analyzes and affirms. Certainly the poet in us is a madman, but his efforts are irreplaceable.

Sacerdotal Madness

Multiplicity and diversity still remain in the soul. There is added therefore the mystery of Dionysus which, by expiation, sacrifices and every form of divine worship, directs the attention of all parts to the Mind, by which God is worshipped. Whence, since the single parts of the soul have been reorganized into one Mind, the soul is now made a single whole out of many.[13]

This second madness of the psyche, focused upon the image of the priest, brings up the extremely complicated issue of the relationship between religion and psychology. That is the topic for another book or series of volumes. We will have to remain here within the confines of Ficino's hints concerning the role of this religious fantasy in the life of the soul. We will not be concerned, therefore, with theological or metaphysical questions; that is, we will not consider religion as any kind of link with a separate metaphysical reality but rather as a psychological phenomenon, as a mode of soul-movement.

As we imagined the poet to be a figure personifying our manner of dealing with images, so the priest is also a personfication of an inner attitude. Through this inner image of the priest we are prepared imaginatively to grasp the sacredness and mystery of ordinary life and to constellate for the soul that spirit which in the past has been accessible through religious ritual and myth. Ficino indicates that the poetic fantasy is not sufficient; in addition to working with images it is necessary to establish a connection with them, and that is fundamentally a religious action.

What I have in mind is essentially an application of the theory Jung proposed in his Terry Lectures given at Yale in 1937. There he defined religion as a function of the psyche:

> Religion appears to me to be a peculiar attitude of mind which could be formulated in accordance with the original use of the world *religio*, which means a careful consideration and observation of certain dynamic factors that are conceived as "powers": spirits, daemons, gods, laws, ideas, ideals, or whatever name man has given to such factors in his world as he has found powerful, dangerous, or helpful enough to be taken into careful consideration, or grand, beautiful, and meaningful enough to be devoutly worshipped and loved.[14]

In the context of "priestly madness," and consistent with the thought of Jung and Ficino, we may say that religion is "a careful consideration and observation" of the fantasies and images unveiled by poetic vision, in the sense we have just detailed, in an attitude of devout worship and love. The religious attitude surpasses simple awareness of the dynamic images at work in experience; it involves a sense of being bound (*religio*) to them, an acknowledgment of their importance, and a means, perhaps ritual, for keeping them in mind and heart. We may interpret many religious practices throughout history and around the world *psychologically* precisely in this way. They are a means of keeping the foundational fantasies of the individual and collective soul in mind and maintaining their efficacious significance. In this way there may indeed come about a certain unifying of the soul: fantasies become focused through an attentive and reverent ego-attitude.

In this sense religion is not just something to take care of on Sundays or Saturdays and in churchs and temples, nor does it depend entirely upon an individual's belief. Religion is a component of psychological life, related to but different from poetic consciousness—perhaps an intensification of it. Psychologi-

cally a person may be quite religious even though he never
steps into a church or professes any literal belief in God.
This is the way Ficino should be understood, when he says:
worship "is as natural for humans almost as neighing is for horses
and barking for dogs."[15] In worship we encounter an image, not
from a distance, but close up; in fact, we participate in the image
itself. Mind, emotion, and imagination are given over in worship
to the atmosphere and eternal pattern represented by that
particular form of worship. To participate in a Good Friday
worship service is to enter deeply into the universal human
phenomenon of self-sacrifice, suffering, and death. Outside of
formal church structures, we can also enter imagery deeply, relate
to it seriously, and enjoy its spiritual rewards.

Our attitude toward dreams, for example, might be poetic or
religious. At the level of poetics a person might be quite serious
about his dream life, keeping an account of his dreams and making
some effort to understand them. But a further step would be to
establish a relationship to the images appearing in dreams, to see
those images as constitutive in some way of psychological status
and posture. In Jungian active imagination these images are
revived and even addressed as persons or perhaps sketched in
water colors or clay—a kind of religious iconography. Like the
Virgin Mary in Roman Catholicism, these figures from dream and
fantasy may be revered and given a position of influence without
being made into idols themselves.

Ficino presents his theory of divine madness in several of his
writings, and each time he uses a different vocabulary.[16] Though
the priestly madness is always attributed to the god Dionysos,
which places it in the context of Dionysian patterns generally, he
names it alternately *"sacerdotium,"* priesthood, and *"mysterium."*
The role of mystery Ficino clarifies somewhat in a letter written in
June 1491 to Piero Divitio. Writing about the four kinds of
madness he comments specifically on the priestly style of
consciousness. "Ancient theologians," he writes, "defined
Dionysian drunkenness as a departure of the mind (*excessus
mentis*), separated from mortal things but penetrating the secret
Mysteries of divinity."[17] To gain entry to the mysteries of the soul,
those elements that are more-than-personal, the soul's cyclic
patterns and unreasonable predilections, one has to depart in
drunkenness, not literal of course, from logical, literal, normal,
reasonable, and linear patterns of thought. As we saw in our
discussion of the elements, the Dionysian factors keep life
dismembered, broken into its fantasy components, and now we

find that this Dionysian process renders accessible transpersonal mysteries.

In some religious contexts a mystery is a sacred secret known only to initiates; the secrecy itself separates followers of the cult from those not initiated. But in the Renaissance period mysteries were believed to be secret bodies of knowledge preserved in highly symbolic and arcane texts and images. Ficino and his friends were fascinated and mystified by the ciphers and symbols they found in the Hermetic texts, and, in fact, they considered the texts significant precisely because of the secret nature of their contents. Some of Ficino's predecessors in the development of "poetic theology" also thought highly of ciphers and emblems. Dionysius the Areopagite, whom Ficino had studied, taught not only the negative way to God but also the way of divine names and images. Joachim of Fiore is another remarkable theologian who expressed his deepest insights in iconographical form. Nicholas of Cusa, too, closest to Ficino in time, sought imagistic containers for his theological intuitions, writing books on the image of the face and even on a ball game (De Ludo Globi) as means of approaching the deepest mysteries. As Edgar Wind observed in his masterful book on Renaissance mysteries: "Pico [Ficino's protégé] held that pagan religions, without exception, had used a 'hieroglyphic' imagery; that they had concealed their revelations in myths and fables which were designed to distract the attention of the multitude, and so protect the divine secrets from profanation."[18]

The true mysteries of the soul, those constant rhythmic movements that rarely seem synchronized with our conscious wishes and plans, are not easily expressed or understood. The psyche moves by a logic different from the reasoning mind; so it is logical to assume that rational logic will not bring us to the heart of these mysteries. We have to depart from that kind of mentality, as Ficino advised Divitio. He makes a similar point in The Planets, where, in the twenty-first chapter, he ranks the seven planets in order, tracing the steps the soul takes in its ascent back to its original home. Seventh and highest is Saturn, representing "simple and hidden knowledge, cut off from movement, joined to divine things, governed by Saturn whom the Hebrews deservedly called by the name 'Quiet'—Sabbath."[19] In order to perceive at all the mysteries deep within the soul, it is necessary to move away from ordinary activities and usual patterns of thought. What is needed is a state of consciousness or an attitude attentive to the eternal rather than the temporal.

Kerenyi has made some observations about mystery which may

elucidate the psychological role of the religious attitude. Mystery for fifth-century Greeks, he says, was centered in the atmosphere of the ceremonial night, focused possibly in the smell of a burning torch. Recall Ficino's aroma of wine, our discussion of the multidimensional image, and personal experiences, perhaps, of ceremonies that have been gripping and memorable because of the "atmosphere." In Greek religion, according to Kerenyi, there was "no serious intention of maintaining the secrecy of the secret. The study of religions of nature shows that in the secret cults it is a question of the same thing found, according to Goethe, in nature itself: a *sacred open secret*."[20] According to Kerenyi what was concealed was the *arreton*, the unutterable. It was secret not because it would not be spoken but because it *could* not be spoken. Only later did this open secret become the *aporreton*, the carefully kept secret.

In Ficinian psychology we can blend these two notions of mystery: sacred open secrets of nature enfolded in the arcane imagery of myth and ritual. But the purpose of opaque imagery may not be to *hide* the secrets; the images themselves may be the best if not the only way to *hold* the secrets adequately. Dreams seem to be expressions of the psyche's secrets. Freud proposed that the reason for the opacity of the dream images is one of repression. Dreamwork covers up the true, rationally conceivable content of the dream in order to protect the dreamer, at least to protect his sleep. Jung's approach to dreams is closer to the attitude of Kerenyi toward religious mysteries. Dreams contain sacred open secrets, not repressed through imgery but contained and revealed to us through images, if only we were more familir with imagery.

The mysteries revealed through Dionysian, priestly consciousness are the eternal patterns of the psyche, the side of the soul that is godlike rather than human, though through ritual a connection is established between personal consciousness and cyclic pattern. Again in the words of Kerenyi, "the cult representation alone can raise my experience toward the universal in such a way that it still remains my very own: my ineffable mystery that I have in common with all men."[21] Expressed another way, if a person can find his way out of the conditioning of logical thought long enough to consider the very different language of imagery, he may begin to perceive the mysterious directions psychological life takes, and he may establish a connection with those movements. In this way, religious consciousness overcomes the sense of alienation and confusion a person might well feel when cut off from the rhythms of the soul. Religious sensibility in this case is a binding, not to another metaphysical world, but to an often neglected dimension of inner life.

Jung believed that external religious forms, such as rites and liturgies, could be quite important for the soul, since in these forms the soul comes intimately into contact with its deep mysteries. The problem here, as usual, is one of literalism—getting stuck in only one psychological viewpoint because of the limited nature of one's religious imagination. The psychological view of religious sensibility all too briefly sketched in this section might also speak to the problem of those who cannot any longer profess literal belief in the religion of their childhood but still sense the value of religious awareness. The world of the psyche may be the better arena for making our bonds with the transpersonal.

Prophetic Madness

Since the single parts of the soul have been reorganized into one Mind, the soul is now made a single whole out of many. But there is needed still a third madness to lead the mind back to the Unity itself, the head of the soul. This Apollo brings about through prophecy, for when the soul rises above Mind into Unity, it sees into the future."[22]

The third significant figure of the soul who brings his own kind of mania is the prophet. Following Ficino's schema we may imagine the prophet within, one who sees far into the future and predicts events. There is no doubt that this is indeed a fascinating figure of imagination and no doubt accounts for some of the success of astrology today. Reading teacups and noticing itchy palms is not what Ficino has in mind for the psyche, but obviously fascination with the future is common to all these claims of prophecy.

In his essay on divine madness Ficino makes it clear that when he speaks of prophecy, which he calls *vaticinium*, he is not referring to logical assumptions about the future. If an individual predicts the future, he says, with "human cleverness and insight" that is not truly prophecy but only conjecture or premonition.[23] True prophecy requires a separation of the soul from the body. Now we have to try to understand what kind of separation this is.

Before looking into the more subtle aspects of this theory of prophecy, bringing it up to date, so to speak, we should be clear that Ficino did believe in prophecy at a very pragmatic level. Kristeller has gathered together some historical facts that are quite telling. He notes that Ficino was particularly impressed by the prophetic powers of his mother, who, for example, foresaw a death and an accident among her relatives.[24] His father, too, was once informed in a dream of a dangerously ill patient. Ficino himself was once seriously ill when he was told in a dream about his recovery. And, of course, Kristeller mentions Ficino's frequent use of astrology for the most ordinary situations, like determining the best time to begin construction on a building. Although his language is often quite abstract and perhaps anachronistically imagistic, Ficino obviously lived his philosophy at its most occult extremes. It all fits in with his psychological viewpoint—pervasive in theoretical and practical affairs.

Back to the theory: before Ficino outlines the theory of the four kinds of madness in his work on Plato's *Symposium*, he mentions the multiplicity of the soul: "Because it has fallen into the body," he says, "it is distributed among many functions, and it looks back upon an infinite multiplicity of corporeal things."[25] Then the higher parts of the soul are dormant and need to be awakened by poetic consciousness, by attention to fantasy. As we have seen, then psyche requires a religious relationship to those fantasies. Now the "unifying" function of prophecy is to draw one's consciousness further from the deadening multiplicity of individual actions and situations to a vision that transcends linear discrete time. The soul has to be brought to a head, as he says, where the categories of time are no longer limiting. The prophet within sees things in way quite different from ego, that is his madness. His perspective blurs time so that the past seems closer to the present and the future not quite so full of surprises. In Ficino's words, "The minds of all these searched through many places and comprehended the three parts of time in one when they separated themselves from the body."[26] If we keep in mind that separation from the body means the avoidance of a materialistic and literalistic attitude, then statements like these make good sense. It is when we have our minds only on the concrete, physical reality that we are so caught up in the categories of time and see events as discrete and sequential. From a higher perspective, patterns emerge, repetitions are noticed, and even future developments can be glimpsed.

To see the three parts of time in one is to see a thing in a perspective of timelessness, to see those characteristics not affected by time directly. The soul is directed to its "head," where the world exists in seed, in primordial and ever-recurring images, stories, wishes, hopes, and fears. The prophet's vision is not really forward but within. We are the prophet when we catch sight of those fundamental fantasies we are continually acting out and when we see how much the past inhabits the present, not as cause, as so many psychologists would like us to believe, but as the traces of patterns that never vanish. When we become more familiar with the rhythms and images of the soul, of our own personal inner life, then truly the borders of time melt, and we can abandon feverish attempts to eradicate the past and build a new future. External circumstances can obviously change, certain potentialities become refined and prominent, and growth of some kind does take place in every human life;[27] but the timing of the psyche is slower than that of ego, and its course is not straight. It makes many loops in the course of a lifetime, many reprises coccur, patterns of character emerge again and again, more and more artfully perhaps, but nonetheless in recognizable form.

To speak so seriously of prophecy in our day may sound absurd, or it may be rather dangerously misleading in view of the irremediable itch so many have for occult powers. Yet, this is an excellent image when properly understood for a genuine need of the soul even today. The eyes of modern men and women continuously dart at the clock and calendar. Time burns itself into consciousness as if it were pasted in neon throughout our environment. Establishing the psychological attitude, the whole point of the psychology we are developing here, necessarily involves a change in one's sense of time. Truths of the soul follow a different clock. Psyche's episodes pile up on each other, so that a pattern we may have acted out last many years ago in childhood appears in a middle-aged marital spat. This is not to say that the past, and especially childhood, determines the future; simply, the pattern may be the same, returning like a large wave on the beach.

Paradoxically, we might imagine that a prophet is someone who has an excellent memory, both with regard to personal past experiences and larger, basic human cycles. His memory may be the kind that knows myth and prehistory, for these are the stories that are timeless. Typically, in traditional stories, the prophet is blind, like Tiresias, to the external world but has twenty-twenty vision of the inner world. In modern life that outward blindness appears in modified form as absent-mindedness, though there is no reason for the prophet to negate the professional person in us. The point is, if one has the psychological savvy proper to the prophet within, one's insight is truly inward and in a sense backward—aware of the past as a treasury of timeless patterns. The nature of this past-sightedness was captured by Martin

Heidegger when he wrote about Sophocles' *Antigone*. He speaks of the "great might and strangeness" of the beginning of history, concluding that "what comes afterward is not development but the flattening that results from mere spreading out."[28] I would not interpret Heidegger too literally here because, for example, the fifteenth time one falls in love may not be all that different from the first. But to see the fantasy at work in all those episodes might well be a revelation of the "might and strangeness" of fantasy.

These unusual factors at work in prophecy, making it appear indeed as a madness, come through most forcefully in dreams—a popular phenomenon among prophets. As might be expected, Ficino was quite ecstatic about dreams. Of individuals who normally live with a psychological attitude he writes: "While these men are awake their Souls are freer [from the body] than those of all others, and while they sleep, [their Souls] are completely free, therefore the higher impulse is easily perceived by them."[29] In dreams the categories of time obviously fall apart. In a dream we may go for a ride with a cousin who died ten years ago and a young man we met yesterday. The literal significance to ego, which is bound to historical time, seems to be peeled off in dreams, and only the significance to psyche remains. In dreams the very patterns of psychic life themselves appear before our prophet's eyes, placing us in touch with the "might and strangeness" of our own seeds, themselves stored in the "head" of our soul where our night visions dance.

This is one reason among many why attention to dreams can be a vital part of psychological awakening: the three parts of time melt into one. It may also help explain both the curious capacity of dreams to reach into the future, and the fascination of so many for the question of dreams and prediction. At the deepest level, prophecy is a vision from the highest perspective—it is the gift of the god Apollo, say tradition and Ficino. It is a celestial viewpoint from where one can behold the cycles that provide the material for our individuality.

That is the final point I wish to make, still following Ficino, about prophecy: in it we find ourselves in our uniqueness. Psychology often moves in the direction of personal history, either dredging for the causes of current problems or making plans for future trouble-free living. But these approaches are never truly satisfying because no causal explanation is fully convincing or efficacious, and troubles never seem to go away. Examining larger patterns one finds rhythmically recurring in personal life, or investigating images popping up in dreams and fantasy, may seem on the surface to head away from individuality, but in fact they do just the opposite. For these possible patterns are many and their combinations innumerable. Tracing our behavior and emotions back to their cyclic fantasies encourages a deeper sense of oneself as an individual. One discovers the things that truly matter, whether they take one form or another in enactment.

Edgar Wind summarized this point rather more philosophically by comparing the attitudes of Ficino and his pupil Pico della Mirandola. Pico spoke of two kinds of happiness: natural happiness, or finding traces of the divine in oneself; and supreme happiness, losing oneself in God. Wind makes this significant observation: "Ficino always held the two ways to be one, because he believed that only by reverting to God do men achieve not falling off from themselves.' Since transcendence was the restorer of immanent virtue, man should find, not merely lose, himself in God."[30]

Without this prophetic sense to gather up the parts of time before our inner eye, we may well "fall off from ourselves," know the ennui and confusion of surface experience, and feel the psychic bruises caused by conflicts between deeper movements and surface expectations. What we call reality may be perceived as a dream: the confluence of many times and places, a multitude of faces and voices, and a strange amalgam of promises and regrets. Looking back on the dream it is often difficult to know if it has to do with current situations, past experience, or future hopes and fears; usually a dream can be the imaginative backdrop for considering all three. A dream seems to hold all of experienced life within itself as within a cloud—the pieces floating around out of sequence but joined by an inner logic. From the point of view of a depth psychology, personal experience as well as cultural developments assume these characteristics of the dream. We can see the heart of the matter, or in Ficino's imagery the head, when we alter our vision, "seeing through" the usual compartments of time, beholding, with the prophet's hindsight and foresight, the dynamic economy of the soul.

Erotic Madness

Finally, when the soul has been made one, one I say which is in itself the very nature and essence of soul, it remains that immediately it recovers itself into the One which is above essence, that is, God. This the heavenly Venus completes through Love, that is, through the desire for the divine beauty, and the passion for Good."[31]

If it seemed strange to talk about poetry, religion, and prophecy as madness, there should be no problem with love. Anyone who has loved knows that it is a madness, a mania whose meaning is elusive, its rules confounding, its goals and outcomes a riddle, and its attractiveness overwhelming. As Ficino suggests, and not too subtly, people who love don't know what they are doing. But he also hints, in poetic language as usual, that there is something *to* love, something behind it not readily visible. Love may be painfully exhilarating and disastrously pleasant, but above all it is necessary for soul—like religion and poetry, it has psychological significance.

In the passage quoted, Ficino defines love as "desire for the divine beauty," and he speaks of ultimate unity and of God. Again, we ought not to get caught up in literal readings of these terms, especially since our goal is to focus on Ficinian psychology. Too often Platonic ideas such as these are rationalized to the point that there is no soul left in them—interpretation contradicts their very content.

For Ficino, "Love has the enjoyment of beauty as its goal."[32] Most Western psychologies have a more Aristotelian character, wanting to know causes and origins, parts and mechanisms, and clear and final reasons why people do the things they do. In short, psychology generally has a desire for the truth; it applauds conclusions reached, while it strongly discourages speculation. Ficino's objective, in contrast, is to be led through beauty to contemplation—no endings, no conclusions, and no final intellectual satisfaction. James Hillman speaks of the goal of psychologizing as a "deepening," but in gaining depth there is no end. It is not a matter of problems solved, but rather mysteries approached more deeply. The lure of beauty leads toward contemplation and fantasy, and in Ficino's view that is the proper goal of the soul.

The core of Ficino's psychology of love, then, thoroughly Plantonic in origin, consists in the capacity of human love to entice the soul away from the mulitiplicity of materialism toward the pleasures of soul-values. As he writes in the *Theologia Platonica*: "the soul is enflamed by the divine splendor, glowing in the beautiful person as in a mirror, and secretly lifted up by it as by a hook in order to become God."[33] Of all the images used by Platonists to describe the lure of love, the hook certainly has to be one of the most mundane. Yet it is not a bad image, especially today when we speak of persons getting "hooked" on something. Lovers, says Ficino, are hooked in a madness which potentially leads them out of the myopia of materialistic vision toward a true care for their souls.

I say "potentially" because not all forms of love represent the movement of soul away from body—obviously. Ficino contrasts noble love with lust, and James Hillman warns against interpreting all forms of love as the movement of anima or soul.[34] Love might well reveal the work of Aphrodite rather than anima, he says, and though both are significant expressions of love, still they are distinct. And there are yet more loves, many ways in which people are drawn to each other, signifying many different movements of soul. Nevertheless, there is a kind of love which does draw the soul toward its "natural" realm, a world quite unnatural to the ego.

If a person could have the peace of mind and self-awareness sufficient to distinguish the different kinds of currents which flow through the psyche when he is "in love," he might find an astonishing variety. He may find a desire for vitality, an urge to fly out of the doldrums, maybe even a spirit of power and violence. The objects in each case may be different, but love is the wind blowing the soul out of present circumstances. As Socrates says in the *Symposium*: "[Love] is a great spirit [daimon], and like all spirits he is intermediate between the divine and the mortal . . . He is the mediator who spans the chasm which divides them, and therefore in him all is bound together."[35] Therefore, although the experience of love reveals some kind of movement taking place between the deep sources of the soul and the ego, it is not always easy to know what the true object and goal is. Ficino expresses this idea in a familiar and effective image:

> Lovers never know what it is they desire or seek, for they do not know God himself, whose subtle incense has infused into his works a certain sweet aroma of Himself; by this aroma we are certainly every day aroused. We sense the aroma certainly, but we cannot distinguish its flavor, and so when we yearn for the indistinguishable flavor itself, being charmed by it sensible aroma, certainly we do not know what we desire and what we suffer."[36]

The madness of being in love clearly shows many characteristics of soul activity: interference with plans and projects, long periods of time spent in daydream and reverie, projection of ideal fantasies onto the loved person (by no means a modern insight),[37] confusion about personal goals and values, a weakening of willpower—all of these reveal an activation of the deeper strata of the soul. But we have great difficulty distinguishing the flavors. If love between two people is not just a matter of relationship, what kind of spirit is being enlivened? And what about the relationship, does this talk of soul-values diminish the relationship, psychologize it away?

The flavors of the aroma hidden in the concrete experience of love can be known only in imagination. As is the case with any concrete situation, its psychological meaning, that is, its significance to the psyche, can only be revealed through the work of "reversion," seeing the situation as a fantasy, against the backdrop of other images. The infatuation and madness of love encourages this work through the spontaneous unfolding of a wealth of images. The main point is, however, that the spirit of love can break open the psyche; the flame of Eros, for that is the God we are talking about, sets off an explosion of fantasies and feelings which may be more significant to the psyche than the relationship.

That could be a difficult statement to accept. Yet most of us must know those occasions when this erotic madness flares up like a blaze of magnesium and quickly dims. Afterward we wonder what happened, why we took our feelings so seriously, perhaps why secure and cherished relationships were threatened or maybe destroyed. Too quickly it becomes clear that it was not the relationship—a conscious union of two persons—that was so important, but rather the significance of the event to the people involved. If poetic flight of mind can be destructive, erotic mania can only be described as brutal. No doubt the soul is seduced by the beauty of Love himself, as the Eros and Psyche story tells so effectively, but as the story also reveals, there is genuine suffering in store for those who give assent to this god's fire.

On the other hand, do we not also justify, explain, and even romanticize a love relationship as a means for the soul-nourish-ment of the persons involved? Jung and some of his followers quite properly warn against the illusions of love, but they also at times suggest that we ought to grow mature and get beyond this adolescent penchant for blind love.[38] We can look at this another way, however. Relationship may well be the container—Eros's boudoir, the alchemical vas—in which Eros and Psyche meet, sleep, wound, chase, and eventually give birth. Such relationships may be episodic—why establish a norm for these vessels? And in fact the value to the individuals might be their satisfaction in creating and sustaining a place of containment for psychic movement. There are indeed illusions and delusions, ecstasies and disappointments in these "aromatic" loves, but that is the madness of it all. One wonders about the quite reasonable, rational, well-conceived relationships, sometimes fixed by written contract, one finds in modern society. Could it be that madness, essential to "true love" and therefore to the containing relationship, has been ruled out by agreement and "mature" judgment?

Of those loves which do not have "divine madness" in their structure Ficino writes rather harshly, although his remedies for getting out of such relationships are quite interesting: he suggests that the person keep busy, have his blood thinned, consume large quantities of wine even to the point of intoxication so that new spirit may come in, work up a heavy sweat, and finally, following Lucretius, have sex frequently.[39] The only advice Ficino doesn't mention that is part of even modern folk wisdom is a cold shower. Of course, Ficino sees these remedies as means toward psychological catharsis, for starting afresh.

Even though the image of erotic madness is tied to the actual experience of love, especially love between a man and a woman, and although this phenomenon still reigns as one of the chief conundrums of life, still we should also see this human love as a metaphor.[40] Our experience of human love creates a multidimensional image, deeply felt in body and soul, that gives us an idea of the movement of the soul away from concreteness and literalism toward image and fantasy. The soul is lured by beauty, for the beauty of the world reflects the beauty of the heavens—a central idea in Ficino's Platonic thinking. Therefore, erotic madness finds its place with the others.

Reviewing the four kinds of madness once more, we can see that the poetic imagination withdraws from literalism, waking the soul and establishing the basis for a psychological attitude. This attitude is given due serious attention through a mode of fantasy we have called "sacerdotal madness." In this second phase, not only fantasies but the deepest structuring patterns of the soul, its true mysteries, are brought into view. Next, in prophetic madness one experiences a shift in time perspective which moves attention away from discrete events taking place in linear time to cyclic patterns and fragments of imagery that do not fit the linear scheme. Finally, eros draws us into contemplation through desire for these soul perspectives. As in Apuleius's story, psyche is initiated into its own "unnatural" world where it remains through union with eros, giving birth to the pleasure suited to body and soul, not merely the senses.

Puffer's Gold

We are now ready, finally to consider the planets themselves. This and the previous chapters have laid foundations for understanding Ficinian astrology and have suggested the relevance of the planets and stars to modern psychology. If those suggestions are still rather thin, they should thicken as we look closely at the planets, one by one. What we must avoid is the astrological equivalent of puffer's gold, the dubious achievement of those alchemists who were more interested in making goldlike metals in their ovens rather than the inner gold of spirit and soul.

In alchemy we saw one remarkable varition on the single theme weaving through all these preliminary studies: the establishment and maintenance of a point of view we have called psychological, meaning the term literally, "the logic of the psyche." Making, or rather accepting from tradition, the all-important distinction between spirit, soul, and body, we could separate and identify the peculiar characteristics of the psychological dimension, especially the central place of imagination and the processes needed to develop a metaphorical view. For metaphor is of the essence of psyche. Attending to the nature and needs of the psyche, we can see that every action is an expression of something else. People comfortable only in a literalistic attitude find this kind of metaphorical thinking maddening, and we have seen that it is indeed madness from the literalizing ego's point of view. Nevertheless, the psyche's occasionally infuriating obstinacy, never allowing a conclusion or a simple, direct statement, leads us onward toward deeper understanding and more intense participation in life.

All of the psychological processes we have examined, all too briefly, aim at keeping psyche in the middle, away from the thin air of spirit and the sticky mud of matter. Since psyche can become fixated in a single fantasy, which thereby tends to become literalized, I have advocated a constellating of the psyche, sustained variety and multiple, fluid fantasies. This process parallels the poetic imagination with its job of keeping the soul alert and awake. I have also suggested, following Ficino closely, an ecology of the soul, a cultivation of the environment with psychological needs in mind. We have seen that the role of alchemical consciousness, an attitude that can be nurtured, by the way, without practicing in a laboratory, also keeps soul in the middle by dissolving materialistic and literalistic attitudes and by congealing spiritual ideas and tendencies. Then, the very fantasy of four elements of spirit supports once again the idea that soul has its own properties and requirements, indeed its own constitutive and nutritive elements. Finally, we have studied four kinds of nonrational consciousness helpful in maintaining the psychological perspective.

If there is overkill and repetition in all of these variations on the theme, it is because psyche is so foreign to most of what modern people take to be true and self-evident. We feel we have emerged in an evolutionary manner out of the need for myth, imagery, metaphor, and other psychological factors. Even, *mirabile dictu*, psychologists resist the psyche, perhaps more than other scholars and professionals. So it seems legitimate to make the point from many angles. But in addition to providing emphasis, the various psychological elements and processes we have examined each provide a unique aspect of psychological reality.

Now we turn to an even greater scandal in the eyes of modern scientific thought: astrology. Investigating the imagery of the planets with Ficino's psychology in mind and with the aid of his sparse, enigmatic comments on them, we will try to understand even more specifically the processes and requirements of the psyche. Our purpose is not to espouse or support the actual practice of astrology, but to *constellate* in our psycholgy some ideas and images which promise to enhance both theory and therapy.

PART II
Radii Planetarum:
Planetary Radiance

Trismegistus said that the Egyptians used to take certain materials of the world and make images, and the souls of daemons would enter them, even the soul of his ancestor Mercury. Apollo, too, and Isis and Osiris would descend into the statues for either the good or ill of mankind.

— Ficino, *The Planets*, chapter 13

According to Goethe, the alchemist discovers that what he has projected into the retort is his own darkness, his unredeemed state, his passion, his struggle to reach the goal, that is, to become what he really is, to fulfill the purpose for which his mother bore him, and, after the peregrinations, of a long life full of confusion and error, to become the *filius regius*, son of the supreme mother.

— Jung, *Psychology of the Transference*

6
Zodiacal Reflections

Although my interest in Ficino's astrological statements was born of a concern to recover a more adequate psychology than the reductive scientific one under which we now suffer, I am also concerned about the attacks of scientists on forms of imagining which lie outside the paradigms of science. Too often these attacks are transparent forays against imagination itself.

On the other hand, of course there are dangers in folk astrology just as there are superstitious tendencies in folk religion. For many the intricate procedures and intriguing interpretations of astrology satisfy the desire for mystery with superficial hocus pocus; or they respond to that wish to be free of choice and responsiblity — surrendering to the influence of the planets; or, finally, they caress the ego, placing it amid cosmic happenings and building up fresh fantasies for personal destiny.

Before dismissing astrology, however, with a knowing, moralistic denial of egoism, perhaps it would be worth while to consider what psychological benefits there might be even in the popular attraction to astrology. Or, if "benefits" is too strong a word, at least we might investigate the fantasies behind the widespread fascination with the stars.

Sun-signs: A Theology of Grace

Discussing one's sun-sign at a cocktail party and finding Cancer and Leo on glasses, towels, charm bracelets, and underwear have "flattened out" the mysteries of these ancient symbols. Yet, even a fad stems from a fantasy, flat though it is, and the fantasy behind sun-signs and planets hints at an otherwise unanswered need.

There was a time when many of us lived within the fantasy of a theology of grace. We believed that there were "wheels in motion" in the universe which threatened us with disaster but also promised the occasional gift from the sky. Believing in grace we assumed an attitude of receptivity, cooperation, gratitude, and dependence. Schleiermacher's descriptions of religion in the nineteenth century chiefly in terms of the sense of dependence are still moving and seem to reach the heart of religion. But in the modern world, where science and technology not only fabricate marvelous instruments and gadgets but also create an imaginative realm of meaning, that sense of dependence and grace is gone. In its place is the narrow open window of statistical probability. We might be the one in a thousand to live a healthy life or enjoy a happy marriage. But we can no longer confidently pray for such a grace or feel that we have any support beyond that which we build and maintain. Even in philosophy the existentialist realism which warns us that we make our own heavens and hells corrodes the sense of grace-full living.

But if my sun-sign is Aries I imagine that by some destiny beyond my own power I will have the passion and initiative to make life a success. I don't really know this, in fact I know that it is not true, but by taking astrology half seriously I can imagine and therefore feel that something in the universe is working for me. Astrology becomes a thin vestige of formerly deeply felt reliance upon grace. God may have disappeared from the sky, but that canopy of infinite space, opened up and made more vast by science, still catches my fancy and carries a share of my destiny.

Although the feeling behind the fad of identifying sun-signs and ruling planets often runs deep, betraying a desire for living life in a larger context, popular astrology, both the kind found in the newspapers and with many professional astrologers, is far from adequate in responding to that desire. Astrology itself is only an indicator of a fantasy and, in the best hands, a partial instrument for picking at the surface of deep desire and longing. Although, as I said, my interest is in using Renaissance astrology as a source for deepening modern psychology, still I think that the ritual of astrology itself, though in no way necessary and not even important, might serve as a useful means for exploring one's fantasies and life patterns.

Besides creating in the individual a sense of connection with a larger world, a world which might well be inside rather than outside, astrological imagery also importantly creates an imaginative awareness of one's own uniqueness. The birth chart, for example, defines identity with images that stretch far beyond ego, but it also emphasizes the unique space and time of one's birth. We saw earlier that Ficino recommended that psychic exploration begin with a sense of one's own daimon and destiny. This daimon may be found in a planet on the horoscope, but the chart as a whole also includes that image of unique individuality. One is not simply a constellation of cosmic factors, one is a person, on earth, with a particular culture determined by time and place. Both the eternal and the temporal conditions of human experience are taken into account; indeed, in true astrological consciousness a person simultaneously imagines his uniqueness and his common heritage.

As I mentioned earlier, going through the process of gathering information for the horoscope, setting up the chart, memorizing positions and aspects, and working it interpretation can be an art of memory, the work of imagination. The concrete process brings forth significant fantasies: historical and family conditions at the time of birth, parents and relatives, the town or house of birth and early years. Qualities of all these factors become intensified when viewed through the prism of planetary aspects and houses and signs. At some time in life it may be a useful experience to go through this rite in order to get one more psychological portrait of oneself. It certainly would have as much validity, and much more imagination, than a psychological, statistical inventory.

The serious psychological danger in astrology, a danger found in all religious and occult systems, is the temptation to lose soul in spiritual literalism. Instead of using astrology as an art of memory, people begin "believing in" astrology, and such belief takes this art of imagination out of the realm of metaphor. "Believers" then might make life decisions—from buying clothes to getting married—according to the planets, not in order to keep their imagination alive, which would be a psychological move, but in order to be successful in their physical life. Spirit and body serve each other, but there is no soul in between.

When we read of American Indians or Castaneda's Don Juan thanking the earth before pulling up a vegetable or flower, we may be impressed at the attitude created by such a practice. An entire fantasy of relatedness to nature is fostered by such a simple rite. But if the purpose of that little prayerlike attitude is to get the best food, we again find spirit serving the belly. The same is true of astrology. It may be one effective imaginative device among many, for some people, to nourish imagination in the specific ways proper to it; but if the focus is not soul, then we dally with faddish fundamentalism and move even further away from a psychological, soul-enhancing attitude.

Planets of the Soul

Having alluded to astrology as fad, an imaginative device, and as a fundamentalist spiritual practice, let us now leave the concrete ritual and concentrate on the metaphorical value of astrological imagery. By referring to the images of astrology, but not advocating the practice, we may be able to unveil otherwise undifferentiated facets of psychological processes. Let us inquire into the fantasies behind Ficinian astropsychology without necessarily mimicking his quaint life-style.

Ficino's attitude toward astrology was ambivalent: he writes against astrologers more than once, yet his writings are filled with allusions to astrology, and *The Planets* is fundamentally an astrological treatise.[2] In a letter to Bembo in 1477 Ficino uses a pun to put astrologers in their place: "As diligently as astronomers measure the heavens [*metiuntur*], astrologers fabricate empty lies [*mentiuntur*] about human life."[3] But, as we have seen, Ficino consults the sky for building projects, for making medicines, and for constructing images. He also saw the general heaviness of his own life marked by the planet Saturn in his horoscope.

One way Ficino theoretically resolves the apparent contradiction in his attitude toward astrology may help us gain a proper perspective on it for ourselves. As Kristeller explains, Ficino's general principle holds that superior beings have power over inferior beings. In Ficino's hierarchical universe the planets and stars are higher than the human body, but not higher than the mind. They could influence, then, the body without having power over the higher faculties. And in fact, *The Planets* is a book on care for the body primarily, though the soul is by no means neglected.

In a similar way, when we imagine the planets within to be images for deep patterns and focal points of psychological life, we do not have to consider these as metaphysical entities or as determining factors in human life, as in the traditional belief in the inescapable *influence* of the planets of the sky. There are indeed felt movements of the psyche obviously not intitiated or even fully controlled by the ego, but there is no need to turn these subjective experiences into self-sufficient entities. In that case psychology becomes an internalized theology, another two-tiered universe turned inside out.[4] Jungians tend to treat the archetype of the Self,[5] for example, as a metaphysical fulcrum holding the psyche in balance, but the planets and the archetypal fantasies of personality are, to interpret Ficino somewhat, images that move the soul without deluding the mind. We can know these images to be metaphors without destroying their power to move us psychologically.

Accommodations and Arrangements

In the second chapter of *The Planets* Ficino describes the world as something alive, like an animal, and in this vital body lower parts draw benefits from higher members. "The more powerful the source," he writes, "the quicker it is to act, the more prone to give. So, if we apply scant additional preparations, that will be sufficient for acquiring celestial benefits. And if someone *accommodates* himself [*se accommodet*] to this [higher world], to him it will be especially subject."[6] To accommodate oneself means, as we have seen before, to expose oneself to those material things rich in the kinds of spirit we need. Ficino expresses this whole process in the following way. The planets are the source of various kinds of spirit needed to nourish the soul. From the planets come rays which strike the earth and are absorbed by objects, either naturally or through human intervention—making images, for example, obviously appropriate to a particular spirit. Living with the needs of soul in mind, we would go about our daily affairs making a special effort to expose ourselves—accommodation—to the proper objects.

Let us develop this idea first by noting carefully Ficino's own description of planetary radiance:

> Rays can impress wonderful occult powers on images, as they do on other things. For they are not inanimate like rays of lamps; rather, they are living and sensate like eyes shining in living bodies. They bring wonderful gifts with them from celestial imaginations and minds, as well as strength and power from the configurations and rapid movement of these bodies. They incite in the spirit, effectively and appropriately, a reproduction of the celestial rays.[7]

If we imagine the planets within as images of deep patterns and movements of the psyche, then, following these imaginative ideas of Ficino, we are to understand that certain objects in our material world will correspond to certain planets, and not only correspond, they will radiate and convey to us the spirit of a particular planet. The material world, both natural and man-made, is a source of various kinds of spirit needed for psychological movement, In

Ficino's psychotherapeutic system, if we could only sort out the objects according to their "planetary" (archetypal) characteristics, we could take better care of the soul in everyday life.

The notion that the material world has an inherent spiritual dimension is to be found throughout religious and occult traditions. For example, it is nicely described by the alchemist Basil Valentine:

> Thus the power of growth I speak of is not imparted by the earth but by the life-giving spirit that is in it. If the earth were deserted by this spirit, it would be dead, and no longer able to afford nourishment to anything.[8]

Indeed, in our modern world, without imagination the earth is dead, we treat the world and our own lives as lifeless pieces of matter to be maintained and gratified. With imagination, however, the spirit inherent in material things becomes evident and efficacious. Roger Bacon made the point mythologically, adding a note that leads us from alchemy to astrology:

> By Proserpine the ancients signified that ethereal spirit which, having been separated by violence from the upper globe, is enclosed and imprisoned beneath the earth (which earth is represented by Pluto) as well as expressed by those lines: Whether that the earth yet fresh, and from the deeps of heaven new-sundered, did some seeds retain, some sparks and motions of its kindred sky.[9]

Bacon, like Ficino, presents the image of the material world containing within it some "seeds" of its relative, the sky. The material world, in other words, holds the fantasies of our inward souls, either in its man-made form or, in Hillman's words, in the fantasies we have about it.

"Accommodation," then, is another psychological process we can add to constellation and cultivation. We accommodate ourselves to the fundamental and varied movements of the soul through our orientaton toward the material world. Astrological consciousness thus becomes a mindfulness of the deeper, archetypal significance of the most mundane events. The otherwise undifferentiated, linear, and literal sequence of events becomes ordered, not through reason alone, but through imagination into patterns the significance of which appeals to the soul more than to the mind. Rather than exert all our energies and give every bit of attention to the mother's materialism, we give the daughter, Persephone/Proserpina her due.[10]

A good portion of *The Planets* consists of advice for accommodating oneself to the various planetary centers. Each planet is described roughly, then the material things associated with each are listed, as we are advised to use the proper material objects. Some of the objects mentioned have obvious physical properties related to a particular planet, such as golden things connected with the sun. Others have stories behind them linking them to the deity of a planet.

Interpreting this procedure of accommodation, we may understand the details metaphorically. There are seven planets in the classical system, but there are many more archetypal possibilities one can imagine for the soul. We may begin to understand the process of accommodation by studying the planets, along with Ficino, as archetypal images, but we do not have to stop there. An imaginative symbol system helps, and there are many to be found in the religions of the world and even in art and psychology, but sometimes we need only an idiosyncratic metaphor against which to view an actual situation and glimpse the fantasies congealed in it. A dream will do, or a novel, or science, or a walk in the woods. Everything is metaphor and food for the soul. All of the material world contains sparks of the kindred sky, flashes of the psychological lumen.

If accommodation is a posturing of oneself toward the world so that the psychological dimension is revealed and put in action, then what happens to the psyche itself is an "arrangement." Recall the title of Ficino's book: *De Vita Coelitus Comparanda*. I am translating *comparanda* as "arrange," though it could also mean "dispose" or "prepare." The title of the book refers, then, to arranging life according to planetary spirit, but we could also think of the arrangement as a constellation of psyche itself, all parts awakened and in place. When one's psychological life reflects the sky, *its* planets are in motion. It is not stuck under the domination of a single planetary focus. We will explore this polycentric image of the psyche in the last chapter; for now we can understand the context of our study of individual planets. The ultimate purpose is to know the varieties of soul-movement so that this variety can become part of psychological life. Movement itself is essential to the soul, for without movement there is no feeling, no valuing, and no vitality.

It is apparent that Ficino's astropsychology suggests a picture of the psyche which embraces many extremes of experience without sacrificing any of them or, worse, rubbing them out through harmonizing or reconciliation of opposites. Ficino affirms both sides of pradoxes consistently, always keeping a Janus face. He affirms the role of cyclic, transpersonal factors (planets) in human life while at the same time emphasizing the important task of disovering one's uniqueness nd individuality. Among the planets he recognizes those which are particularly painful to the soul, like Mars and Saturn, but he doesn't suggest flight from these influences—they are part of life. True to his pervasive Platonism he strongly advocates a dying to materialistic attitudes, yet his theory remarkably places great value on the ordinary, the mundane, and the worldly.

One final point should be made about the interpretation of the planets and their characters. I am suggesting that we read all of this astrology in terms of a sky within. The planets correspond, then, to deeply felt movements of the soul and not to either ego attitudes, that is, conscious values and positions, or to persona qualities. I mean the latter in the Jungian sense: social, gender, and ego roles we play. Mars is not simply a surface tendency toward anger, nor is Venus the trappings of body awareness. These planetary centers are deep in the psyche, generating many complexes, fantasies, and behaviors. They sky within truly seems as vast as the sky without, and the planets are just as massive, mysterious, and unearthly.

7
Sol

Of all the heavenly bodies revolving rhythmically around our physical world (astrologically speaking we on earth are still in the center of the universe), the one so important for maintaining life, so visible in its brilliance and influential in its warmth, and so obvious as to be taken for granted, is the sun. These days we are especially aware of the generosity of the sun as it daily showers us with raw energy, but we probably rarely consider the impact of this huge, golden brilliance upon our psyches. If everything in the world, including pencils and ants and chicken soup, find themselves "metaphorized" into our unconscious stores of images, the sun cannot rise and set with such grandeur and color our skins and expose our world without having immense psychological impact. Worldwide devoted worship of the sun attests to its spiritual significance, and this inner influence was not lost on Ficino and his forerunners. Ficino not only refers to Sol frequently in all of his writings, and especially in his direct astrological passages, he also wrote a seprate monograph on light (*De Lumine*) and another on the sun itself (*De Sole*).

As we study the various planets in search of their psychological significnce, we will be particularly interested in distinguishing the kind of spirit they represent, in Ficino's imagery, the kind of rays they shine into our lives. Each planet will be seen to depict a distinct spirit, but the sun, in addition to having some unique distinguishing features, represents spirit itself. So we can say that Ficinian psychology is above all *solar* in character on account of its emphasis on the role of spirit in the care of psyche. Ficino develops this idea in *The Planets*:

> Our soul, besides maintaining the particular powers of its members, promotes the common power of life all through us, but especially through the heart, source of the intimate fire of the soul. Similarly, the World Soul flourishes everywhere, but especially through the sun, as it indiscriminately unfolds its common power of life. (Chap.1.)

127

Then, in the fourth chapter, Ficino offers a step-by-step plan for the care of body and soul and comments there on the healing power of Sol. Cure begins with the separation of infecting vapors and their banishment by means of purging medicines. Next, the patient is illumined by bright objects. Third, he is cared for so that he might become stronger. And finally, he is exposed to heavenly rays and to the direct influence of the sun. "In this way," advises Ficino, "the spirit, though in us, pours heavenly benefits into our body first and then into our soul—benefits, I might mention, that are entirely celestial, for *everything is contained in the sun*."

The sun is an image, then, of spiritual power itself, the "heart" of the life of psyche. Like the gold of alchemy, it is the spirit to be found in all things spiritual. In Ficino's words, "gold is like the sun: it is present in all metals just as Sol is in all planets and stars."[1] Sol is the center of the planetary system, not as a geometric focal point, but as an ever-present quality. In the Hermetic texts Ficino had read an intriguing description of God, one quoted many times in later literature: God is the center of a circle whose center is everywhere and whose circumference is nowhere. A poet directly and deeply influenced by Ficino, Guy le Febvre de la Boderie, who had translated Ficino's *Libri de Vita Tres*, including *The Planets*, applied this definition of divinity to the sun:

> The infinite sun, whose prime roundness
> Perennially produces rays of light:
> Thus from the roundness as well as from the precious ray
> Comes forth eternally the eternal warmth.
> It is the unlimited Round, of which the central point
> Is found in every place, whose spherical contour
> Is found nowhere, and from whose center and circuit
> The rims or rays ensue all around.[2]

Solar spirit comes, interestingly, from the roundness of the sun as well as from its rays. Like the soul, circular when not in personal human form, spirit is round; that is, spirit is not something produced or even educed directly by human intention and effort. It is transpersonal and transhuman.

Jung had many occasions to discuss the role of Sol in alchemy, and, pairing Sol with the alchemical Luna, he tends to identify the former with consciousness and the later with unconsciousness.[3] In this interpretation Sol is the light of consciousness shed on the dark mysteries of nature, so that an increase of solar influence corresponds to a heightening of consciousness. According to Jung, "Thus the concept of Sol has not a little to do with the growth of modern consciousness, which in the last two centuries has relied more and more on the observation and experience of natural objects."[4] Jung has much more to say about Sol, but this is the gist of his comments on the bright side of the sun—he makes other interesting remarks on the shadow of the sun and the sun in the center of the earth, *Sol Niger*. In the peculiar Ficinian notion of spirit, one we have studied at some length, Sol is imagined as spirituality itself, not unlike the alchemical elixir, the secret of secrets, the most mysterious yet most open secret of all. From the heart of spiritual conciousness radiates the transforming spirit of the sun. Given solar consciousness, all the other varieties of spirit may follow, but general attention must be given to spirit itself first and above all.

Although Ficino's psychology is primarily "celestial," concerned above all to effect a "tempered" psyche, he frequently emphasizes the role of solar spirit so much that his theory might well be called "solar" as well. For example, he claimed to follow the Arabian philosophers who considered Sol to be the fundamental "human" planet. We can see this, Ficino writes, in man's beauty, the subtlety of his humors, his clarity of spirit, and his insight and imagination.[5] These qualities of human beings, similar to those of the objects he lists in *The Planets* as solar, are all signs of spirit, an evanescence of the person beyond materialism. His solar psychology, then, is aimed primarily at developing this human imagination so that it can use the material world for its spiritual potentiality.

Now we have to distinguish this kind of solar, spiritual approach to psychology from others that have solar charac-teristics but are essentially different. Roberto Assagioli's "psy-chosynthesis," for example, is a solar psychology in many ways. He himself called his approach "height" psychology in order to distinguish it from depth psychology. In his diagram of the personality, he depicts the "higher Self" as a sun, the source of insight and creativity for the ego.[6] In practice, this solar, higher Self is treated as an oracular source (the Delphic oracle in Apollonian psychology?) of fantasies to which one turns for guidance in life decisions. Other aspects of the psychosynthesis regimen, its meditation techniques for example, ally this approach with spiritual disciplines in which the notion of spirit is quite different from that of Ficino. For them spirit is an upward region removed from body and often preferably set apart from fantasy and emotion, an arena of the mind and intellect similar to Ficino's *Mens*—a mentality quite removed from the concrete. The humanistic movement in psychology instigated by Maslow and others has in recent years spawned a "transpersonal psychology,' a movement interested largely in assimilating meditative techniques and other spiritual practices from the world's religions. Psychosynthesis and the other transpersonal psychologies, eager to transcend the "inferior" problematics of ordinary psychological reality, pursue spirit in a manner Ficino would label "intellectual," although they probably would not, since the awareness they seek is beyond conceptualization. At any rate, transpersonal psychologies and their devotees employ solar imagery and often speak in the imagery of "light" in order to denote the high regions of spirit, whereas Ficino conceives of spirit as an emanation of the material world. For him spiritual increase is truly a psychological process, necessarily attached to the concrete life and to the entanglements of soul. Therefore, his solar spirit is immanent, a sun whose center is everywhere *within* our most mundane experiences, and decidedly not a reach above the mid-realm of psyche. In practical terms, then, one cultivates Ficinian solar psychology by attending to the spirit or atmosphere of everyday affairs, extracting fantasies and concretizing vague moods and lofty ideas; one does not practice yoga or mediation, as useful and these might be for other purposes, in order to move beyond the ordinary.

Sun and Earth, Soul and Body

This peculiar way of dealing with spirit lies at the heart of Ficinian psychology and more than any other aspect of his theory makes his approach valuable in our modern world, where we have more psychologies than we need and more spiritual paths becoming popular than any individual can assimilate. With the split between spirit and body and passionate advocates of each, we have no soul. Ficino's notion of spirit is truly psychological, as I have said, and therefore gives us a way of imagining and effecting a union, finally, of body, soul, and spirit. We can picture this union yet another way, borrowing a schema from Bachofen, the nineteenth-century anthropologist and mythologist. Even if his historical opinions are now questionable, his mythic paradigm of solar consciousness still has heuristic value.

Bachofen delineates three stages in the evolution of solar consciousness. In the first phase, the radiant son (sun) is ruled by mother (earth), and day is like night. Spirit is dominated by matter. The second stage is Dionysian, an era of father-right, an age of the god who fecundates the earth, a phallic Sol forever seeking receptive matter in order to give it life. The third stage is Apollonian, of which Bachofen writes:

> The phallic sun, forever fluctuating between rising and setting, coming into being and passing away, is transformed into the immutable source of light. It enters the realm of solar being, leaving behind it all idea of fecundation, all yearning for mixture with feminine matter . . . . Apollo frees himself entirely from any bond with woman.[7]

Bachofen's first phase or image of solar consciousness clearly is one Ficino is arguing against most strongly. Values of the spirit are not perceived because they are blocked by materialistic shortsightedness. Individuals, neglecting soul, are compelled by unknown movements of the psyche, as Jung so often complained, not knowing why they feel empty inside, never satisfied with their incomes, unhappy in relationships, drawn to alchohol, or gambling or some other compulsion.

The third phase of Bachofen's paradigm I have already discussed—an ascent into spirituality cut off from psyche. This ascent generally takes one of two forms: escape into intellectualism or into spiritual discipline. In traditional mythological language, Apollo's immaterial masculinity would have no commerce with the feminine material world. In this mentality there may be concern for the body, but not a psychological concern. A person can be a body-builder and at the same time a devoted practitioner of transcendental meditation, but that isn't sufficient for soul. In another way of keeping the mind clean, emotion, which can give body to ideas, may be ruled out as feminine, a stain on pure thought.

Bachofen's second stage is closest to Fician solar psychology. Though Bachofen places this sensibility in the domain of Dionysos and Ficino consistently speaks of solar consciousness as Apollonian, still we can recall that these two deities in Ficino's mind are brothers, inseparable. Bachofen describes spirit in this phase as fecundating, though it remains at some distance. Psychologically, the individual neither flees contact with body and feminine reality, nor does he immerse himself in the material world to the neglect of spirit. Ficino himself employs imagery compatible with that of Bachofen:

Heaven, the bridegroom of earth, does not touch her, as is commonly thought, nor does he embrace her; he regards (illuminates) her by the mere rays of his stars which are, as it were, his eyes; and in regarding her he fructifies her and so begets life.[8]

Solar consciousness, an awareness of the spiritual values in material things, brings these things to life, fertilizing them, animating them, giving them soul; for spirit is the food of soul. Consciousness then, or imagination, is efficacious; to behold spirit is to take a step toward receiving the benefits of spirit. But in addition to having the ability to discriminate spirits, one still has to get in touch with the world in order to make life fertile. It may be necessary to take action on fantasies; if they are merely entertained in one's fancy, their full character may never to revealed and their spirit may never be communicated. A Dionysian abandon must overcome Apollonian distance and defensiveness if the spirit is to be assimilated. Gnawing fascinations and compulsive infatuations cannot easily be dismissed in favor of the clean, white life without sacrifice of spirit. Or so the imagery of Ficino and Bachofen suggests. Psyche needs the sexual touch of spirit and matter if it is to be fed, fertilized, and embodied.

Sources of Solar Spirit

Several chapters in *The Planets* make the reader feel that he has entered a bizarre apothecary, filled with rare and aromatic substances and sparkling with radiant stones and gems. Indeed, in the preface to the book Ficino pretends that this volume is a laboratory: "Our laboratory here—this book—offers for different kinds of people a variety of antidotes, drugs, poultices, salves and remedies. If any should be unpleasing to you, I will skip over those and include others."[9] He was particularly concerned about resistance to astrological matters, but the modern reader might also have trouble with most of his examples of spiritual, solar objects. For example, among the substances he mentions as particularly solar is nutmeg, a spice whose color and tang suggest the spirit of the sun. Peppermint, by the way, he says contains the spirit of Jupiter. The list of solar objects gets even more interesting:

Anything which is from stones and plants called heliotropes because they turn toward the sun is solar. So too are gold, gold pigment, gold colors, chrysolite, carbuncle, myrrh, incense, moss, amber, balsam, honey, aromatic reed, crocus, corn, cinnamon, aloes, and other aromatic materials; Aries, Astur, chicken, swan, lion, beetle, crocodile; yellow-skinned people; people who are curly-haired, bald, and magnanimous.[10]

In the case of most of these items it is fairly easy to see why they would be considered solar. Usually they are either sun-colored or aromatic—exuding spirit. Others need some clarification. But we should not overlook the basic point, Ficino's "natural magic," which is really a school of imagination. By surrounding ourselves with objects which look *like* something as profound as solar spirit, we keep that spirit in mind. As if by sympathetic magic, these metaphorical objects can in fact bring to us the spirit they represent. We can either bring imagination to the natural world (to spices and gems) or make things resembling the spirit with which we are concerned. It is the *image* that effectively communicates the spirit.

Obviously, it is not necessary, as I have said before, to imitate Ficino exactly and surround our bedrooms and studies with spices and herbs, although I wouldn't rule that out. But there are other similar ways to tutor imagination—paintings, hangings, plants, records, books, colors, architecture, furnishings, clothes, and so on. Our physical enviroment can be cultivated even in this way with psyche in mind. Activities and people around us, not just bald or curly-haired friends, can bring into our lives needed spirit, naturally. Conscious of these spiritual values in the ordinary we become, like Ficino, a modern magus, a magician of the soul, working marvels not for profit or recognition but for psychological animation.

Let us take a look at some of the less transparent items Ficino has on his list of solar objects.

Chrysolite is an example of a substance related both to gold and to spirit. The name comes from the Greek *chrysos*, gold. In the fifteenth-century *North Midland Lapidary* it is said that chrysolite signifies the gifts of the Holy Ghost and that it is the color of water and of gold. The lapidary refers us to the *Book of Revelations* (21:15) where the seventh precious stone of the New Jerusalem's foundation is identified as chrysolite. The brightness of this stone, associated with the "aroma of the Holy Ghost," signifies not only spirit emanating from matter, a basic solar image, but also the pristine, archetypal nature of that spirit—a foundational element in the City of God. Like Bacon's earth, which retains some sparks from the sundered sky, matter like this holds traces of the spirit of an even higher heaven. In other words, spirit we may glimpse or "smell" in the things of ordinary living may have a place at a much deeper level, at the very foundation of the psyche's character.

Other substances on the list suggest some dangers in the basically positive "heliotropic" attitude. The rays of the sun, powerful and all-encompassing, have great amplitude, and although, says Ficino, they are basically beneficial, they can be toxic. "They may have a drying effect in the closed hollows of dry matter."[11] To be too much in the sun is to have an overdose of spirit. Spirit can be desiccating, producing arid universities, tinder-dry lectures and books, experts of spirit high and dry in ivory towers, and parched personalities. This highly desirable quality of solar spirit needs to be doused in moist darkness now and then.

There is in fact a curious relationship among some of the solar objects listed in the solar apothecary between sun and water. For example, according to the *Sloane Lapidary* carbuncle or the ruby "driveth away all taches [blemishes] and ill conditions. It is sayd yt this stone is in ye fleme [river] of paradise."[12] Furthermore, three of the animals listed are amphibious; like the sun (according to many traditions among people living by the sea) they spend part of the time in water, part in air. These animals are the swan, the beetle, and the crocodile.

The thirteenth-century bestiary of Guillaume Le Clerc says of the crocodile:

> Never was seen another such beast, for it lives on land and in water. At night it is submerged in water, and during the day it reposes upon the land. If it meets and overcomes a man, it swallows him entire, so that nothing remains. But ever after it laments him as long as it lives.[13]

In spite of all we have seen in support of a consciousness of spirit, the sun cannot always shine; night fortunately comes along with its refreshing darkness and relief from the heat of day. Psychologically, there are times for unconsciousness, for not giving a care about the spiritual rewards involved in what you are doing. There is a time for pure experience, for plain physical absorption and enjoyment, and, again in spite of what was said earlier, a time for entertainment. These times offer a rest from solar heat and light, establishing a natural rhythm, like the imagined path of the sun across the heavens and under the sea. Without this rhythm the spirit can swallow a person up "so that nothing remains." Excessively spiritualized persons walk about disembodied, like Echo of the frail voice and wasted body, or like the Cheshire Cat. More often the "refreshment" is indeed darkness, not so pleasant, but a necessary counterpoint to the light of the sun.

One can think of other connectious between sun and water: water as the matrix of the unconscious from which spirit comes, water as emotion to balance the thinking of solar attitudes, water as the nighttime of dreams and the reflecting pond of the Narcissus-like soul, water as the sea of the hero-sun's night journey. Like an amphibious animal the soul must learn to live in different habitats and to tread on unusual and varied soils and waters.

Another allusion to the nighttime of the sun is the swan which moves brightly and gracefully over the water during the day and is also known to pull the sun's barge at night, as it towed the knight's boat in the Lohengrin story. Its serpent-shaped neck also hints at its dark, chthonic side. There is a time for the sunset of the soul, a dark period where, as Jung points out, the sun is black. In his essay on the sun, Ficino notes that when the sun is ascending to the mid-heaven, there is increase of vital and animal spirit, but when the sun descends these spirits are diminished.[14] Here we find another advantage to the astrological image-system: it takes into account the movements of the heavenly bodies, their rhythms of ascent and descent, increase and decrease.

The story of the lion, another solar animal, hints too at the dark side of the sun. Le Clerc tells us that the lion has three outstanding characteristics; it lives on a high mountain, it sleeps with its eyes open, and "when the lioness brings forth her young, it falls to the ground, and gives no sign of life until the third day, when the lion breathes upon it and in this way brings it back to life again."[15] During the Middle Ages this last characteristic of the lion was interpreted as a reference to Jesus' three days in the tomb before his resurrection, but it undoubtdly also refers to the sun giving birth to the moon after three days absence—the time before the new moon.

The three days before the birth of the young lion, the new sun, represent the three days Jesus spent in hell, in the underworld working for the freedom of souls in limbo. An anonymous alchemist of the sixteenth century saw this analogy:

> All men had to descend into the underworld, where they were imprisoned for ever. But Christ Jesus unlocked the gate of the heavenly Olympus and threw open the realm of Pluto, that the souls might be freed.[16]

The night of spirit, the sinking of consciousness, the "dark night of the soul," is a necessary movement in the rhythm of light and darkness. Included in solar sensibility, and therefore in a solar psychology, is this downward movement toward twilight of understanding and the sunset of brilliant spirit. When Heraclitus made the obvious but profound remark "The sun is new each day," he implied the death of the old sun. Even though the sun is that planet illuminating all others with its light, it too has its rhythm of descent.

Finally, Jung points to another negative side of the sun. Alchemists, he reminds us, associated the sun with sulphur, the corrupting material of decay and transformation. We should note too that the sun not only nourishes and supports life, has its times of descent, and threatens with spiritual dryness; it also causes decay and fermentation with its heat. Here arise intimations of the Dionysian factor once again: a principle which corrupts in the service of new forms of life. Solar consciousness, sulphuric sometimes in its capacity to dissolve the objects it illuminates, brings endings as well as beginnings. Some of the solar psychologies we noticed in passing seem to suggest the romantic notion that spirit is always life-affirming, whereas in fact solar sensibility has many points of contact with dissolution, darkness, and death. Dionysos and Apollo are brothers. The goal of solar therapy is not simply eternal happiness. It is not a "no-hassle" approach to psychology. On the contrary, to enter the light of solar spirit is to know the depths as well as the heights, to risk the danger of that crocodile's mouth and to feel the sting of sulphur as well as the tang of nutmeg.

Thus the very central radiance of Ficino's model of the psyche embraces opposites and suggests a realistic approach to therapy. In the sun's light we see the houses of spirit which sustain the soul, we feel the nourishing and corrupting processes of psyche's movement, and we enter more deeply into the round of planets. Therapy often appears as an attempt to avoid the unpleasantness and the madness of one "planet" or another. But the solar sensibility suggested by Ficino leads us deeper into these inexplicable movements with their highs and lows, ecstasies and depressions, fullness and emptiness. Each planet has its own brand of such experiences, but all participate in the vicissitudes of the central solar pattern.

8

Venus

Ficino begins the nineteenth chapter of *The Planets* with instructions on how to make an archetypal model of the universe—*formam quadam mundi totius archetypam*. It should be made of silver, and gold and contain and three colors of the cosmos: green, gold and sapphire, the colors of the Three Graces. The craftsman should begin work on the model when Sol enters Aries, and he should finish it in Venus. Astrologers, says Ficino, believe that the world began in Aries, and for that reason the model should be begun then. Naturally it should be completed under the guidance of the goddess of beauty.

In this particular case, Frances Yates supports the idea I have been suggesting throughout our study of Ficino's images: this archetypal model of the world was to be used as a means of educating the memory.[1] Yates suggests that if a person had such a model or picture in his bedroom he could go through a day's activities interpreting them through that familiar image. Jean Seznec, in a study of astrological images of classical deities, mentions that private homes, public buildings, and even churches, indeed the Vatican itself at this period, often had detailed and exact horoscopes painted on their ceilings and walls.[2] What once may have begun as a mnemonic technique to help orators remember their speeches turned into an enterprise of natural magic, or, as I have been suggesting, a school of imagination. Yates suggests that Botticelli's famous painting of flowing bodies and florid dresses—the *Primavera*—was precisely an image to be used in the practice of natural magic, a means of exposure to the spirit of Venus, especially useful, she says in full accordance with Ficino's own thought, to circumvent the ravaging spirit of Saturn.[3]

I propose, then, to look closely at this painting in order to grasp the essential qualities of Venusian spirit as imagined by Fincino's circle. We have already seen how intimately familiar Botticelli must have been with Ficino's ideas, and we know that he painted

Sandro Botticelli, *La Primavera*. (Uffizi Gallery, Florence)

this portrait of the goddess for a Medici, Lorenzo di Pierfrancesco. Art critics and historians have been as fascinated by this work as has the public, and they have provided more interpretive information than we need. In my remarks I rely heavily upon the summary statements of Edgar Wind concerning traditional interpretations of the work and upon his own ideas.[4] However, I am interested in the psychological significance of the image, in its power to tutor the imagination in preparation for onslaughts and deficiencies of Venus's benefits and pains.

Let us regard the *Primavera*, then, as one of Ficino's amulets and talismans, an image not just to admire aesthetically but to contemplate and use for spiritual increase. Pursuing this approach to the planet and its goddess, we will be engaged in a mode of learning prized by men of Renaissance Florence, for whom nothing could be more stimulating than a cipher—an image packed with mysterious symbols, waiting to be cracked open and explored.

Botticelli's *Primavera*

The number "three" was one favored by poets, theologians, and musicians of the Middle Ages and Renaissance, whether or not they were Neoplatonists. Music texts of the period, for example, refer to triple meter as "perfect" time, as we still sometimes do today. Ficino, too, in Neoplatonic fashion frequently divides his philosophical paradigms into threes and multiples of three. It is not surprising, then, to find on Botticelli's canvas a trio of threes: three nature spirits, three Graces, and three deities.

On the far right side of the painting the wind of spring, Zephyr, blows and pursues the earth-nymph Chloris. Frances Yates quite properly sees this wind as Ficino's own *spiritus mundi*, the spirit we have been trying to explicate all along.[5] From the breath of Chloris come forth flowers, as she is transformed into Flora, in a kind of photographic stop-action in oil. Flora is the herald of spring, the season of Venus. On the other side of the canvas the three Graces do their round dance—Chastity in the middle with her hair close-bound and a wistful look on her face; Pleasure, to the left, has snakelike hair and loose garments; and close to Venus is Beauty, moderately dressed. The three deities are: first Venus herself, pictured with heavy breasts and swelling belly. Rather maternal in appearance, she seems to be giving her approval for what is taking place around her. Blinded Cupid is above her, taking aim with his burning arrow. And Mercury stands at the far left, pointing to the clouds.

Concerning love and the process of life Ficino had written: "There is one continuous attraction, beginning with God, going to the world, and ending at last in God, an attraction which returns to the same place where it began as though in a kind of circle."[6] The painting shows this three-part circle, one of the circuits of the soul: the spring wind blows in the beauty of the earth as it brings forth its vegetation; the Graces dance in enjoyment of the world, blessed by the fond gaze of a motherly Venus; and Cupid aims his arrow at Chastity, who is already attracted by Mercury. There is a strong feeling of movement from right to left. One can imagine that music is an element in the Graces' dance and in the movement across the canvas.

If there is music implied, it is doubtless played in the tonality of Venus, though there has been some doubt expressed concerning that point. One respected art historian, Erwin Panofsky, sees Mercury as a dissonant note. In his opinion, Mercury represents reason and has no direct access to the sphere of Venus. He turns his back on Cupid, the Graces, the gifts of spring, and Venus herself. "He may be said," says Panofsky, "to express the dignity, but also the loneliness of the one psychological power which is exlcuded from the precincts of *Amor divinus* and excludes itself from those of *Amor humanus.*"[7]

This reference to the two kinds of love, human and divine, brings forward the distinction Ficino and others drew from Plato, a distinguishing of two Venuses. The heavenly Venus was said to be the daughter of Uranus, the sky. She is immaterial, having neither mother nor the limitations of matter. According to Ficino's Platonism she lives in the Cosmic Mind. The common, earthly Venus, on the other hand, was believed to be the daughter of Jupiter and Juno. She lives between the Cosmic Mind and the sublunar world—the Venus of earth rendering beauty perceptible and imaginable.

At first, accepting the idea of the two natures of Venus, it may appear that Botticelli has painted the earthly Venus. Typically the celestical Venus is depicted nude, while the earthly Venus is clothed with garments, representing her bodily incarnation. Only relatively late in history do Stoic and Christian morality cause an inversion of this tradition. In the *Primavera*, at any rate, Venus is clothed and she is surrounded by trees and flowers. She seems to preside over the fertility of the earth, and, if this is the case, Mercury could well turn his back on all of it and raise his eyes to the clouds, to the region of pure spirit. The movement on the canvas would then appear as a swift rush to the left side, off to the clouds, to a more spiritual place. Implied would be the suggestion that while earthly love and beauty are lush and fertile in a physical way, there is something better. Earthly love would appear as a contrast to the realm of the heavenly Venus, a region heralded quite properly by Mercury.

Isolated statements of Ficino would tend to support the view that the Venus of the *Primavera* is indeed the Venus of heaven, or that she is the goddess advocating a movement away from earth toward heaven. For example, in his commentary on Plato's *Symposium* he writes: "True love is nothing but a certain urge striving to fly up to the divine beauty." But Ficino's writing, considered as a whole, does not simply advocate an escape from earthly existence, as we saw in our reflections on solar spirit. To the sentence just quoted he adds: "divine beauty aroused by the sight of bodily beauty." Full, sensuous involvement in the beauty of body and nature "arouses" one to move to the higher regions of spirit, but both are necessary. The Plato scholar Paul Friendländer alludes to this difference in viewpoint, suggesting that in Plato the movement toward beauty does not slight the body. Contrasting Plato with later interpreters he writes: "in Plato, everyone taking the right path must first love one beautiful body and 'generate in it beautiful words'; then recognize the one beauty in all beautiful bodies, becoming a lover of all. No one may omit these preliminary stages, beyond which leads the soul's path to beauty and upward."[8] It would appear that Ficino, like his soul-guide, Plato, affirms both heaven and earth, both sides of Venus.

Perhaps we can find a hint in Botticelli's Venus of the dual realm of this complex goddess. In another painting, the *Birth of Venus*, the nude heavenly goddess seems to emerge from the sea, where she was born, and is about to be clothed in material flesh symbolized by the colorful garment held out for her. In the *Primavera*, too, we can find images of both natures. The lower part of the goddess's body is clothed in rich material, while the upper part is covered by a transparent cloth which clearly reveals her breasts and the contours of her body, much as the sheer gowns on the spirits—the Graces and Chloris—show their figures.

The Venus of the *Primavera* is love in its celestial *and* terrestrial aspects. If it contained only the latter, one might look for another painting, a companion canvas, to show the heavenly side of things. But the *Primavera* is both. It is a complete circle. There is no need for Mercury to spurn anyone, not the spirits of the earth, not Venus in either of her aspects. Mercury is there to keep the circle in motion, to keep the music playing. He works with Venus and plays an intimate role in her divine functions. Here Venus and Mercury are in conjunction, as astrologers would say. They form a combination, a union of two deities, two planetary centers giving each other mutual support. The image of dual deities is a common one in Ficino's writing

Part of the scene upon which Venus gazes with apparent pleasure is the dance of the Graces, an archaic image of the dance of life embracing life's pleasure, beauty, and inherent reserve. All three seem appropriate in Venus's wooded realm, signifying a time and place in the festivities for the steps of beauty and pleasure, two factors we have discovered to be important for the psyche, and for Chastity, that grace of human life offering a natural, timely limitation on affection for the material world. Chastity prevents the soul from "embracing the body too much," as she watches against the temptation to become excessively charmed by the pleasures of the senses. She doesn't oppose the embrace of body and things sensual, but she watches for the opportunity to glance at Mercury, the god of understanding and insight. Chastity's posture is one of full participation in the dance but with an eye beyond it.

Chastity's glance is directed toward Mercury, Hermes Trismegistus, the grand interpreter, the one who knows the exciting secrets held within simple material objects and pastimes. Chastity, attracted to Mercury, offers a way, not out of the graceful dance of life experience, but further into it. She leads the dance to Mercury, the interpreter. He looks to the clouds, not because he has no place in the scene or is not interested in life's graces, but because it is his office and function to see behind the facade of things, to find the signficance and value which lay hidden in the folds of ordinary existence.

The Venus of heaven and earth, then, guides and watches over that realm of life which includes both full sensuous enjoyment and understanding. She takes care of the two affections of the soul, for body and for spirit. She performs her tasks through pleasure and beauty, and she also nourishes an inner reserve that gracefully turns the soul away from absorption in sensuality, directing it toward insight and meaningfulness. Ficino's young friend, Pico, had written of Venus: "Whoever understands deeply and intelligently the division of Venus's unity into a trinity of graces will find the proper way of advancing into Orphic theology."[9] To be "in Venus," to be under the psychological influence of this deep fantasy and pattern, is to discover and treasure the kinds of spirit and insight accessible through sensual celebration of life. This need not be materialistic and deadening; on the contrary, entering the dance of beauty and pleasure, without need of external repression since Chastity is there too, unique spiritual rewards are made available. Venus leads the soul into the body and through the body to spirit. From spirit, to body, back to spirit—Venus's season entails the circle of the psyche Ficino admired.

The Spirit of Venus

The spirit of Venus has its unique character described imagistically in the ancient categories of hot, cold, dry, and moist. Venus's character is the last, associated as she is with moisture of many kinds. Heraclitus, that enigmatic philosopher of the sixth century B.C., has left us some sayings which pertain to the moisture of the psyche. For example, in one extant fragment he says: "Psyche is vaporized from what is moist." If moisture is imagined as a lower element, signifying the matrix of life and psychologically the source of our fantasies and the body of our emotions, then according to Heraclitus soul is made when this down-to-earth element is vaporized, sublimated in the language of the alchemists. The reflectiveness and depth of sensibility we call soul emerges from the material world felt sensually and experienced emotionally. Psyche is not that world so sensed, but it arises from it. Alchemical pictures show the retorts being heated as vapor forms on the upper part of the glass, a vapor described in their texts as the upper firmament of the Genesis story of creation. This sublimated vapor is not unlike the clouds Mercury points to in the *Primavera*, a vaporization of the sensual world of Venus. Heraclitus also warns that although soul takes pleasure in becoming moist, nevertheless a dry soul is best—an observation that requires little comment.

In *The Planets* Ficino ranks the planets according to the degree of moisture they exhibit.[10] He lists them in combinations from low on the scale to high. Mercury with Jupiter is a moist combination —an example of which might be social and political life interpreted with imagination and intelligence. Next and more moist is Venus with Luna. Luna, closest to earth, the lowest of the spheres surrounding the arena of human endeavor, would clearly be moist. In iconography Luna's moisture is quite simplistically depicted as drops falling from the moon, as in the Tarot portrait of the Moon. Venus is moist in herself, saturated with emotion and sensation, but joined to Luna she becomes even more earthy and wet. Third in the hierarchy is Luna with Venus, Luna the main ruler with Venusian elements added: a dark; fickle world moved by pleasure and beauty. Finally, the most moist combination of all consists of Luna with Venus and Mercury. Mercury's interpretive abilities add imaginative understanding to the Luna-Venus combination, but his insight is moist, close to earth, involved with experience, not distant like that of Apollo. Mercury's vapor of concrete insight is added here to Luna's dew and Venus's body fluids.

Venus's gift, then, *is* spirit, but it is a peculiar kind of spirituality, one quite sensual. There is spirit to be gained from her sensuality, sexuality, and absorption in pleasure, and therefore her domain is good for soul. Obviously Venus can entice the soul toward full absorption in sensuality, and there are plenty of stories in mythology to warn us against this aspect of the love goddess. But here we are interested not in the whole story, but in Ficino's particular insights into great realms of soul experience. He paints a subtle portrait of the Venusian territory and season, and he highlights the beneficial side of this tendency of the soul. Without such an appraisal, we may be moved to suppress all that this goddess stands for, recognizing her allurements toward unconsciousness and disaster. But if Chastity and Mercury do indeed have a place in Venus's dark woods, then there is no need for external repression, only a watchful eye on the movement toward spirit.

Ficino notes that there is an opposition between Venus and Sol: "if we devote ourselves properly to Venus, we will not easily have the sun. But if we are properly concerned with Sol, we will not have done Venus well."[11] This comment incidentally suggests the problems involved in the polytheistic psyche; Ficino had no illusion of psychic harmony and peace. But more specifically the point is that Venus's moisture seems incompatible with the drying effect of solar consciousness. It is difficult to think clearly and rationally when a Venusian mood brings fantasies of moist pleasures, for example. But the soul must host both planets regularly.

Ficino's cautionary observation suggests that in those times when we are in the confusing, entangling grips of Venus, when relationships swamp us in feeling and reason appears to be fogged and powerless, it is useless to pretend that we are at the same time in Sol—rational and clear. We cannot simply sublimate such Venusian feelings into nicely shaped thoughts and thereby escape the unhappy side of Venus. True sublimation, by which the soul gains needed spirit and depth, is a vaporization out of moisture, requiring patient endurance of the moist season. Psyche needs moisture as well as dryness.

Sandor Ferenczi, an early pupil of Freud, discusses this point in his book on sexuality entitled *Thalassa* ("sea"): "The first and foremost danger encountered by organisms which were all originally water-inhabiting was not that of inundation but of desiccation."[12] Ferenczi's comment may be applied to the psyche as well, since psychic desiccation is as much a threat as excess of moisture. Ego often prefers to remain dry because then it enjoys full control; we wish to avoid being overtaken by feeling, we search for ways of moderating our feelings and channeling their currents. A fluid psyche, experienced as moodiness, a sense of being swept away as by a wave, the flow of many fantasies and wishes, and a strong physical awareness of these changes, may not please an ego that enjoys a firm grip on the rudder. But on the positive side, water is the river of vitality and the stream of possibilities; to be in touch with it is to be close to the currents of life, as dangerous and unpredictable as they may be. Water is also an amniotic fluid or an ocean from which arise all forms of life; to be dried up, by excessive spiritual flight for example, is to lose contact with that matrix.

Ficino recognized the connection between moisture and fantasy; so it is quite consistent with his theory to imagine the realm of Venus as a state of luscious growth in imagery. In one of his letters he makes the connection between vapor, fantasy, and the loss of rationality: "We experience not only daily but almost hourly the phenomenon of a little vapor, rather crass and humid, exuding from the lower parts of the body. When it reaches the head and fills the path of the brain, we are made heavy with sleep and are soon deluded with images and dreams [*in somniis imaginibusque deludi*]. Sometimes we also experience (if the vapor of black bile, what the Greeks call melancholy, invades and takes hold of the fortress of the body), our queen, reason itself, sink, and people are overwhelmed with obvious insanity."[13] The descent from dry rationality to moist Venusian fantasy is indeed sensed as a downward motion, and perhaps, as in Ficino's imagery, we may feel our normally fortified and defended ego invaded and overwhelmed. This state of consciousness, experienced as invasion, may also be valued as an enemy and as an inferior condition. It is always best, we say, to keep a clear head and "steer clear" of trouble. But these moist fantasies have as much validity in psychic experience as dry thoughts, and in fact they are important for granting Venus's proper spirit to one's overall psychological condition: her psychic body, sensation, aesthetic sense, growth, pleasure, and concrete understanding.

Although the domain of Venus transcends human limits, insofar as she is the goddess of the generation and growth of all life, Ficino gives her a special place, along with Sol and Jupiter, in human experience. She not only watches over the fertile spring wind, she also moderates the dance of the Graces—human grace. She allows her own sphere to turn inward through Mercury, showing how the gods work in tandem, and demonstrating that her domain has a certain transparency and a degree of interiority, not bright like the sun, but dark like the shady grove of the *Primavera*.

Moreover, the numinosity associated with this goddess, that atmosphere created by her spirit and influence, is not that of a divine mind or creator; its mystery is more akin to that of sex, the mystery of the body, dark wonder about the "private parts" of the human body and of earth, the body of the world. But this peculiar numinosity, sustained by fantasy and feeling when not scattered by liberal rationality, is not superficial. The child's question—Where do I come from?—marks an emergent quest for meaning, an inquiry into origins other than plain physical. So, too, the soul in Venusian curiosity asks: Where am I coming from? What are my origins? Where is my spring? The soul seeks itself out amid the foliage of its own fantasies and mysteries, in the Venusian green, where it is always spring—*primavera*.

Venusian psychology may well be caught up in fantasies of growth and freshness. In the last two decades humanistic psychology seems to have blown in on the wind of Zephyr, from the West Coast, bringing endless fantasies of "personal growth," sexual exploration, absorption in feelings—imaged more concretely in hot tubs, concern for relationships and especially groups and marriage, and play with imagination itself.[14] As one fantasy of doing psychology among many, this clearly has its place, but as a dominant image, and certainly as an exclusive spirit, even Venus becomes an overbearing monarch.

In other of Ficino's images all the characteristics we have seen appear. Venus's minerals are corneolus, a fleshlike stone the lapidaries say should be used to staunch the flow of blood in men and menstruating women; and coral, useful for increasing the yield of fruit (growth) and whose origin is in the morning dew (pristine moisture). Her animals are turtles and turtledoves, known for their powers of fertility (sexuality and growth). Ficino stops short, unfortunately, of giving a full list of Venusian objects, commenting: "the rest decency does not allow me to say." We can easily imagine those fluids and facets of life too "indecent" for Ficino to explore. His observation merely raises another of the fantasies associated with this goddess—indecency, shame, and dark secrecy.

Hillman has suggested that the reason for our current compulsive fascination with Venus stems from our long neglect of her, perhaps because of our prudishness and her indecency.[15] If that is the case, we might imagine a possible world climate which gives the goddess her due. What I said about the university being more Venusian would apply to life at large: it would be more conscious of beauty, relationship, body, feeling, and fantasy; and its troubles would be jealousy, overpopulation, excessive growth, dimming of rationality, and venereal disease of body and mind.

Regardless, she is a goddess to be reckoned with, lest, like Hippolytus of Greek tragedy, we find ourselves trampled by our own decency.

9

Mercury

In Botticelli's lavish portrayal of the season of Venus, a moving counterpoint between a sensual presentation of nature's resurgence and that regular inner season of the soul when it experiences Venus's green, Mercury plays a role of crucial importance. He points up and beyond the garden of the senses, turning the display of color and texture inside out, exposing its interiority. Now we can focus directly on this fascinating figure and consider more precisely the nature of his office and the style of consciousness of represents.

Although Mercury offers a kind of knowledge, insight, and understanding, his form of soul activity differs strikingly from that of other deities associated with knowledge. Saturn, for example, offers deep intuitive insight, but the way of Saturn is distant, aloof, cold, heavy, and dark. Mercury, in contrast, is most often depicted as bright, quick, and light; these are in fact the very qualities which account for his peculiar kinds of insight. In the Renaissance period Mercury's intelligence was also contrasted with that of Minerva-Athena, goddess of intellectual speculation.[1] As in the *Primavera*, Mercury is close to the action, pointing beyond it perhaps, but still in the picture. Mercury can lift the soul out of the limitations of a materialistic view of things, but in that regard his role is limited. He is a relatively moist planet, close to experience and feeling, and as he looks to the vaporous clouds his feet are on the ground. Nor does Mercurial understanding involve maniacal Dionysian penetration of experience or an irrational inner voyage.

Ficino observes, rather suprisingly, that Mercury is always "filled with Apollo."[2] There is a certain Apollonian brilliance and levity in Mercurial knowledge, but the small wings usually attributed to this god loft him only a short distance into the air. Of course, in Greek mythology Hermes and Apollo had a rather close, if not trouble-free, relationship. The Homeric Hymns tell of the infant Hermes stealing Apollo's cattle with precocious ingenuity, resolved when Hermes teaches Apollo the art of music. In Ficino's mind it would seem that Apollo teaches Mercury something about knowledge: perhaps how to use the light of reason, and the reason of light, while keeping some distance from the literal.

For Renaissance polytheists Mercury is more closely related to the Egyptian Thoth, god of secret wisdom, and to the Babylonian Nebo, god of writing. Indeed, in late medieval and early Renaissance iconography, Mercury is pictured as a scribe and sometimes as a bishop.[3] Writing and speaking with clarity and wit was regarded as a Mercurial gift, one Ficino especially acknowledged in others, since he spoke with a lisp or a stammer. In a typically quaint letter to a cardinal's secretary, in which by the way he admits his stammer, Ficino gives an unusually concrete example of how he saw the gods and goddesses personified in daily life. After playing, in Mercurial fashion, on the name of the secretary, Calderino, with references to heat (caldus), he tells the scribe: "You are my Mercury. You speak, you interpret, you persuade, you counsel, you explain."[4] And in an earlier letter to the cardinal himself Ficino is more specific: "Venerable Father, it is no secret to you that Mercury is concerned not only with the communication of words but also with the interpretation of the speaker's mind."[5] Interpretation—hermeneutics—is of the essence of the Mercurial spirit. Ficino goes on: "To Mercury is attributed the fortunate gift of reminiscence—in no way an injustice. For when he stimulates perception in the animus, one is seen to speak. But when he provokes reason, one interprets. When he excites memory, one raises up a reminiscence. What about all this? Our friend Calderino seems to fulfill all the functions of Mercury for us: for he not only writes your letters to me and conveys your words, he also interprets your mind for me." Ficino closes this letter with a hint at the difference between Mercurial wisdom and two other forms: "What Mercury cannot explain," he writes," Apollo can present in vaticinium (the prophetic state of consciousness) and Jupiter can fulfill by deed."

From Greek messenger of the gods Mercury descends to Renaissance secretary of noble pronouncements. But of course the image runs much deeper; for, the soul is served by the virtues associated with Mercury: eloquence, versatility, wit, acuteness, genius, artfulness, imagination, and cleverness. These attitudes of mind work events into images and remake images themselves, without necessarily transforming fantasy into rationality and images into concepts. A kernel of this facility appears in the Greek story of the infant Hermes. Very soon ,after his birth the little god finds a turtle, kills him, and makes of his shell a lyre. Now one can let imagination fly and speculate on the turtle shell as a version of the cosmic egg, plucked into Orphic vibrations, but my point is simpler. Little Hermes sees through the literal animal immediately and imagines music, much as the famous anonymous sculptor of philosophy beholds his statue in the marble while it is still untouched. Hermetic knowledge is truly "in-sightful," imagining possibilities fully invisible. Mercury enjoys the power of using the concrete world for invention, which literally means "finding." He finds the images congealed in the density of matter, and then he tricks them out into the open; for Hermes is the crafty trickster god whose magic and oratory can persuade to extraordinary effect with little resource.

The god Mercury supports in his imagery the basic intuitive psychology of Ficino, for Mercury reveals an inner realm of things without depriving them of their concreteness. If, in the *Primavera*, he were pointing to a world beyond, suggesting that there is something better on another "canvas," the richness and beauty of Botticelli's image of Venus would be disqualified. Mercury, on the contrary, affords a sublimation in which the movement "upward" has limits. This kind of sublimation, now a form of interpretation, Norman O. Brown defines as metamorphosis in the way of Daphne. Daphne was the nymph desired and chased by Apollo. As the god drew close to her in the chase she cried for help and was changed into the laurel tree. Psychologically, this story is very suggestive,[6] and Brown sees it as a description of sublimation: in our pursuit of sensate objects, their inherent spiritual value may become evident. Brown elaborates:

> The spiritualization of sensuality is love. . . . Sensuality is not abolished, but fulfilled. . . . When our eyes are opened, we perceive that in sexuality the object is not the literal girl; but the symbolic girl, the tree. It is always something else we want. The object is always transcendent.[7]

As in the alchemical triangulation, the solid world becomes body, soul and spirit—body is not lost, but soul and spirit are gained.

The most common mode of interpretation, in some circles the only way, is to dissect and analyze, freezing the components of an insight into brittle pieces which are then easy to manipulate. But the crafty sleight-of-hand of Mercury interprets without killing, transforming our view of one image through another. The child Hermes saw the shape of the lyre in the turtle shell, and similarly the consciousness and imaginativeness he represents allows us to see a wealth of images congealed in the concrete forms of everyday life. Mercurial insight, then, is a tricky, crafty, clever, witty vision, where wordplays abound and puns have profound value. A character in Joseph Heller's *Catch-22* has a Mercurial malady we all might wish for. Every once in a while he yells out: "I see everything twice!" Mercurial vision is multiple. Through it I see everything many times, because through Mercury I see the many fantasies which pile up on each other in my dreams and in my actions.

Mercurial Awakening

Soul comes to life in the turn from the literal into the imaginal, a twist Mercury effects. Literalism, as we have already seen, is tantamount to sleep, for in literalism the psyche doesn't have to do its job of seeing everything twice, working for significance and digging for depth. The wand of Mercury, visible in the *Primavera*, points to the clouds, perfect examples of the shifting shapes of fantasy, as on a windy day they produce a tableau of dreams before our eyes. Ficino expresses this Mercurial power in a manner perfectly compatible with the cloud imagery:

> Mercury has the power to put souls to sleep or waken them with his staff; that is, in some way or another, by *putting himself into a certain shape*, he can dull or sharpen the mind, or weaken or strengthen it, or upset or calm it.[8]

In Mercurial consciousness form is everything, the shape a thing takes in our imagination betrays its significance. The words we use to describe experience (eloquence and rhetoric), for example; the image we bring to situations (imagination); the double entendres that bubble up into our minds (craft and cleverness); the buried meanings we discover (interpretation)—all these are the means by which Mercurial consciousness wakens soul, turns ordinary literal events into psychological realities. Ficino suggests that if we wish to make an image reflecting the nature of Mercury, we should portray a man sitting on a throne, dressed in a multicolored garment, witnessing to the many colors of Mercurial vision.[9]

A basic law of psychological understanding is the Mercurial one of keeping images in motion, letting them generate each other. This leads to depth of vision, not in a logical, linear kind of reasoning but in the richness of texture[10] that emerges from such a process. Once again we can refer to Brown, a Mercurial thinker himself, for a description of this divine quick-change artist:

> . . .it is important to keep changing the subject. The subject changes before our very eyes. It is important to keep changing our mind—

> > The mind, that ocean where each kind
> > Does straight its own resemblance find.

The mind, or the imagination, the original shape-shifter: Thrice-Greatest Hermes.[11]

"In Mercury," the ruler of the sign gemini, one eye can remain glued to the facts while the other constantly changes perspective. Through him one can exercise double vision without sacrificing its duplicity. There is no final interpretation in the hermeneutic of Mercury, no satisfying conclusion; for there is always a new viewpoint, another color in the motley garb of this consciousness, another angle to consider. There is no ending and therefore always the promise of more—deeper insight, further implication, other applications, unexplored suggestiveness, hidden nuances, and unexpected surprises. Of course, this perspective goes against the grain of all that is true and scientific, but it *is* an option, one with surprising results if given some practice.

The idea of coming across unexpected surprises is Ficino's idea, not mine, or, more accurately, it was an idea suggested by Ficino's brilliant pupil, Pico, who believed it was important to surprise the soul through interpretations of images and stories.[12] Since interpretation consists chiefly in discovering new images among the old, the surprise Mercury brings is a new image or a new idea, a gift from the cunning god who knows how to stir the soul.

In the passage from Ficino quoted earlier, he pointed out that Mercury's power to waken the soul may upset it. Therefore, Mercurial wit is not the kind that pleases with its own cleverness. Anyone can play with puns, twist words around, the produce a veritable euphony of language without disturbing a dormant psyche. It would be a mistake to confuse the god Mercury with the simple human talent for wordplay. The play of words and its possible accompanying eloquence is important in Mercurial consciousness as a means of turning images so that their significance may be revealed; for the soul feeds on images. But cleverness for its own sake is a mere egoistic exercise.

Wallace Stevens defined poetry as "a pheasant disappearing behind a bush," and that is as good a description of Mercurial insight as any and has the advantage of suggesting the alchemical mercury, the slippery silver substance so important to the alchemist's endeavors.[13] In Mercury, words are like crystals whose facets are revealed in their turning, in the various perspectives brought upon them. Whatever keeps our ideas and fantasies turning and shifting, eluding our rational grasp and defying conclusive definition, is Mercurial. When we are the deft, interpretive, eloquent secretaries of our own actions and ideas, then we are Mercury; for then we interpret our own minds.

This is an age generally unhappy with Mercurial insights. We want conclusions and facts, not openings into never-ending mysteries. College students, for example, love one-dimensional definitions. Give them a multiple-choice examination, and they are demonstrably happy and grateful, but confront them with a thought to be reflected upon, to be turned in imagination, and they almost unanimously complain that such knowledge is only personal opinion and therefore of no value. They strongly resist interpretation, even in the area of literature. Every interpretive suggestion is "reading into" the author's work. They insist that the final test of a reading of a poem or novel is the author's own intention, conscious and recorded. They prefer endings to beginnings, conclusions to suggestions, a definition to an exploration, a hard fact to a nuance. Mercury's motley coat is not in fashion.

Yet the great advantage of Mercurial intelligence is its power to keep the soul in motion, spiraling down toward a vortex of significance. Mercury keeps the carousel of interpretation moving, feeding wonder and curiosity instead of granting the stupor of final conquest.

With our fixed and sober image of the mind it may be difficult to imagine all this while that the god we are looking at, complete with his infant precociousness and adult instability, is truly a metaphor for a way of perceiving the life we live and the world we inhabit, that he authentically represents an unconscious and untutored pattern of awareness. Yet we have only to open our eyes, as Kerenyi suggests in his example of missed trains and found books, and find that life itself is tricky. Kerenyi's further words on the subject are worth quoting at some length:

There is much trickery at large in the world, all sorts of sly and
cunning tricks among human beings, animals and even
plants. . . .

The sum of the ways as the Hermetic arena; chance and
mischance the Hermetic substance; its transformation through
'finding and thieving' into Hermetic art (not mixed with
artifice), into riches, love, poetry, and all the ways of escape
from the narrow confines of law, custom, circumstance, fate; all
these are not just psychic realities, they are the world around us,
and, at the same time, a world revealed to us by Hermes.[14]

Through his craft and thievery Mercury wakens the soul, finds
holes in "law, custom, circumstance, fate." His many turnings and
the many paths over which he watches do not subscribe to rational
and moral limits—it was Hermes who laughed at the scene described in the *Odyssey* of Aphrodite caught in adultery with Ares
and who wished to be there himself.

While Kerenyi gives us an intriguing theology of Hermes/Mer-
cury, Rafael Lopez-Pedraza offers a wonderful psychology
founded in this god. Among the many inviting notions of Hermetic reality he uncovers, perhaps the one most appropriate in this
context is the idea of "stealing from memory." Recall Ficino's
remark that Mercury stimulates a reminiscence out of memory. In
Pedraza's analysis, Mercurial consciousness "thieves" ideas and
suggestions from two places: from other people, for example in
conversation; and from the complexes and archetypes of the
psyche itself. We steal from ourselves in our Mercurial
regression,[15] we pilfer a reminiscence from memory that enriches
the present and opens and wakens the soul.

Dreams are often Mercurial in this way: an image of one thing
tricks us into recalling another. Fascinations and infatuations, of
course, can do the same thing—trick us into an impressive world
of feeling, and just when we are in the heat of passion we may
discover that we have not seen the real object of our desire all
along: Brown's Daphne as the tree. Ficino meant something similar
when he observed that lovers can't distinguish the flavors of the
aroma they pursue and enjoy. It is all a trick, a joke encouraging
the laughter of the gods, Hermes' the most hearty. Mercury's
legerdemain breaks open psychic depth by means of the most profound puns and illusions of all. It is remarkable that perhaps one
of the most important qualities in a good psychologist is a taste for
wit and a talent for the double entendre; for only in such multiple
vision are the significant facets of life exposed to the reason of
light.

We could develop the idea of Mercurial vision by exploring the Greek mythological stories of Hermes as guide of souls to the underworld. We would then see that Hermetic insight brings a perspective of death, in the sense that the psyche's reality is lived in the death of the literal. But Ficino's more mundane imagery makes the same point: by discovering within ourselves that structure of consciousness by which we see the many dimensions of significance that dwell in and through the literal, then psychological consciousness is wakened. Ficino's imagery of secretaries and scribes may give too light an impression of this planetary center of the psyche; for Mercurial vision is something quite profound and abiding. "In Mercury" we can habitually discover that things are not always or usually what they seem to be; behind an apparently simple act there may reside a deeply felt fantasy. To catch a glimpse of that fantasy would be to grasp the soul-dimension, and to do this habitually would establish a psychological attitude, the sine qua non of care of the soul or psychotherapy in the broadest sense.

Mercurial consciousness, than, quite legitimately is placed as a major focus in the psyche's round of planetary centers. Sol provides the necessary spirit and Venus the required sensual experience, while Mercury provides the channel for Apollonian light, allowing us to bring the psychological stratum of meaning into our purview.

10

Luna

Of all the mysterious heavenly bodies that fill the clear night sky, the most intriguing and beguiling to the earthbound naked-eye observer has to be the moon. Because it is usually watched as part of the night scene, taking onto itself some of the eerie atmostphere of the dark, and because it changes so much and so often in color, size, and shape, Luna has impressed the human imagination even more than its companion the sun. Poetry and song, superstition and religion, mythology and symbology have all found in the moon an ideal object for stimulating and fertilizing the fantasy. For that reason there is a wealth of imagery connected with the moon, suggesting several different psychological directions and focused upon various aspects of the moon itself. We will concentrate on those suggestive qualities which caught the attention of Ficino and his circle and again see the image of this "planet" within the context of Ficinian psychology.

The Moon's Moistness

While we were discussing the "humidity" of Venus, we had occasion to notice lunar moisture as well, noting that Luna is the most moist of the planets, implying that she is close to earth, far removed from the dryness of abstraction and thought, in touch with experience, saturated with the feelings of the concrete, and participant in other functions of moisture in nature and in the soul. In *The Planets* Ficino makes this clear: "Since Lunar qualities are more crass and moist than the subtle and volatile nature of spirit, they are quite alien to it."[1] Spirit is represented more aptly in the sparkle emanating from a brilliant stone or in the fragrance issuing from a bunch of flowers; Luna, on the other hand, chiefly because of her position close to earth, is imagined to be more dense and less spiritual. As modern astrologers assert, Luna has much to do with the human body and with the processes of nature.

156

In legend and tradition Luna is a planet important to farmers, since her influence is responsible for agricultural increase or failure. In the days when the planets were closely observed, farmers used to plant according to the condition of the moon—sow when the moon is waxing, harvest when it is waning. Ficino, too, observed this natural significance of the moon, as when in *The Planets* he writes: "Venus and Luna pertain to natural and generative power and spirit and to growing things."[2] We will see later how lunar nature embraces the rhythms of growth and decay, but first we ought to notice the particular kind of generative power Ficino is talking about and the role that power plays in psychology.

As Kristeller explains, generation in Ficino's thinking is an idea drawn from natural science and applied to philosophy,[3] or, as I might extend that notion, Ficino observes generation in nature, associates it along traditional lines with the moon, then conceives of this generativity in regard to the soul. His idea is expressed most clearly, perhaps, in a letter to Lorenzo de' Medici. It was in Ficino's correspondence with Lorenzo, by the way, that he seemed most free to give astrological advice and to consider the implications of the various planetary characters. In this letter Ficino addresses the important relationship between lunar nature and the other planetary systems:

> Ancient theologians said that souls (*animae*) go into lower things through Cancer, the domicile of Luna. For, since by a disposition to generation they come into a region subject to generation, appropriately they were thought to make their way through the zone of Luna which favors generation. Therefore, the ancients called Cancer the gateway of mortals. On the other hand, they called Capricorn the gateway of the Gods, for through it souls, once cleansed, were believed to return to their heavenly fatherland.[4]

Psychologically, Luna is the gateway to embodiment and personalization of fantasies, complexes, and archetypal possibilities. She stands, true to her typical *anima* or soul image, as a bridge between the personal and the archetypal. Bachofen suggests this when he calls Luna "the purest of tellurian bodies, the impurest of uranian luminaries."[5] From our personal perspective our Luna within is sensed as that consciousness of suprapersonal or unconscious realities which play a role in life but are not conscious creations; therefore, Luna seems "uranian" or celestial, though close to earth. From an archetypal viewpoint, the connections between archetypal possibilities and personal experience seem so uniquely individual that lunar consciousness itself appears personal— tellurian. In any case, this lunar activity by which collective fantasies are made personal is a downward movement, a tendency toward the concrete and individual.

We find throughout Ficino's writing heavy emphasis upon Luna, constant advice about keeping an eye on this fast-moving planet. A good lunar aspect, he urges, is essential for the proper constellation of the other planets. This lunar watchfulness ensures good timing and a full awareness of both body and soul, their individual movements and their motion in relation to each other. Luna consists in a certain savvy about just when and how to bring some movement of soul into action and imprint it with individual embodiment. For both soul and nature Luna is a guide to propitious rhythms and seasons.

Ficino's letter to Lorenzo, merely suggestive as usual, also shows the two-way street connecting the world of archetypal possibilities with life experience. Fantasies become concrete in the moist, feeling-toned, earthy zone of Luna, whereas the concrete world of action and experience becomes psychological—soul returns to its proper place—through the doorway of Capricorn, a sign ruled by Saturn, god of contemplation and profound imagination. This function of Luna forms the background for further discussion now of other lunar processes: they all serve the basic purpose of generation.

Lunar Motions and Emotions

In another letter to Lorenzo, Ficino makes an observation quoted at the outset of this book: "We have an entire sky within us: Luna symbolizing the continuous motion of soul and body."[6] Anyone who has worked with astrological charts knows that of all the planets Luna moves fastest; it takes careful reckoning of time to be assured that Luna's position on the chart is accurate. This speed of Luna's circuit on the Zodiac highlights a significant facet of the relationship between body and soul: the ordinary time of experience, the time of the ego and ordinary behaviour, seems to move at a rate faster than that of the deeper movements of the psyche represented by the other planets. The sublunar world spins at a faster pace than does the deeper psyche.

We can see this phenomenon in typical ego impatience with the timing of the soul in contrast to its sublunar haste. Psyche grinds away slowly. We find themes in dreams developing slowly over a period of weeks, months, or even years, and at the conscious level we feel an urge to do something about the situation, take some action, arrive at some conclusions and resolutions. But soul in its heaven seems to move like the larger planets and not like Luna. The moon's orbit is close to earth and takes its timing from earth, while the other planetary rhythms are broader, playing largo to Luna's allegro. Lunar consciousness implies an awareness of the time zones of body and soul. Embodiment of fantasies may be quite feverish in tempo, but soul's movements are more like those of a clock, definite but hardly noticeable in their passing.

As Ficino mentions in his letter about generation, we live celestially in two circles, the Tropic of Cancer and the Tropic of Capricorn, one the circle of generation and action, the other the circle of spirit. To get these two circles synchronized is the trick of lunar consciousness. For Ficino this meant keeping an eye on the movements of the moon; for us it could mean keeping close watch on our personal lives and on those rather personal and intimate fantasies which serve as bridges between possibility and reality. Much of the unnecessary pain of living comes from a lack of coordination between these two circles, which is not too surprising since we generally neglect the Tropic of Capricorn.

An individual psychologically constellated, with a Luna within, has a feel for the "natural" rhythms of soul, different from ego, keeping watch as did the farmers who knew the importance of the moon. Ficino goes so far as to say that "except for God, living beings have no life except through Sol and Luna,"[7] a statement he clarifies, so to speak, by saying: "However safe the way may be, nothing can be done without the benefit of Luna, because what is called the "Other Sun" commonly, frequently, and easily sends celestial things downward, making in any month the four seasons of the year."[8] The conditions of personal existence may not reflect accurately deeper soul-movements. What makes sense on the surface may be folly within. And that last phrase of Ficino's is particularly intriguing, confirming the notion that when through lunar activity deep fantasies are incarnated in experience, the slow rhythms of psyche are transformed into the faster tempos of life—the seasons of the year squeezed into one month.

If we think of psychotherapy for a moment, not as it is often practiced, as an aid to personal adjustment, but rather as a program for becoming more "celestial," in Ficinian language, more aware of the processes of the psyche in modern terms, then the importance of lunar consciousness becomes evident. A signficant early step in therapy might be to gain a sense of the soul's seasons and rhythms, its timing and tempo. Therapy itself, as care for soul, requires patience and time precisely because of this difference in pace. This lunar sense itself may well constitute a foundational plank in the construction of a psychological attitude which takes into serious consideration archetypal motions. To begin to hear the polyrhythms of psyche and experience is to begin to live psychologically, with the good of soul in mind.

Waxing and Waning

As is sometimes pointed out in discussions of the image of the moon, lunar time exhibits not only unusally quick time quantities, but also specific qualities of time. The moon waxes and wanes. It is full, new, quarter, and crescent. During the Renaissance period and earlier, astrologers and others found various ways to show graphically the parallel between celestial phenomena and human experience. We can see this correspondence in paintings and woodcuts, for example, that show each planet corresponding to a part of the human body. Ficino assumes this kind of correspondence throughout his three books on medicine and health. But in *The Planets* he suggests another parallel, between the phases of the moon and the stages in human life. In chapter seven he writes:

> From the new moon to the first quarter is youth. From the first quarter to the full moon is youth and maturity. From then to the fourth quarter is maturity and old age. From then to the conjunction is old age.[9]

As with most observations of this nature, we need not choose between the surface meaning and the metaphorical possibilities, but rather affirm both. The moon does indeed reflect in her striking and obvious transformations the progress of a personal life time: human life itself exhibits this lunar character. But it also suggests the dynamics of episodes in the personal life—the waxing and waning, the fullness and emptiness, the beginnings and endings which shape and tone the ways in which we embody the movements of soul. Becoming involved more intimately with the processes of psyche entails familiarity with these lunar phases: knowing the colors and aromas of beginning and of ending, recognizing fullness for what is is—part of a rhythm, not a goal; and appreciating emptiness.

These particular qualities of lunar consciousness appear in the image Ficino recommends for attracting lunar spirit: "a young woman with horned head, on a dragon or bull, with serpents over her head and under her feet."[10] This image is reminiscent of the Cretan women we find depicted in Minoan art, a culture in which moon, bull, and serpent appear prominently in imagination. Moon and snake have often been closely related because of the moon's dying and rising and the snake's capacity to slough its skin in an image of dying and rising. Moon and bull come together in their power to fertilize nature and in their common visage—the cradling crescent taking the shape of bull's horns. Bullish power, like Luna's, is directed toward nature and the material side of culture building.

The Reflecting Moon

Connected with the rhythms of Luna is the obvious fact that Luna's light is the light of the sun. Ficino says it plainly in *The Planets*, and in that context we must read his statement with more than a literal mind: "There can be no doubt that the moon's light is the *lumen* of Sol."[11] Lunar consciousness is by nature reflective, leaving the intiative to Sol, in whom are held all the planetary spirits. Though always in motion, Luna's function is to receive the light of Sol, therefore she is rather passive and reflective. This would be a point easy to misinterpret, but it seems that our lunar nature, the gateway to embodiment, must essentially take a receptive and reflective stance. Personality and all the moist aspects of life reflect the deeper sources of spirit and channel these spirits into personal life. There is something essentially indirect about psychological awareness and "action." Ego does not take the initiative except to prepare itself to receive the spirit. In this sense the constellation of lunar consciousness might temper the tyranny of the usual Saturnian ego, which always wants to build and rule. One of the two feminine planets, Luna offers a necessary comple- ment to ego's potentially useful but easily destructive Saturnian tendencies. Open to the influence of Luna, the ego would by nature receive energy and direction from the depths instead of the surface, and those depths would be varied, for Luna channels the spirits of all the planets through her zone.

When we imagine the spirit of the planets passing through Luna, who channels and reflects them, then personal experience does indeed appear to be a shadow of shadows: one of Plato's funda-

mental intuitions. And if that is the case, then the way back to the
light and to psychological awareness is through these shadows,
tracing them back to their origins. The purpose of studying
imagery and the often farfetched speculations of a Ficino is to find
a broader context for experience, to see unique events against the
background of more embracing images. If, as Ficino implies at
every step, personal experience is a reflection of a larger spirit,
then perhaps we can speculate (*speculum*: mirror) and reflect on
our reflections. Magic, they say, is accomplished by means of
mirrors. If we could find that imagined depth behind the mirror,
we might find that of which our lives are a reflection.

Another feature of the moon, related to its reflecting powers, is
its tendency to pour itself out. Traditionally the moon is believed
to empty itself as it approaches the sun and begins to wane.
Among the emblems of the alchemist, Michael Meier, for example,
is one showing a toad sucking a woman's breast. The motto
accompanying the picture reads: "Put a toad to the breasts of a
woman, that she may feed it, and the women may die, and the
toad grows big from the milk."[12] This is an image of lunar
emptying—*kenosis*. The idea is not one of self-sacrifice in the
heroic sense, a giving up of personal pleasure for an ascetic need,
nor is it even a denial of self. Fantasies of self-denial usually betray
their deeper roots in images of inferiority and a striving for recognition and self-importance. *Kenosis*, a lunar activity and therefore
a natural rhythm of the psyche, consists in an imaginative
acknowledgment and appreciation of processes of ending: wane,
rot, entropy, decay, and death. Unlike Saturnian obsession with
these processes, lunar sensibility acknowledges them as part of a
larger pattern. For Luna, as opposed to Saturn, it is the emptying
itself that is important. Lunar realism allows itself to imagine the
ugly toad sucking the woman dry and letting her die. The heroic
ego would step in and fight the threat of death, and Saturnian
fantasies might lead to an effort of preservation, keeping life the
same forever, which is not too different from eternal death.

In lunar consciousness personal life is emptied as well as filled, a
round that has as much darkness as light. Luna would empty us of
those purposes and plans, as well as the interpretations and
explanations, that keep life busy on the surface with no guarantee
that there is movement within. Emptying, naturally, does not feel
as good as filling up; it seems uncreative and unproductive; nevertheless, the cycle of the psyche's moon requires an acknowledgment of decay and death. Farmers who watch the moon know
when to let things ripen, fall off the tree, cure, and ferment. The

psychologically attuned person observes the soil of his soul with equal sensitivity, knowing that nature wanes with the moon and falls into total darkness.

Lunar imagination has been romanticized as a half-conscious idyllic openness to the oracular messages of inner voices: the moon's darkness as a bath of inspiration. But mythology tells too of Hekate and other terrifying moon goddesses who assure us in their savagery that lunar death is not always sweet. Imagination, participating in the lunar pattern, is not to be equated fully with glowing creativity, playful inventiveness, and inspiring reverie. It, too, has its waning moon, drawing toward the three-day darkness of death. Part of a fertile imagination is the capacity for enduring the death of what has already been achieved.

As we noticed in our allusions to Ficino's historical setting, death is always close to creativity. We may imagine it metaphorically, in images of Persephone and the underworld, for example, as a state or a quality of attitude. In a sense, all of life experience that has been "psychologized," or stored in memory and viewed from the perspective of soul, is dead. But this lunar dying is more a process, a movement in the direction of emptiness, accompanied by appropriate feelings of ending and loss. At any one time in life one might expect feelings and fantasies engendered by the waning of some spirit in oneself. In that case the image of the toad sucking out the life of the young woman seems quite appropriate; for the waning of what has been a vital spirit feels like a violation and an ugly crime.

This lunar sensibility that forms part of the celestial temperament differs strikingly from that fostered by psychologies based on evolutionary and developmental models.[12] Here psychological life is not seen as a steady progress away from childishness and ignorance toward maturity and happiness. Part of being celestial is to experience cycles of growth and decay, of light and darkness. The implication for therapy is obvious: expect movements of decay as well as growth and don't interpret them as inappropriate. In fact, a therapist with this planetary scheme in mind might look for a loss of Luna, experienced as resistance to natural decay and waning. Without the phase of emptying, there can be no vital fullness. Besides, the moon is full for only a brief moment in its month; yet we so often imagine an ideal state of psychological health when one's moon is always full. And finally, as I already mentioned, we do not have to imagine these lunar rhythms as sequential plots in time but rather view them as archetypal images of the psyche. Waning or waxing, full moon or sliver-crescent may be sensed at any time with reference to one of the many motions of the psyche.

In *The Book of Secrets* of Albertus Magnus, a collection of legends about the planets, among other things, we find a description of Luna. The moon, it says, is the conveyor of the virtue of all the planets—a Ficinian notion as well—it promotes qualities of honesty and honor, but it is also inconstant and loves wet and moist places.[13] The danger in moist planets, of course, is the tendency to "embrace the body too much," to become preoccupied with the physical and the personal. But, as Albertus assures us, Luna also keeps us honest, down to earth, blessed with the common sense of the farmer. These are all virtues psychology as a discipline too often lacks. The best psychotherapists, in my opinion, are those rare people who have the down-home horse sense of the farmer, who can put their fingers to the wind or glance at the sky without any instruments and know the weather well. They know some secrets of common living that are irreducible to conceptual formulation. They are not anti-intellectual by any means, but in addition to sharp thinking they have a talent for catching sight of obvious but extremely subtle signs of spirit in its progress, like a seasoned farmer noticing without much display the tawniness and dip of an evening moon.

11

Saturn

Among the seven planets that form the circuit of psychological processes, two in particular offer dangers to the soul—Mars and Saturn. We have already seen the ominous disposition of Saturn in Ficino's own natal chart and have noted his obsession with the implications of that disposition. In his three books on life, *De Vita Triplici*, he keeps returning to the motif of Saturnian malevolence, although it is in these books that he also brings back to life the ancient idea that within Saturn's heaviness lay the treasures of deep religious contemplation and artistic genius. Both of these tendencies in Saturn, associated with the peculiar Saturnian malady, melancholy, have been studied historically, interpretively, and with a substantial discussion of Ficinian theory by Fritz Saxl, Erwin Panofsky, and Raymond Klibansky.[1] James Hillman, too, has used the insights of Ficino as he has been developing over the years a highly differentiated image of *senex*, the Old Man of the psyche so influential in modern personal and social life, and imaged especially in the mythology and iconography of the god Saturn.[2] With so much excellent work already done elaborating this dominant image in Ficinian psychology, it remains for us here to explore a few more images of Saturn we find in Ficino's correspondence and in his medical books, place his theory of melancholy within the context of earlier chapters of this book, and possibly suggest some concrete ways this promising but ominous planet influences modern life.

Atra bilis: The Black Humor

Saturn is the god of Roman religion and mythology about whom little is known except that he was the deity presiding over winter sowing, the winter solstice, the festival of late December, and agricultural activities in general. In medieval and Renaissance iconography we find more elaborate portraits of "Saturn's children," those people who in their habits and occupations reflect the spirit of this planetary deity. Among these children of the hoary god are geometers, carpenters, latrine cleaners, and grave diggers—all occupations we will see indicating a facet of Saturn's spiritual influence.

Saturn was identified in the syncretistic amalgamation of Greek and Roman religion with the Greek Kronos, from whose story were derived many of Saturn's positive and negative characteristics. Kronos began as a young man rebelling against his father, assisting the revenge of his mother, Gaia, by taking a sickle in hand and castrating his father, Ouranos, the sky. Ouranos had offended his wife by shoving back into her womb the children she was bearing, causing her great pain, naturally, and planting in her the feeling of hate and a fantasy of revenge. The sickle by which Kronos separated the union of father and mother, sky and earth, remains with him and appears later in pictures of Old Man Time and in the astrological glyph or symbol of Saturn, a crescent shape beneath a cross.

Even in this early story, therefore, we find extreme ambivalence in the character of Saturn; for, when he grows old and becomes father and king, he swallows his sons with the same motive with which his father had violated his mother—in order to maintain his rule and authority. When he finally lost that position through the trickery of his wife, Rhea, and his son Zeus took command of the Greek pantheon, Kronos was left to rule the kingdom of the Golden Age. So Saturn has in his story elements of *puer*, the young man as rebellious son, and *senex*, the senile old king jealous of his authority and monarch of a golden past.[3]

The relationship between the puerile and senile aspects of Saturn is not simply one of opposites in tension or even of paradox, though a sense of ambivalence is sustained consistently. Ficino is quite specific about the attitude we ought to take toward this planetary center: we must at all costs avoid his harmful influence and especially his power to desiccate the soul; on the other hand, it is only by going through Saturn, experiencing his spirit to the hilt, that we can gain the positive benefit he has to offer. Just as within the story of Kronos we find the young man who dares to create a space between sky and earth, opening up a middle realm where perhaps the soul can exist, so in other stories and images of Saturn we find a shining reward within the darkness of his malevolence.

Dark hues surround the image of Saturn: in alchemy Saturn was identified with the process of putrefaction and as the Black Sun,

Sol Niger, of the *nigredo*, the phase of blackening, psychologically that phase of the soul's work when the mess that has been made is allowed to settle, rot, and putrefy. Among the classical humors of the body, Saturn is *atra bilis*, the black bile responsible for depression and melancholy. Death and darkness penetrate the realm of Saturn, and, as Ficino warns, either blackness will attract the influence of Saturn, or Saturn will bring with him feelings of death and decay.

A young woman I had just met once told me of a strange dream she had had. She dreamed that she saw the sun in the sky, only it was all black except for a yellow glow around the edges. For her this black sun appeared after a long siege of depression, an image of her darkness but with a promising indication of the gold that lay within the black mass of melancholy. More recently, a young man came to me complaining of incessant feelings of depression and an inescapable proximity to death. Just before he came to see me he had gone into the city to walk through a park, hoping to find some relief from his heaviness, but he no sooner walked into the park than he tripped over the body of a vagrant, an old man who had apparently died right on the street. When this young man came to talk to me, he was wearing a black shirt and black pants, and his hair was long and black, meeting a flowing black beard. Planetary imagery is often subtle, but sometimes it blares, clearly and unmistakably.

Not surprisingly, Saturn's metal is lead, a traditional notion readily proven when depression comes along and we feel "heavy" and weighed down. Saturn is also always at the edge, far away and distant, as when in depression our eyes tell those around us that though our bodies are present our spirit is far removed, turned inward. Ficino points out this isolation of the melancholic in *The Planets*: "Saturn does not easily symbolize a quality and power common to the human race, but a person cut off from others—divine or bestial, blessed or overwhelmed with extreme misfortune."[4] In the story of Kronos, his final fate is to rule at the end of the world, far from the activities of ordinary life.

Carpentry and Construction

Clinically, depression may include a sense of powerlessness, not only in relation to the outside world but also with regard to thought, memory, and introspection. At least on the surface, it appears that the melancholic can do nothing; all his energy and ability to focus his attention seems dissipated. Yet, as Freud pointed out, melancholy denotes a time of external inactivity and internal labor.[5] Deep within, it would seem that something is going on, attention is being taken from the outside world and applied elsewhere.

We may get some idea of what kind of work occupies Saturnian consciousness, either in its form of melancholy or in its less striking manifestation as dry conservatism, control, rigidity, and orderliness in ordinary life, through some simple comparisons with other planets. Ficino observes that both Saturn and Mercury are constellated through study and work in literature and science, but Mercury is not nearly as *dry* as Saturn.[6] We might also notice that though Saturn was not known as a God of the harvest, as such, he looks much like the "Grim Reaper," and his sickle is used to cut down growing things for the harvest. In this respect he is quite opposite Venus in spirit, another moist planet whose unbounded fertility can well use the blade of old Saturn. But what Venus grows in her moist soil Saturn leaves dead in his own barren ground. Not having the moisture that supports new growth, Saturn is compelled to live on what has long been rooted and flourishing.

True to his conservatism and dryness, Saturn lives on old and outdated fantasies, which, since they have no inherent signs of vitality, he must bolster, patch, and defend. So Saturnian souls, like those carpenters who are his children in the ancient woodcuts, are quite involved in construction: building, ordering, collecting, analyzing, planning. Could this be a fantasy behind the binding fascination people have with collections of bottles, stamps, classic automobiles, and just about everything else that can be brought together? Behavior that has no clear object among ego-values must be nevertheless the enactment of serious business. Are collectors trying to put order in their cosmos, and is their god Saturn? And what about more practical construction jobs—city-building, the voracious attempt to eat up nature (Gaia), to swallow her children, transforming them into the body of Saturn himself in his own conservative image?[7] Deprived of the moisture of fresh fantasy, we are forced to build worlds out of old and dry ideas, giving a definite Saturnian cast to much of our culture. The stone buildings, geometrical forms, and styles from an idealized past, features found on many campuses and government complexes, betray signs of Saturn's rule.

For the individual, internal work is similar: an attempt to build on archaic materials and to survive without life-giving moisture.

The turn inward in melancholy is a move to a distant place within, to the cemetery of the soul. Cemeteries are usually located at the edge of cities, and that is where Saturn takes the soul. In alchemy he was imagined as a tomb, and his children were grave diggers, as we have seen. Not only is there construction taking place "in Saturn," but also burying. The melancholic feels the grim task of working in the land of the dead, dry soil all around, all vital spirits gone underground. Freud says that melancholy is essentially a feeling of loss, and though he takes us through too many contortions to find out what is lost, that feeling is an important part of the complex.[8] Being in Saturn, we have lost touch with the movements of soul: the planets, lunar reality, and the surface of earth. We are far away within, in Saturn, the most remote of the planets and the coldest. We have not lost something so much as we ourselves are lost at the rim of our inner zodiac, at the end of the world.

Now we may consider, as usual, the image Ficino presents in order to draw down the spirit of Saturn:

> The ancients made an image of Saturn for long life in Feyrizech stone, that is, in Sapphire, at the hour of Saturn, with Saturn ascending and well disposed. Its form was this: an old man sitting in a high chair or on a dragon, his head covered with a dark linen cloth, his hands extending above his head, holding in his hand a sickle or fish, clothed in a dark garment.[9]

Here we find images for all the qualities of Saturn we've discussed so far. First and foremost, Saturn is an old man, felt in the mentality we may associate with old men. Though it would be absurdly literalistic to label all real old men Saturnian, they often fit the role. One only has to look at a photograph of our assembled senators and congressmen to find the leading image of our society—Saturn on his throne, dry and cold. He sits on a chair as on a throne, or on a dragon—both images of the mother as earth and nature. The Old Man side of Saturn would dominate the chthonic and earthly powers of Mother Nature; though, as we have seen, he doesn't hesitate to engulf the children of nature for his own purposes. His head is covered with a dark linen cloth, an image of death. Onians, that insightful historian of ancient imagery, informs us that the Romans veiled their heads if they knew they were about to die, and they covered the heads of the dead with a cloth, believing that psyche was housed in the head.[10]

A fascinating modern source for Saturnian imagery is the work of Samuel Beckett, who, among other things, depicts the dry and barren quality of a culture cut off from its fertilizing roots. His settings, in novels and plays, are often, in accordance with the nature of Saturn, stark and pale, lonely, and indeed melancholic. We could look at several of his works from this viewpoint, but it is in the drama *Endgame* that we get the clearest portrait of Saturn. As the play begins, Hamm, ancient as the son of Noah his name suggests, sits in a chair with a bloody handkerchief covering his face. During the course of the drama his action is limited, as, never leaving his chair, he moves about geometrically on the chessboard of the stage, giving harsh directions to his young companion and speaking cruelly to his parents who pop up out of trash cans. He represents that tyrannical consciousness that dominates all times of ending—endings of a life phase, a belief system, a body of values, and an attitude toward onself. He wants full control over the past and the future, and his first and often repeated words—"it is finished"—identify him with a dying god, an eternal moment of death.

Saturn is indeed the god of a closing time, of endgame, when what has been in play for a fruitful period ought to end; but, as in Beckett's play the game never ends, so in Saturn there is no ending point, no conclusion, only a frozen, dried-out state of death.

Saturn's Gold

Saxl, Panofsky, and Klibansky's *Saturn and Melancholy* began as an attempt to show that Dürer's engraving *Melancholia I* crystallizes a tradition, revived by Ficino, according to which there is treasure to be found in the foul wastes of Saturn and in the heaviness of his leaden weight. Much of Hillman's work, too, shows that depression and other manifestations of Saturn play a productive role in the economy of the psyche. Both of these directions are prefigured in the work of Ficino whose allusions we will consider now in order to understand where Saturn's malevolence leads.

First, however, we must underscore Ficino's insistence that Saturn is to be avoided when his spirit would dry out the soul and adversely affect the body. We have already seen that he recommended the practice of the Pythagoreans—to wear white clothes especially when engaged in study to offset Saturn's dark influence. He also suggests turning to Jupiter, god of civil and social life: "Jupiter arms us against Saturn's influence which is generally foreign to and somehow unsuitable for mankind."[11] Recall the fundamental principle that guides Ficino in all of these recommendations: certain activities tend to draw to the soul particular kinds of spirit associated with that activity. In the first and third books of *De Vita Triplici* he addresses the literati, warning scholars and others who spend energy and time on ideas to watch out for Saturn's spirit. They should turn to more jovial pursuits now and then and become involved with society and social affairs in a remedial process of constellation.

Ficino's statement, however, continues: "But those who escape the baneful influence of Saturn, and enjoy his benevolent influence, are not only those who flee to Jupiter but also those who give themselves over with heart and soul to divine contemplation, which gains distinction from the example of Saturn himself."[12] So, besides running away from the painful conditions of Saturnian melancholy, one can profitably stay with them and find, in Saturn himself, a degree of contemplation equal to the severity of his malevolence. Stated simply, Ficino is advising us to get deep into our depressions, stay with them long enough to allow their work to have an effect. But we still must inquire into the manner in which depression and melancholy can offer a gift. It is not sufficient merely to accept the legend that the greatest authors and artists have been by nature melancholic. What is there in depression that can offer the soul not only a useful benefit but something extraordinarily positive?

James Hillman was once lecturing to university students when he was asked about depression. Why is it, the students inquired, that his psychology refers so often to depression in a supportive manner, to the point that some critics think that he and his followers must be depressive types? Hillman's response was that depression is an answer to widespread manic activism and is a dying to the wild world of literalism. Feeling low and heavy we are forced to move inward, turning to fantasy rather than the literal action of the ego. And that turn inward is necessary for the soul, for it creates psychic space, a container for deeper reflection where soul increases and the surface of events becomes less important. This response connects with his essay on *senex* consciousness, where he says that Saturn pushes us to the edge where our imagery becomes primordial, refined, and removed from our usual patterns of reflection, our accustomed imagery, and personal reference.[13] The comment on Hillman's followers being depressive recalls a curious fact about Ficino and *his* friends. Their inner circle called themselves "Saturnians," and they knew their place of meeting as *Mons Saturnus*, the Mountain of Saturn.[14]

The authors of *Saturn and Melancholy* seem to have caught the spirit of this Ficinian insight, for they write: "As enemy and oppressor of all life in any way subject to the present world, Saturn generates melancholy; but as friend and protector of a higher and purely intellectual existence he can also cure it."[15] I would take exception only to the world "intellectual," given the very first statement in *The Planets*: intellect without soul has no relationship to the body. Soul must stand in the middle. More accurately, therefore, Saturn takes us to the higher regions of the soul.

Ficino, too, makes some observations which complement Hillman's idea about depression leading us away from the surface realm of particulars. In *De Vita Sana* he writes:

It seems to be a natural phenomenon that pursuing difficult studies it is necessary for the spirit [*animus*] to go from the external world, within, to move from the circumference to the center, and while reflecting in itself to remain securely in the center of the person. But to gather oneself from the circumference and move to the center is like earth, to which black bile is quite similar. Therefore, black bile provokes the spirit to gather itself together, remain together, and assiduously contemplate. Like the center of the world, it draws to the center of each thing to be investigated and stretches to the heights those things to be comprehended, when it is most like Saturn, the highest of the planets.[16]

There seems to be a contradiction here: Saturn takes the soul to the edge of its inner firmament, to the end of the world, away from human life; yet here we see Saturn described as a movement to the center. But of course the center here is not the midpoint of the psyche but rather the center of "each thing to be investigated." In Saturnian heaviness and deep fantasy we are drawn deep into the imagery of the soul—not always vivid visual pictures, often simply the vague image of a mood or atmosphere. The concerns of ego and an active imagination no longer hold attention. In Ficino's theory of knowledge Saturnian consciousness is proper to *Mens*, the highest part of the soul, that function farthest removed from the material world. This is neither the spirituality of Sol nor the rationality of Mercury, but rather a function of deep contemplation, distant from the concrete, and it is an achievement in consciousness which Ficino celebrates highly:

Those lunar people whom Socrates describes in the *Phaedo*, inhabiting the highest surface of the earth and still higher in the clouds, watching prudently and content, in moderation, and dedicated to the study of secret wisdom and to religion, enjoy the happiness of Saturn. They live a prosperous and long life, so that they are considered not so much mortal persons as immortal daemons, whom many call heroes and the Golden Race enjoying the age and reign of Saturn.[17]

Elsewhere Ficino writes in a similar vein: "Instead of earthly life from which Saturn himself is removed, he confers celestial and eternal life on you."[18] In his own way Saturn brings us out of the world of the literal, away from plain life experience, into the realm of eternal patterns, the true home of the soul, or more plainly, to a state of consciousness in which the psychological dimension in its purest can be perceived and appreciated. When the gnawing painfulness of Saturn is avoided and his influence appears simply as senile crustiness and imperial control, we do not find our way to these primordial fantasies so far removed from moist experience. The Golden Age then is simply some idealized personal past. But when we submit to this god and endure his melancholy, that Golden Age pushes past personal history to a consciousness of much larger patterns. Our heroes this in his collective, archetypal memory are not merely important persons of youth and child-hood, but true heroes and ancestors, much bigger than life. The melancholic feeling associated with this fantasy may well be, as Freud intuited, a feeling of loss occasioned by the abandonment of one's personal history as source of meaning. A person becomes more concerned with the images than with the people who occasioned them and becomes more centered in those images than centering the images in himself. This, says Ficino in many contexts, is the very height of soul involvement, the ultimate meaning of contemplation, and in a genuine sense a religious phenomenon.

The reward to be found in feelings of melancholy, depression and heaviness stems directly from the withdrawal from life those feelings encourage. This is evident in the list of experiences Ficino provides in *The Planets* as examples of conditions that might elicit Saturnian spirit. "We are subjected to Saturn," he writes, "through leisure, solitude, and sickness; through theology, secret philos-ophy, superstition, magic farming, and through mourning."[19] All of these involve a withdrawal from ordinary offairs, either physically through leisure and solitude, or bodily through sickness, or through the study of things that are themselves far removed from what we would consider ordinary and usual. Saturn weakens energy and enthusiasm for the common life in order to highlight the extraordinary, the very depths of the soul.

When the power of ordinary living to provide a sense of meaning and vitality fails, feelings of sadness and temptations toward withdrawal invade consciousness. This is a natural move of the psyche, a turn in the round of planets; for that sadness may be a call for deeper roots. Jung claimed that every significant psychological problem presented in this day of confusion and meaninglessness is fundamentally a religious distress.[20] In one sense at least it may be a Saturnian situation, religion at its deepest in Ficino's view, because we finally confront, in our melancholy, the finite potential of the ordinary and personal, and search out something transcendent. This is not to say that only in depression do we find religious significance and satisfaction, but we find it also there. Saturn is not simply a troublesome planet to be avoided; with perseverance and endurance we may find in his dark, heavy, ambivalent moods a way through and beyond the shallowness of the present.

12

Jupiter

The last two planets we have to consider bear the names of deities that have a rich history in mythology but in Ficino's system called forth little elaboration. Jupiter and Mars both represent areas of psychological significance no less important than the others, but their functions appear so direct and straightforward in the Ficinian zodiac that one finds little resource for imaginative development. The two are quite opposite in character; indeed, in Ficino's writings Jupiter is simply called upon as a benefactor to solve all problems and Mars is presented consistently as a threatening power to be avoided. Therefore, we cannot expect very much in the way of suggestions for a Jovial psychology.

Seeds of Fantasy

If we found in Saturn a way of withdrawal from the ordinary life, we find in Jupiter entry into precisely that which is most common and ordinary. He is, in Ficinian astrology, the god of the common life, the deity who represents, above all, those things which keep life moderate, especially laws and government, the maintenance of social and civic life. Among Ficino's letters we find a brief statement on Jupiter, written interestingly enough in 1492. Here he gives some advice for making an image of Jupiter and in the process tells something of Jovial character and spirit. "Jupiter is intellect," he writes, "from which the universe is produced";[1] therefore, he may be symbolized with spheres or round forms. Or, he may be imaged as a man, since essentially he is mind (*mens*) and "produces all things with the 'seminal *ratio*.'"

This is the "seminal *ratio*" Ficino describes in the opening lines of *The Planets* in quite convoluted language,[2] and because this notion is basic to his astrological theory, it deserves a brief comment here. According to Ficino, the World Soul, essential at the cosmic level for uniting mind and body, has as many "seminal *rationes*" as there are ideas in the divine mind. Species of things take their forms from these ratios in the soul, and in fact when things degenerate they may be revived through the soul's seeds, and further, this process can be accomplished through material forms in which these gifts of the World Soul have been stored. These material forms which correspond to the seeds in the World Soul Ficino advises us were called "divine allurements" by Zoroaster and "magic decoys" by Synesius. Ficino goes on to explain that we can make such "decoys" in material forms capable of attracting the influx of the cosmic soul; they work either as exemplars or like generative seeds.

One of the guiding principles in this study has been a shift in perspective: seeing soul as a quality rather than a substance. It is one thing to place psyche within a metaphysical scheme and quite another to imagine soul as a dimension of consciousness. If it is true, as I suggested earlier following Hillman, that the World Soul is the world itself enlivened through fantasy, then we may read these abstruse statements of Ficino as having to do with fantasy. Indeed, it would be quite appropriate to translate *"ratio"* in this context as "fantasy." "Seminal *rationes*" then become the seed fantasies that germinate in imagination and fertilize life. To say that they are cosmic fantasies takes them out of the personalistic realm, placing them in the circular astral body.

What Ficino seems to suggest is that life can become routine and unconsciously stuck in materialistic projects; it *degenerates* because it has been cut off from its *generative* fantasies. But life can be revived and ensouled again, says Ficino, through the skillful use of images; for it is in images that we will find the seed-fantasies. Reflecting on Jupiter we return once again to that Ficinian leitmotif: soul is re-created and nourished through the spirit contained in material forms, in the images that permeate life. The things of this world, so obvious and overlooked, are the "magic decoys" that can lure us back to a psychological perspective and once again put us in touch with the very seeds of experience, the deep fantasies we have about our world and ourselves.

Jupiter's role is to provide the specific intelligence needed to build a culture and to keep it vital. He is that form of imagination by which we transform our visions into the realities of collective living. Ficino says that our images of him should show that his power is stable and unchanging, that his creative intelligence is visible to intelligent and superior beings but hidden to inferior creatures. His is, in fact, "the most spiritual [*spiritualissimum*] domicile of life."[3] Ordinarily we might think of culture building and maintenance as simple hard-core pragmatism; a project of physical survival. But in Ficino's view culture is a source of spirit and the imaginative creation of fantasy, and that is not to say that culture is automatically a wonderful source of psychological creativity. The spirit and fantasy may be quite negative and flat. Nevertheless, Ficino is suggesting that we do have in Jupiter a planet within, a "vivifying spirit of the world," the capacity to create a social environment that is psychologically nourishing.

The seedlike intentions that fill our minds as we build our cities and nations, care for the world's government and commerce, establish structures of education, law, politics, communications, and other forms of the common life—all these are not merely "natural" products of reasoning people, they also have deep roots in the psyche; they can be traced to a god who is the profound spirit that gives birth to culture and sustains it.

A Grace of Human Life

It was in the spirit of Jupiter that Ficino saw his own age and culture as an outstanding achievement; in a letter he called his era "the age of gold." "We have brought back to light," he boasted, "the liberal disciplines: grammar, poetry, oratory, painting, sculpture, architecture, music, and ancient songs sung to the Orphic lyre."[4] These are doubtless not the kind of claims twentieth-century enthusiasts would boast; they are all "solar" achievements, full of spiritual significance, nourishing to the soul and not just aimed at the mind and body as so many of our successes are. So it is for Ficino a Jovial extravagance to cheer his time so enthusiastically; for he considered Jupiter the source of the most humanly significant spirit. Along with Mercury and Sol he is among the most human of the planets, or so Ficino says in *The Planets*. In a letter to Lorenzo he adds Venus to the list and, by coupling Jupiter with Mercury, ends up with three planetary "Graces." The letter is worth quoting at some length:

> At first the poets among us depicted the Graces as three young women embracing each other. These three are most powerful among the highest planets: Mercury with Jove, that is, disposed to the gift of Jove, Phoebus, and Venus, companions together in the heavenly circuit with mutual advantage. The names of the three Graces are: Viriditas (Green), Lux (light) and Laetitia

(Joy), most suited to the same stars. So disposed in the heavens, these stars especially favor human temperament. For that reason, they are called the Graces, not of animals but of humans. In fact, they are not the servants of Venus but of Minerva. When you hear that the first of the Graces is Jove, you should not think of Jupiter but of Mercury-Jove. For Mercury incites Jupiter with his lively and timely mobility, so you should carefully investigate these things. Sol makes accessible every discovery to you who are searching by his light. Finally, Venus always adorns whatever is found with the most gracious charm.[5]

This letter, written at Careggi on October 18, 1481, several years before the publication of *The Planets* (1489), gives us an important insight into Ficino's understanding of these planets. He was especially conscious of their interrelationships, which is to say, he knew how various patterns of consciousness interact. Jupiter's concern for culture-making requires the services of the spirit of Mercury in order to "keep changing shape," to see behind the work of culture so as not to get stuck in empty structures. Venus's green, Sol's spiritual light, and Mercury-Jupiter's optimism and joy all fit together to create a nourishing human climate. They are the three Graces who dance together and embrace each other. And they are servants of Minerva, says Ficino, therefore close to Jupiter; for Minerva-Athena is the intelligence of the *polis*, the genius of the city and state, who knows how to charm both passion and reason into a civil setting conducive to human life.

According to the title of the fifth chapter of *The Planets* Jupiter is the middle sister of the Graces, the Grace most suited to us (*maxime nobis accommodata*).[6] Jupiter is that spirit most important to human life because it both shares in the spirit of other nourishing planets and moderates them for human tolerance. For example, through Jupiter the spiritual intensity of Sol is mollified. In *The Planets* we read:

Although Sol accomplishes the same things more effectively, Jupiter does them with Sol's power, In both heat thrives and overcomes moisture, though in Jupiter the effect is moderate while in Sol it is powerful. However, in both the effect is beneficial."[7]

Solar people find innumerable ways to touch directly upon the world of spirit. They may join a monastery or climb a mountain, hook up with a political cause, learn some system of meditation, or join a church. Others prefer the indirect path to spirit, the way of Jupiter. Restoring old houses in a city may not look much like a spiritual activity, but it is in fact an involvement spiced with the peppermint of Jupiter. Whatever contributes to gracefulness in life and rebounds that grace upon the psyche is essentially Jovial in Ficino's typology. This is a spirit that enjoys favorable "conjunctions" with Mercury, the more moist planet. There is less danger in Jupiter than in Sol of drying out the soul in its lofty aims; Jupiter remains close to the flow of life, the excitement and traumas of social involvement, and the mundane, concrete details of fabricating and fashioning culture.

Jupiter not only has these solar capacities, worked out in his own moderate style, he also tempers the lower tendencies of the soul. As Ficino says, this spirit contains elements of Sol on the one hand and Venus and Luna on the other. In *The Planets* he says:

> While the rays of Venus continuously join Sol's light, and transform it, Sol's rays, since they are warmer, temper her moisture. But Jove's rays require no tempering; for what is Jupiter but Sol tempered especially from the beginning for the well-being of human affairs? Or what else but Luna and Venus made warmer and more powerful?[8]

Human culture, founded in this image of the planet Jupiter, aims at fulfilling the two extremes of human concern — spirit and body — and it gathers them at a midpoint that is psychological. Thus, the "moderating" that Jupiter accomplishes is essentially a psychologizing; the extremes of solar spirit are mixed with the earthy, feeling-toned fantasies of Luna and Venus. Jupiter, then, in his way accomplishes exactly what so many of the other processes we have examined intend: establishing a space for psyche, as in the alchemical dissolving and congealing and the triangulating of the square. In the case of Jupiter the process is the making of culture, a blend of spiritual concern with fantasy and body. In Ficino's imagistic words, "Mix solar things with the things of Venus, and you will have made a Jovial figure from both."[9]

The crucial point, however, in constellating a Jovial spirit is the level of consciousness at which culture-making goes on. We saw earlier that an American Indian thanking the earth for a piece of fruit might do it with a mind toward getting more food for his body, or, more likely, he performs this little ritual in order to maintain his consciousness of a relationship he has to the earth. In the latter case his action is psychological, feeding his psyche more than his body. So it is with the work of culture — making laws, building cities and cultural institutions and so on — this work may be done with a psychological attitude, with care for the psyche foremost in mind. Now this may be quite a rare phenomenon in our modern world, but such an attention to psyche does show itself clearly now and then. An example might be the work of architects who build their constructions for human beings, and not just functionally but with human feeling and values in mind. Architects, for instance, who are building hospices for the dying are obviously concerned with physical comfort and care, but they are more preoccupied with the significance of space to the psyches of the people they are working for. They may take into consideration the need for privacy, the fantasy of death the building suggests, the gradual approach of relatives and friends to the dying.[10] This kind of work on behalf of a social institution may be done in a Jovial spirit, serving the psyche, so that we might well imagine not only music and people with soul, but buildings and social institutions as well.

The functional, pragmatic attitude so prevalent in modern times screens other more important tasks of the culture. Society is not only a collection of people, it is also a theater of images. When we put up buildings or establish a social agency, we are also creating an image. I don't refer to the kind of persona image advertising people speak of. Even in our functional attitudes, in spite of ourselves, we make images everywhere, and those images determine to some extent the quality of psychological life of a people. A city's plan or lack of it speaks not merely to the physical requirements of its people, it adds or detracts form its life of psyche. A city that has soul will nourish the psyche of its inhabitants, and one without soul might well suck the life out of its people.

Ficino's descriptions of "seminal *ratio*" and the World Soul may sound like so much Neoplatonic mysticism, but in fact his insights are quite relevant and down to earth. The things of culture are indeed "magic decoys" that draw forth a spirit that strikes deep in the psyche, deep enough to be represented by a cultic deity. The images we find all around us in our manufactured world do serve as exemplars and as generative fantasies for our personal consciousness. It is almost a truism to note that we are to a large extent an internalization of our culture. Our values and wishes and fears develop from our imaginative encounter with the human world around us. So, Ficino suggests, why not cultivate that world for soul. Why not recognize the role of this planet Jupiter in the rhythms of the psyche? Society itself can be a source of psychological creativity, but, as we have seen before, in order to get soul we have to bring soul with us. In order to do that we have to have imagination, and . that is the purpose of Ficino's astrological therapy: to enliven imagination so that we might be conscious of the psychological implications of all that we make and do. Ficino calls Jupiter "the helping father to all people living the common life."[11] He is such a father because he provides the impetus for a cultural accommodation of spirit and body in a final psychological milieu.

In Jean Seznec's study of the Renaissance gods, an image of Jupiter is reproduced, a picture taken from Mantegna's *Tarocchi*, a series of engraved cards believed to have been made in the mid-fifteenth century for a group of ecclesiastical dignitaries, including Nicholas of Cusa.[13] Jupiter is pictured as a king, his eagle just over his head. Instead of a lightning bolt he holds an arrow, and beneath him on the ground lie vanquished soldiers. Jupiter sits within a mandorla, a geometrical figure made from the intersecting of two circles, and within the mandorla, just beneath his feet, is a young child, apparently protected by Jupiter.

This portrait of Jupiter, from Ficino's time and place, reveals the essence of Jovial spirit. The two spheres of spirit and matter meet in the middle realm, the space of the mandorla, which is the containing space of psyche. Jupiter's eagle, as Ficino informs us in several places, represents his close connection with the sun and his authority over all beings; but, like the lightning bolt or arrow, the eagle also shows that Jupiter can traverse the distance between earth and sky. With this middle region established, the child, that defenseless growing part of the psyche, is protected and the threats of heroic fantasies are set aside. This last point is especially significant. When the work of culture is not understood in its psychological dimension, that is, as a work for and by the psyche, then an unfettered spirit of militancy and heroism is let loose. Nationalism replaces concern for a human society; money and energy go into projects whose aim is to overcome the powers or mysteries of nature, but with no depth purpose.

Stated simplistically, Ficino's social psychology runs like this: What we do is what we get. If we set to the task of cultural activities with soul in our minds (memoria), even if we have to paint our horoscope on our bedroom ceiling so as not to forget, then soul will be nourished by the "magic decoys" we have made. If all of culture were to be a "magic decoy" or a "divine allurement," then psyche would be fully cared for and we wouldn't suffer the separation of mind from body. Perhaps then our churches and universities — now serving mind in itself or a refined sense of spirit — would mesh more closely with the worries of politics, now for the most part materialistic. Perhaps what we need, among the processes of the psyche, is the mandorla of Jupiter where these two circles intersect.

What Ficino suggests in a few subtle, enigmatic references to Jupiter is a social psychology that far outweighs that discipline as we know it today. In the Ficinian context, social psychology has to do with the impact society has upon the soul and the means of giving soul back to society. The implications of both for the task of culture-building and for the discipline of psychology are immense.

And amid all this discussion of Jupiter's role in the psyche's tour of the planets, we should not neglect the common-sense meaning of "Jovial." In the social setting just described, in a society that has soul, one might indeed expect to find a jovial climate, one perhaps both alluring and magical.

13

Mars

After summarizing Ficino's *De Vita Triplici* in her book on Renaissance hermeticism, Frances Yates offers her own fantasy of what Ficino's therapeutic practice might have been like: "We might be in the consulting room of a rather expensive psychiatrist," she says with the acumen of an imaginative historian, "who knows that his patients can afford plenty of gold and holidays in the country, and flowers out of season."[1] The "Laetus in praesens" atmosphere of Ficino's villa, the wealthy patronage of the Medici, and the kinds of remedies Ficino recommends support this picture Yates suggests. It would also seem that Ficino and his friends would fit well in the atmosphere of those far western counties of California. Surrounded by artists, intellectuals, travelers from the East, touring aficionados of things occult and mystical; finding every excuse for festivals; available for private psychotherapy, especially for wealthier patrons; and finally equipped with what today would be an electronic acoustical Orphic lyre, Ficino, for all his physical unhandsomeness, would cut a striking figure. Perhaps this updated picture gives a hint as to why Mars should be the last and least of the planets studied in this *circulatio* of the zodiac.

Like some modern psychologies which might have "flowers out of season" as their logo, Ficino's mind found little place for this god of anger, violence, and audacity. Throughout his writings, whether in *The Planets*, in his philosophical works, or in his letters, he warns against the influence of Mars the relatively few times this planet is mentioned. He often groups Mars together with Saturn, but in the case of the god of melancholy he was able to find positive traits, as well as negative. Mars remains for the most part a negative factor in the life of the psyche, to be avoided or at least mollified.

Ficino had good reason to warn against Mars: anger, violence, hatred, war, aggression of all kinds, bitterness, and heroism — these are the manifestations of the god. Ficino clearly knew these in the flesh during his lifelong sojourn in Florence, where intrigue and murder, civil strife and war were common problems. His patron Cosimo had been imprisoned and threatened with death before he was banished from the city.

In our world, too, one can go on to find the positive side of Mars only after facing the full potential of his other side. War and violence are still so widespread and are pursued with such self-righteous spirit as to threaten our very existence daily. Unrestrained heroism accompanies ideological fervor to such an extent that the religious nature of Mars-worship lies thinly concealed, especially in terrorism politically motivated. In domestic settings too we read daily of spouses, parents, lovers, friends, and neighbors crazed by an onslaught of anger, a possession by Mars, turning into violently mad creatures. Finally and more subtly still, one comes across so many instances where apparently a person is truly at war with himself. Ficino himself said it: "A person rages against himself in Mars."[2] It is not only the pressure of a well-armed superego that torments the ego, although superego does seem to have a tough Martian spirit and power, but conflict between many parts of self have the flavor of warfare.

The records of twentieth-century life often read as accounts of Martian turmoil. Newsreels and newscasts that chronicle the century sometimes stream before our eyes endless varieties of war materials and weapons. Newspapers, as I said, tell the stories of murders, sometimes as interesting as detective stories, but more often plain narratives of blind rage and regrets. Even many of the century's memoirs and diaries shock us with their revelations of the rage that burns inwardly, gutting out the interior of a life that looked serene from the outside. Mars, too, is a planet to reckon with.

In the next chapter we will consider some ways of dealing with the fierce negative side of the various planetary spirits, suggesting with Ficino that "tempering" might be a solution. But here, in the case of Mars especially, let us recall a fundamental rule. Jung held that any unconscious factor, if neglected and repressed, would become so overwhelming that it might wipe away all ego involvement. It might appear at times that Mars himself takes over a body and commits murder, or Venus swamps the ego and drives esteemed senators to burlesque stages and massage parlors. Jung's solution is to establish a relationship with our dark fantasies, find those little people — the complexes — who inhabit the flophouse of our mind, and see if we can make some deals.[3] In order to do that it is necessary first to become acquainted with those inner personified figures who appear nightly in our dreams and occasionally pop out in uncharacteristic behavior and action. Often people not accustomed to outbursts of anger will find themselves hurled into a rage and afterward they invariably say: "What came over me?" Maybe the proper question is: "Who came over me? Who overcame me?"[4] The figure within who rages may be a composite of many things: past experiences, identifications with friends, or perhaps an uninvited but proper resident in the house of the personal psyche. Beneath and beyond these personal factors there is the archetypal, essentially human and transhuman force of conflict, battle, and rage — Mars himself.

Mars is a collective fantasy at work in the lives of us all as a natural force — Strife, a most fundamental reality posited by early Greek naturalist philosophers. Mars is the collective culprit of the psyche, who causes much havoc but who also plays an irreduciable role in the total economy of the soul. We find hints in Ficino concerning the nature of that role, although, as I said, Ficino leaves Mars for the most part among the outlaws of Olympus, a spirit to be avoided more often than confronted. Nevertheless, he does suggest some important functions for this fiery deity.

Fortifier of the Soul

While investigating the service Mars renders psyche in his place among the planets, we do not want to sidestep his true character and change his burning red to a delicate pink. Ficino shows us the proper way in *The Planets*. First, he says, "Martian things are like poison, natural enemies to spirit."[5] Then he warns that Mars can have a disastrous effect on the intestines; "You ought to avoid a bad aspecting of Saturn or Mars with Luna; the former bothers the stomach, while the latter destroys [*dissolvit*] the intestines."[6] It is usually better not to interpret Ficino literally when he makes statements like this; in astrology the body itself serves as a metaphorical system. But it might be worth investigating a possible connection between intestinal problems and the work of Mars. In any case, the spirit of Mars is a fiery spice, not easily digested into the body of psyche.

Then Ficino gives us a way into a more positive evaluation of Martian spirit: "If anyone believes that Saturn and Mars are poisonous by nature, I would not agree, for these too should be used just as physicians sometimes use toxic materials."[7] Therefore, even though the spirit of Mars is essentially toxic and often harmful, it too has its place. Jung's celebrated theory of the "shadow" parallels this statement of Ficino's; for, even though a psychic element may be offensive and even a severe threat, at least from the ego point of view, it may have a significant role to play in the total constellation of the psyche. We may tend to keep Martian spirit out of our "temperament" because we find it morally toxic; yet, perhaps by keeping anger outside the realm of moral possibility, we allow for incursions of more violent forms of Martian spirit. Mars contains a great deal of shadow, at least for some. This is especially true among people whose religious upbringing has led them to such a pacific general attitude that any sign of Martian red rage or militant force is a sure signal of evil. Today Mars is warded off by phrases such as "I didn't want to hurt anyone." Martian spirit is indeed forceful and feelings can be hurt when his spirit is present, but often the result of keeping feelings placid is simply another form of Mars, the rage against self. It is curious that Mars and Saturn are often linked together, for they correspond to two kinds of depression: melancholy as we have studied it, a manifestation of Saturn's lead; and rage against self, the feeling of having been vanquished by our own power.

Ficino provides an appropriate astrological comment on these problems: "To offset timidity, at the first hour of Mars, with Scorpio rising, make images of Mars armed and crowned."[8] To that part of the population in whom Mars is well constellated, it may seem strange and even questionable advice to suggest means for acquiring Martian spirit. But not everyone has such a vital Mars; indeed, in a culture which often rewards passivity and obedience in the extreme, Mars may be far removed, to the detriment of individuals and the society at large. Recent psychological studies have recorded the capacity of our society to remain passive in the face of absurdity, crime, and personal violation. Granted that these phenomena are complex, could it not be that a failure to acknowledge Mars in the pantheon of the psyche accounts for a measure of this unrealistic tranquillity?

The Fire of Audacity

The color of Mars is red, of course; his metal iron, his element fire, and his temperature hot — he is the hottest of the planets in Ficino's paradigm. This red hot spirit not only provides directly for an attitude of militancy, overcoming timidity and passivity, it also intensifies the spirits of other planets. In *The Planets*, Ficino claims that "Mars warms the coldest things and energizes the sluggish."[9] In a letter he says that "Mars, ruler of Ares, inflames the fervent spirit."[10] And in his essay *De Amore*, Ficino ascribes to Mars the power to "excite the winds."[11] Ficino often recommends a combination of the spirits of the Sun and of Mars in any human endeavor requiring intensity. In general, then, we might imagine this intensifying power of the red planet to be rooted in the same source from which come our problems with violence and rage, but when the God is acknowledged and given his due, his heat and energy turn toward more creative ends. Once again, then, we find in Ficino not a theory of repression and therapeutic advice to "cool it," but rather another way of imagining, and therefore experiencing, what can easily be a toxic spirit.

In the relations of the planets, the one most curious from the point of view of Mars is Venus. These two have long been considered opposites whose reconciliation would be one of the miracles of all time. In mythology the two deities unite and have a child, Harmonia; but as Edgar Wind wisely warns, we should not think that in this coitus the spirit of Mars is swamped by the moisture of Venus.[12] Ficino, in a passage noted by Wind, elaborates on this, adding some further insights into Martian character. I quote this passage at some length:

Who is bolder than a lover fighting for his loved one? Mars surpasses the other Gods in fortitude since he makes people strong. Venus tames. For when Mars is aspected, or in the second house of nativity, or in the eighth, he portends evil. Venus, often in conjunction, or opposition, or reception, or in sextile or trine with Mars, as we say, checks his malignity. When Mars rules a person's birth, he bestows greatness of spirit as well as irascibility. If Venus comes near, *she does not impede* that greatness of spirit given by Mars, but she represses the strength of the anger. She seems to tame Mars and make him more mild. But Mars does not tame Venus. If she is leader, she provides the affect of love. If Mars leads nearby, he renders the heat of Venus's power more ardent. So, if anyone is born with Mars in a house of Venus, in Libra or Taurus, because of the presence of Mars whoever so born will enjoy the most passionate loves. But Mars follows Venus, Venus does not follow Mars, since audacity is the lackey of love, love is not the servant of audacity.[13]

Renaissance painters took pleasure evidently in showing us how easily Venus tames Mars, but, as Ficino points out, she does not interfere with the magnanimity he provides. Aphrodite's love can obviously wield immense power, charming our senses and souls, but she need not root out our magnanimity, the presence of Mars. Mars can intensify love and embolden the lover, says Ficino, but Venus does not serve Martian spirit. On the whole, then, we see here a beneficial spirit that "makes people strong," even fortifies our love. Love and strength are not incompatible, though love tempers the emotions of Mars. Indeed, without the troublesome, undervalued attitude of Mars, love might well shrink the spirit, numbing the feeling of strength Mars bestows and cooling his desirable heat and passion. A modern psychology of love and of marriage might take this ancient couple into account, reviving the tradition that would give Venus priority without loss of Martian vigor. It would appear that in love relationships, when the needed role of Mars is excluded on the grounds of morality or sentimentality, his ugly side rises in fits of anger, spouse beating, and verbal abuse. Yet it would be quite unusual to find a minister blessing a wedding with a prayer to Mars, or the equivalent thereof. We seem consciously dedicated to the ideal of the placid life, and all those couples in attendance at weddings, knowing full well the temptations of Mars, keep the doors shut on him. Would it not be better, in true polytheistic fashion, to render him his due in ritual and celebration so that his inevitable presence as an archetype of the psyche would not shatter the house Venus built?

A Thrust toward Multiplicity

Finally, in Ficino's commentary on Plato's *Philebus* he gives Mars a role in the act of reasoning. Mercury, he says, defines, Saturn resolves, and Mars divides.[14] He does't explain this further, to my knowledge, but in the context of Martian spirit in general we may interpret his role in rationality.

In spite of all the positive points we have seen, Mars is still poison, even if the kind doctors use to cure ailments. For many the process of division in imagination and thought, especially in matters psychological, is a highly suspect notion. We readily join the bandwagon of integration and wholeness and neglect the forceful realism of Martian multipicity. Harmony, the daughter of Mars and Venus, is not a pleasant blend of the two. She is more like the taut string of the lyre Rilke describes in his *Sonnets to Orpheus*; she is the tension between the two poles, created out of their opposing force, not from their blending. Mars does provide a kind of *harmonia*, but one we shall see in the following chapter to be in its essence a spread of multiplicities. Mars in his fiery realism counters sentimental ideals of integration and wholeness, and he allows the psyche to exist in the brilliance of its many centers. The planets themselves are multiple, reflective of the many facets of the psyche which resist harmonization. It takes, it seems, the forcefulness of Mars, with his shadowy nature and toxic spirit, to affirm this fundamental pluralism of the psyche. His strength splits the psyche like a diamond into its glittering parts, allowing wishes, moods, feelings, and thoughts to sustain their creative conflict instead of finding a soporific peace in harmony.

We will turn now, in the final section, to a direct study of psychological polytheism. This is an idea not directly approached by Ficino at the level of philosophy and psychology in *The Planets*, but one suggested in his chapter on music. Mars, strangely perhaps, leads us on to musical harmony and a discussion of the gods as tones on a scale. Mars plays a significant role in establishing that harmony and in creating the magnanimity of spirit equal to a polytheistic psyche. Indeed, all the planets, as we have seen, bring their own gift to the creation of the psychological attitude, or soul. They all have potential extremes, and some are on the surface malefic, like Saturn and Mars. But all are to be given their due if this attitude of soul-consciousness and psychological imagination is to be nourished and supported. In Ficinian imagination the psyche is pictured as a round of planets, all simultaneously contributing to the music of the soul.

PART III

Musical Humana:
Music of the Soul

The united personality will never quite lose the painful
sense of innate discord. Complete redemption from the
sufferings of this world is and must remain in illusion.
The goal is important only as an idea; the essential thing
is the opus which leads to the goal: that is the goal of a
lifetime.
　　　　　　—Jung, *Psychology of the Transference*

Gods should be iridescent, like the rainbow in the
storm. Man creates a God in his own image, and the
gods grow old along with the men that made them. But
storms sway in heaven, and the god-stuff sways high
and angry over our heads. Gods die with men who have
conceived them. But the god-stuff roars eternally, like
the sea, with too vast a sound to be heard.
　　　　　　—D. H. Lawrence, *The Plumed Serpent*

14

The Well-Tempered Life

We may collect our thoughts on astrological sensibility and summarize Ficino's idea of psychotherapy by giving close attention to the metaphor of music, as Ficino does in the twenty-first and twenty-second chapters of *The Planets*. I do not intend to turn to music as some grand romantic image for the soul, making of psychotherapy a powerful orchestration of life's diversity or picturing the psyche as a symphony of possibilities. The art of music contains some precise forms and structures which reflect the life of the soul with a high degree of differentiation. Furthermore, music inherently expresses the dynamics of life, so that the metaphorical value of music is not something external to it or added on. To participate aurally in the complex patterns of a piece of music is to enter deeply into an image that conveys sensations and perceptible patterns in life itself.

This close connection between the mobile patterns of life and the structural forms of music was once widely acknowledged, but that connection was lost in the turn in Western history from a mythological to a scientific view of the world. It is apparent to many people interested in mythology, art, and religious systems that in two fields we have studied, astronomy and chemistry, a rationalistic, scientific reduction began to take place toward the end of the medieval era. Astronomy was drawn pure and clear from the murky myths of astrology, and chemistry developed in precision and mathematical rigor, leaving behind the occult hallucinations of the alchemists. It is less recognized that music suffered a similar purification, losing its religious and mythological foundations to become a refined art. From the point of view of a psychologist who values imagery, of course, these developments were hardly evolutionary in any positive, progressive sense. What was lost is at least equal in importance to what was gained.

In the case of music, in the development of the fine art as we know it today, we lost two-thirds of its scope as it was practiced and theorized in the medieval and early Renaissance period. We have already had occasion to note the three fold paradigm offered by Boethius in the sixth century and held firmly in musical treatises down to the time of Ficino and beyond. In that scheme *musica instrumentalis*, or music in sound as we know it today, was rated lowest in the hierarchy. More important manifestations of music were *musica mundana*, the music of the cosmos played in the seasons of the year and in the rhythms of the planets; and *musica humana*, human music or the music of the soul, sensed in the moving patterns of subjective experience: in moods, feelings, thoughts, values, and, in the minds of medieval churchmen, virtues—in short, in human temperament.

Naturally, Ficino emphasizes *musica humana*, but the connection with cosmic music is natural and clear. If we have a sky within and planets making their "music of the spheres" in our very soul, then music is to be found in the rhythms of these planets. "As above, so below," the alchemists were fond of saying. As the planets of the soul enter and fade and play through the psyche in varying counterpoints, their movements, felt in emotion and fantasy, give musical form to the very structures of our consciousness. Seeing this correspondence between music and the planets, Ficino was only following his mentor, Plato, who in the *Republic* (book 7) called astronomy and music "sister sciences." Socrates makes the claim: "As the eyes are designed to look up at the stars, so are the ears to hear harmonious motions; and these are sister sciences." Ficino would capitalize too on the long-appreciated coincidence by which the number of planets equalled the number of tones in a musical scale.

The idea that music has a close relationship to soul would not startle anyone; music obviously affects the emotions and "calms the savage breast." Aristotle provides an early detailed description of the psychology of music:

> Rhythms and melodies contain representations of anger and mildness, and also of courage and temperance and all their opposites and the other moral qualities, that most closely correspond to the true natures of these qualities (and this is clear from the facts of what occurs—when we listen to such representations we change in our soul).[1]

Later, in the sixth century, Cassiodorus speaks of these virtues and moral qualities as musical in themselves, making the psyche itself musical.[2] For him music of the soul consists in the harmony of good habits and virtues—a virtuous life is a musical life.

Ficino takes into account and enhances both of these approaches, bringing the ancient tradition of *musica humana* in line with his theory of spirit.[3] He conceives human music as the proper arrangement of one's life so that all concrete experiences resonate, like overtones, the fundamental octave of possibilities represented by the planet-tones. Psychotherapy would be musical then insofar as one would temper and tune the planetary tonal centers so that each would hum within the surface events of life.[4] This key notion of "tempering" calls for further analysis, but first it will be necessary to examine another difficult musical term, harmony.

Pythagorean Harmonia

The goal of Ficinian theory and practice is a kind of spiritual and psychological harmony; qualities of the soul as well as the body need to be "tempered to a celestial consonance (*ad coelestem consonantiam temperato*)"[5] But the notion of harmony implied in Ficino's vision differs from that popularly conceived. Ordinarily, in music theory harmony is a blending of several tones sounding simultaneously to form a chord. In such a blending, for most ears individual tones lose their identities as they contribute to the overall sound. The harmonic aspect of the chord concerns this blended unit and not the sounding or movement of the individual tones. The idea is expanded metaphorically when we speak of ideals of "world harmony," "living in harmony with nature," and "being in harmony with oneself." We usually imply a lack of conflict and dissonance. Ficinian harmony flows from a different conception, specifically the musical theory traditionally attributed to Pythagoras.

We can find the essence of the Pythagorean meaning of harmonia, a term we may now use to distinguish this from the popular view of harmony just discussed, in a passage from the *Odyssey* (5.248). Homer describes the timbers Odysseus "joins together" (*harmonia*) in order to construct the platform of his sailing vessel or raft. This image of lashing together several logs is closer to Pythagorean harmonia than memories of fifty-voice choirs singing rich, pleasant chord progressions. Harmonia in the Pythagorean sense consists of a lateral or horizontal arrangement of tones, while later harmony is a vertical phenomenon.

Ficino evidently drew his musical ideas from his study of Greek literature rather than from the music theory and practice of his day. In Ficino's Florence the rich polyphony of the Burgundian composers could be heard; for example, a Dufay motet was sung to inaugurate the cathedral in Florence in 1436.[6] Also, the great Flemish composer, Henricus Isaac, whose *Choralis Constantinus* constituted the first complete cycle of religious motets, was at the court of Lorenzo de Medici around 1480.[7] Nevertheless, the older notion of lateral harmony was much in evidence in the texts Ficino was reading, translating, and commenting upon.

The discovery of the relationship between musical intervals— the "distance" between tones—and certain numerical ratios is credited by legend to Pythagoras. The story was told that he was passing a blacksmith hammering on anvils when the insight suddenly hit him. He is also said to have experimented with tones and numbers on a simple musical instrument, the monochord, a single-string instrument. Basically he discovered that small-number ratios correspond in music to the consonant intervals, an awesome finding for someone predisposed toward finding a unifying principle in the universe.[8] The entire problem of temperament and tuning is much more complex in modern music, and even working out the Pythagorean scales and ratios is not so simple; still the basic idea of Pythagorean harmonia rests on the simple ratios "sounding" with purity of tone. The art of making the proper ratios is the essence of all later Pythagorean systems,[9] and we find this art applied in such diverse areas as architecture, writing, philosophy, magic, and even psychology.[10]

Out of the simple ratios and their corresponding pure intervals, the Pythagorean scale was formed; and it is this scale, a careful arrangement of tones in which each is tuned to be distinct from its neighbor, that I am identifying as Pythagorean "harmonia." A few specific characteristics of this scale account for its metaphorical importance as an image for the tempered psyche: (1) each tone is distinct, not lost in the blend of a chord; (2) the scale is theoretical, not a piece of music in itself; (3) the ratios have a certain natural or given purity about them; and (4) the final pleasing effect is achieved by keeping the tones distinct and multiple. If we imagine the planetary psychological processes we have examined to be tones on a scale, then these four points apply to the psyche as well: (1) each of the planets must be given due regard, they cannot be blended in some overarching ego-plan; (2) as Jung claimed, archetypes of human life do not exist in themselves, we only assume their natures from concrete situations; (3) the planets are poetic images for processes we find at the foundation of life, they are not ego-products; and finally, (4) to keep the music playing we have to keep these processes in tune, accessible, and active.

Many medieval and Renaissance philosophers and theologians grasped this notion of a world constructed according to simple ratios, saw its beauty, and worked out their own applications of the theory, attributing the basic insight always to Pythagoras. This is true of writers like Athenaeus, Cassiodorus, Boethius, and Isidore of Seville,[11] and of Ficino's followers, notably Robert Fludd.[12] Ficino himself frequently acknowledged his debt to the Pythagoreans and characteristically ranked the study of ratios in a curious hierarchy: he conceived a progression from arithmetic to plane geometry to solid geometry to music. Music has to do with figures and bodies in movement.[13] Music, then, in this Ficinian hierarchy is a fourth dimension, one that takes into consideration both the importance of proportion and the peculiar problems of movement. In *The Planets* he makes it clear how broad his concept of music is:

> But let us return to the proposition that music consists first in the ratio, second in the fantasy, third in speech, followed by song, making music with the fingers, the music of the whole body in gymnastics or in dance.... The Pythagoreans, the Platonists, Mercurius, Aristoxenus—they all say that the soul and body of the world and of all animals consist in musical ratios. Even the sacred writings of the Hebrews hold that God disposes all things in number, weight, and measure.[14]

Music of the psyche, at least in this Pythagorean aspect, is made by giving each process of the soul its place on the scale. In tuning a musical instrument, each tone has to be given an exact proportion of vibrations if it is to ring true and clear. So with the psyche, it resounds with the cosmic music when each planet sounds its true pitch through the experiences of life. If one is in Saturn, his heaviness is acknowledged clearly and given space and time to resonate; if Venus presses, her voice is allowed to sing through with its own timbre, not made presentable through some pretense that Venus is other than she is. A musical soul is tempered, not tampered with.

Tempering the Instrument of Soul

In order to fulfill the Ficinian ideal, then, of becoming "as celestial as possible," one also has to become profoundly musical—well-tempered and tuned. The question remains, how do we get ourselves in tune so that our lives have resonance and harmony of the Pythagorean type?

Ficino gives us a few ideas how we might go about tempering the soul:

> Whoever imitates by devotion, study, life and habits celestial benefits, activities, or order, insofar as he is more like the heavens he will receive more abundant gifts. But people unnaturally dissimilar to the heavens and *discordant* [*discordes*] are secretly miserable, though publicly they may not appear unhappy.[15]

Each of these kinds of "imitation" deserve some attention, since it is through them that the planets are constellated.

"Devotion" once again raises the issue of religion. Obviously, it is not necessary to worship the planetary deities as did the Greeks and Romans; yet they do call for a certain amount of dedication and absorption. The traditional way of speaking of these gods is for an individual to say that he is "in Mercury" or "in Venus." The idea is that the mood and atmosphere accompanying the archetypal posture of the god take hold of the person, commanding his attention and coloring all his perceptions. One does not simply waken Mercury in one's soul by writing some doggerel or playing at dream interpretation. It is Mercury who wakens the soul, urging one on toward understanding and insight. The gods are not out in the sky but neither are they merely poetic terms for personal experiences. Ego senses the shadow of the larger embrace of the god, though the god is a psychological reality. A person can, then, truly take a religious attitude toward these movements of the psyche, acknowledging their influence and power, and drawing their spirit into the fabric of life. As Jung said in his definition of religion, religious sensibility involves giving attention to the contents of psychic life, whether they be known as spirits, gods, demons, or unconscious fantasies.

A second way of tempering the soul is through study, a simple technique almost too obvious to be taken seriously. Yet, it appears quite certain that Ficino blended in his mind and practice forms of education and therapy. As he wrote, "it is a special discipline to understand properly which spirit, force, or powers these planets symbolize." Then he goes on to warn against "adoring" the stars; rather we are to "imitate them and through imitation capture them."[16] In a limited sense, study of the planets would include reading about these seven deities, knowing what they represent and which spheres of life they influence. In a more general sense, one way to temper one's life is to become familiar with imagery, through reading in mythology and religious traditions, giving some attention to poetry, fiction, and the other arts, noticing the imagery of dreams and waking fantasies. The goal is to get to know the imagistic expressions of soul. In our society we think it terrible if a person cannot read, spell, and perform basic mathematical procedures; but even our adult population is illiterate when it comes to imagery. Yet images crowd our consciousness day and night, provide religion and art with most of its content, and determine our values and understanding of our world.

Giving some time and attention to dreams is another effective way to temper the soul, for through study of our dream images our own personal mythology, complete with heroes, villains, demons, and deities, is brought into consciousness. Often serious attention to dreams is considered superstitious, or it is left to psychotherapy, where dreams are typically interpreted entirely with reference to personal history. But anyone may take note, literally, of his dreams and find, over a priod of time, recurring images and themes. It is not necessary to look to the dream for guidance (Ficino warns against such adoration) or to find conclusive interpretations of them; it is sufficient to give them attention, study them, turn them over in imagination, and have them at least vaguely in mind as we go about our daily business. Such "devotion" to the figures of dream tempers the soul by providing imaginative references for our feelings, fantasies, and expriences. If, for example, a theme of being abandoned appears in dreams over a period of time, that seed fantasy may organize in imagination a series of experiences, moods, wishes, or the like. We may "hear" the tonality of abandonment sounding through a number of otherwise opaque events.

One of the results of giving some care to dreams is the discovery of the importance of images in experience. One finds that there is not the broad breach between dream and reality one always assumed. Indeed, appreciation for the images that shape life has an effect on our very sense of self; for one discovers rather quickly how fluid this "self" is, how fantasies are fought, befriended, and identified with quite regularly, either internally or in projection. Ficino observed that tempering not only highlights the world's variety and its imaginative depths, it also affects the person.

But you may make a finer image in *yourself*. Since you understand that nothing is more ordered than heaven and that nothing can be considered more tempered than Jupiter, you may expect that eventually the benefits of the heavens and of Jupiter will follow if you show yourself ordered and tempered in your thoughts, feelings, activities, and way of life.[17]

Here, the particular example concerns Jupiter and Jovial spirit: when one imitates Jupiter's characteristics, one's sense of self takes on qualities of that image. In Ficino's language we may not feel the full impact of what he is suggesting; for once we begin to realize the power of images, we discover that not only the world at large but our very identity is determined by imagination. My perspective on the world and on myself determines who I am, the way I act, and the significance of events that happen in my life. Nothing exists free of my imagination, including myself. Therefore, careful tuning of the images and processes that go to make up my psychological activity tempers my own soul.

Ficino's example is complicated, since Jupiter is the God of tempering. With Jupiter's image constellated in the psyche, the ego loses its *senex* desire for control and defense and becomes more imaginal and flexible. It tolerates ambiguity, contradiction, and movement precisely because these are the processes of temperament. Jupiter is that dimension of consciousness through which we find concrete images for our experience without aiming for a single dominant image. Jupiter tempers by constellating all the major processes of the psyche, tuning them to be distinct and effectual. A tempering consciousness does not preclude the dissonant rub of paradox and contradiction that is bound to arise from multiplicity in perspective.[18] In music the bite of a good discord is always sharpest on a well-tuned instrument, and a well-placed dissonant note enhances rather than detracts from the music. So, too, in psychological temperament, tuning not only does not rule out dissonance—suffering, confusion, enigmas—it actually emphasizes them.[19]

Although dissonance is desirable in the composition of the psyche, nevertheless the soul can be poorly tempered, and this distemper *is* a sickness of soul. Distemper may be simply a lack of tuning due to faulty imagination: life makes no sense, there is little sense of value, internalized social values substitute for individuality, and so on. Or, perhaps more common, one perspective dominates to the point that consciousness may be considered monotheistic.

Alcmaeon of Croton, a Pythagorean physician of 500 B. C., held that "equality of rights between the qualities of moist, dry, cold, hot, bitter, sweet, and the rest, preserved health, but the rule of one among them [*monarchia*] produced sickness."[20] We have seen that these are qualities associated in various degrees with specific planets, so we may apply Alcmaeon's observation to the planets as well. The dominance of one signals the sickness of soul known as *monarchia*, a tyranny that serves to exclude multiple perspectives. Ficino declared outright, in a similar way, that "in heaven there is no excess of any single elemental quality." Nor is there any excess of spirit issuing from any one planet, for in such a case psychological life would have no music, it would be the incessant drone of a single tone—monotony.

Polytonality: The Music of the Gods

It would doubtless be fruitful, but beyond our scope here, to go more deeply into the psychological correlates of specific phenomena in music history and theory. For example, it is curious that in Western history, during the period of enlightenment and rationality, almost all music was founded in what theorists call "functional harmony." Every phrase and note in a piece, no matter how long, could be heard and interpreted as a "function" of the tonic note. Everything that happens musically in a symphony in C is integrated by its relationship to that note. In the twentieth century, during a time of upheaval in society and in personal understanding, Arnold Schoenberg developed his "atonal" music and his system of "serial" composition. In this music, complicated rules and procedures are followed precisely to avoid giving any note dominance over the others. Schoenberg's music is truly polytonal: each note is a center unto itself."[21]

Schoenberg's "polytonality" reflects the Ficinian tempered psyche better than the traditional tonal system; for each tone (god) is given its due, and it is the ratios or intervals of the precompositional scales that determine the unfolding of the piece. In the hands of some modern composers, Schoenberg's twelve-tone system gave birth to arid, intellectual music, lacking as much in expressiveness as it gained in technical complexity. But it can be eminently expessive, and that is a quality one would want to carry over analogously into the music of the psyche.

One advantage among many of the polytheistic/polytonal psyche is the variety of psychological experience it allows. As Ficino remarks in the language of astrology and natural magic: "Since different stars have various powers, their rays too are differentiated. When these rays fall, making an impact here and there, distinct powers are brought into being."[22] A tempered, polytheistic psyche, containing all the planets and their rays/spirits, enjoys a variety of powers otherwise precluded by a monarchical consciousness or simply by lack of imaginative depth. All the processes we have seen associated with the planets are accessible in such a constellated, tempered soul, regenerating in their various ways soul itself. From the moist pleasures of Venus to the dry intensity of Mars, soul thrives on the variety of sensibility and perspective available to it.

Another advantage we have seen several times in passing is release from moralism of all kinds. Religious and ethical moralism can often suffocate soul when it is rigid and narrow, but modern forms of psychological morality can be worse. Today individuals whose consciousness is awakening feel unusual modern pressures to grow, self-actualize, let their feelings hang out, enjoy a liberated sex life, keep no secrets, be happy and active all the time, produce something creative, raise children without "hang-ups," and so on. A polytheistic psychology, in which all the gods and all sides of them, are tempered or tuned in, does not appear so insanely wholesome and positive, and in fact it does not impose such a glorious yet demanding morality. James Hillman has summarized the values of the polytheistic approach, underscoring its virtue of tolerance:

> Polytheistic psychology obliges consciousness to *circulate* among a field of powers. *Each god has his due* as each complex deserves its respect in its own right. In this circularity there seem no preferred positions, no sure statements about positive and negative, and therefore no need to rule out some events as "pathological." When the idea of progress through hierarchical stages is suspended there will be more tolerance for the non-growth, ono-upward and non-ordered components of the psyche.[23]

The implications for therapy are extensive. Without concern for maturing, development according to some norm, a hierarchy of psychic values, expectations of advance and change, projects and goals of self-improvement, and a deeply rooted fantasy of adjustment to a *senex* society, then the therapist is free to let imagination do its work. The god of tempering, Jupiter, a deep inner tolerance and appreciation for multiplicity, might better bring imaginal order to fantasies and feelings than the patient, the therapist, or the society. Ficino was rather indirect as a therapist, to put it mildly. He played his lyre, dispensed spices and perfumes, directed his clients on walks through the countryside, and chose for them just the right amulets and stones. Even taken quite literally, his example is a good one to follow; for he knew intuitively and in theory that psyche needs imagination. By natural magic—that channel of spirit flowing between objects and consciousness—psyche loses its distemper.

A modern Ficinian therapist might well follow the master's example and find all kinds of things that might turn imagination on psychological experience. Nothing is out of range: herbs, photography, music, dance, travel, plants, perfumes, artworks of all kinds, museums, airplane rides, novels, meditation, massage, isolation, school, reading, drama, acting, construction, sports, astronomy, and astrology. All of these or none of them may be used in tempering the psyche, depending upon the presence of imagination and a genuine concern for soul. Whatever the psyche presents in dream, fantasy, wish, desire, fear, longing, dread, regret, or love may be imagined and thereby drawn deeper. Such is the process of tempering, and such is the meaning of psychotherapy, care for soul, in the Ficinian context.

The imagining psychotherapist looks with his client into the skein of images contained in the skin of events. He may play the alchemist helping his client cook up the garbage that has been lying around half-rotting for years. He may be the astrologer mapping the planets and charting the constellations. He may be the magus practicing some ancient or modern art of memory by which the "sacred open secrets" hidden in the images that permeate life and crowd consciousness lie revealed.

Most psychologists, of course, favor a well-integrated ego and a life without loose ends; some criticize polytheistic psychology as an irresponsible, *laissez-faire* approach to psychological suffering. They interpret it as advocating the dissociated personality, schizophrenia, and all forms of "flipping out."[24] But the imaginal[25] or aesthetic ego inhabits a middle ground, usually unappreciated, between the strong-willed ego and an ego overwhelmed by its alienated fantasies. Many of the problems people present in therapy are precisely the symptoms of a rigid ego, typical and expected in a *senex* culture such as ours. Surface values of the society demand order and conformity and the guardians of sanity can even hospitalize those who do not measure up. Therapies bent on will power, ego strength, and social adjustment only compound the problem, adding another layer of denial upon the urge toward polymodal expression of the psyche.

The therapist concerned more with imagination, deepening and true insight into behavior and fantasy, can encourage flexibility and a softening of self-judgment, thus favoring both increased consciousness and acknowledgment of pressing fantasies. The mere process of becoming familiar with the powers that move us and drive us into compulsive actions and weigh on our souls eases their destructive power. Knowing the incubi that haunt the hollows of our hearts, we may move with them rather than engage them in useless struggle. Unless we enter into some kind of dialogue with these inner demons, we have no way to discriminate among them and deal with them. Without imagination, ego is too far removed from these inner figures to know threat from promise.

Tempering therefore requires a light touch, whether it occurs in formal or informal therapy or in the course of dealing with one's own fantasies. Unlike most psychologies, this Ficinian approach neither advocates repression nor advises compensation, both *senex* measures. Faced with a variety of dynamics in the psyche, it seeks to gain the benefits of all. Ficino encouraged this accepting attitude by referring in several of this writings to the story of the Judgment of Paris.

According to the myth, Paris was to choose among three goddesses: Hera, Aphrodite, and Athena. When Aphrodite simply loosened the clasp on her tunic, that was enough for him. He chose her and won Helen and the Trojan War. Ficino interpreted the goddesses as allegories of wisdom, pleasure, and power, and the warned his friend and patron, Lorenzo, that those who favor one deity over others end up paying a penalty. Socrates himself, says Ficino, chose Minerva and won his death. But Lorenzo "may disdain none of these higher beings. He may behold three and worship three for their gifts."[26] When confronted with a choice among the gods, choose them all. That is Ficino's practical, polytheistic advice. Put up with the ambiguity, confusion, and illogic of the polytheistic vision; for one wins clarity and control, integration and a sense of wholeness at the cost of psychological vigor.

Sympathetic Overtones

More in the spirit of modern psychology, Ficino directs his musical attention to empirical studies. In *The Planets* he advises a careful use of music as a form of treatment, a practice he not only advocated but became involved in himself with his lyre. Certain kinds of music, he thought, would capture the spirit of a particular planet and make it accessible to the person in need of that spirit. He offers three rules for determining the planetary nature of a piece of music: (1) find out characteristics of the planets and insert these into the text of a song; (2) find out which planet rules a certain region, study the music of that region, and incorporate these elements into the music required; (3) find out how people are affected by various astrological patterns and incorporate these findings into the songs.[27] Here is an early form of music therapy, an efficacious art of memory by which the spirit of the planets would be infused into the psyche of the listener, tempering his soul with its tempered tunes.

Musica instrumentalis serves in this method as a means of establishing *musica humana*, and its theoretical basis is thoroughly polytheistic. Now if we would shift to a metaphorical viewpoint we would see that the therapist as *musicus*, musician of the soul, has to know the gods extremely well—their characters, the effects they have on people, their rhythms and patterns. Thus the therapist becomes the guide of a musical psyche, sensitive especially to the multiplicity of its deep structures.

One further "musical" talent is required of the Ficinian therapist: he must have a good ear for the subtle tones of the psyche. After offering the three rules for an astrological music therapy, Ficino makes the following observation:

> You will procure one of these four (the four musical planets) by his or her songs, especially if you apply music fitting the songs, so that when you call by singing and playing in their style, they will seem to respond immediately, like Echo, or like certain strings on a cithara vibrating when other strings are struck and tuned alike.[28]

Ficino is referring here, of course, to the acoustical phenomenon known as "sympathetic vibration," and he uses this as one more example of natural magic—the power of causing a spiritual effect through material means. Sympathetic vibration occurs when two strings are tuned to the same pitch, or when one is tuned so as to contain strong overtones of the other. Then when just one of the strings is plucked, the other will vibrate "in sympathy." Ficino's point is that when the music characteritic of a certain planet is played, that planetary spirit will be set in motion and make its way to the listener.

Robert Fludd developed the metaphor of overtones further, and, joined to Ficino's sympathetic vibration image, it suggests a subtle but truly significant notion abut psychotherapy. In one of Fludd's charts, "On the Internal Numbers and Harmony of Man," a human body lies within a circle labeled "Earth." Above him are the other three elements, water, air and fire, all encompassing what Fludd calls *"diapason materiale"*—the material octave. This is the level of matter, the arena of physical events perceptible by our senses. A second octave extends, however, above the first, like a series of overtones that sound faintly but perceptibly in any musical scale. This is, according to Fludd, the *"diapason medium"* or "mediating octave," the realm of soul. Fludd divides this into the seven planets, the stars, and the Prime Mover. So here we have a correspondence between this image and Ficino's theory of musical planets. Finally, there is a third and even more subtle octave, *"diapason spirituale,"* the spiritual overtones which emanate more faintly from bodily events. Here Fludd places the nine choirs of angels. Embracing all three octaves is the following inscription: "The essential harmony by which the human soul takes for its own constitution a portion of the three regions of the world."[29]

Fludd's diagram is fully consistent with Ficino's view of the soul and its musical structure, and it presents a useful image for psychotherapy. We have seen several tasks a Ficinian psychotherapist might engage in when confronting the problems of a client. Here it is suggested that a therapist must have an "ear" for the overtones of crass, physical behavior. In his role as musician of the soul and magus, he may see with his eyes the problem presented to him but hear with a special talent the overtones of psyche and spirit. These overtones are essentially the same as the aromas and fragrances we found among the elements of the soul, and the sublimated vapors released through alchemical operations. The overtones complete the fertile musical analogy and bring us back to the fundamental Ficinian principle of psychology: the soul is a hidden but perceptible dimension of material existence. Soul lies in those strong vibrations, the overtones of the material world, the mediating octave. Attuned to those moderately subtle overtones we hear the music of the spheres, the seven planets which represent the multiple powers of the psyche, and achieve a degree of psychological sensibility.

In music the tones of the scale lose their rigid ordering and turn and twist in all directions as they combine to make melodies, harmonies, and counterpoints. In serial music it is even clearer that the fundamental scales revolve in unending variation, creating the unique expressive quality of the music and its own inner logic. In the music of the psyche, too, variation goes on without end. The many planets and their combinations provide countless perspectives, so that in polytheistic psychology there can be no final point of view, no one reason for anything, no ending in therapy, and no goal achieved. Though it is most difficult for a *senex* ego to accept such continuous variation, an imaginal ego finds in variety both logic and beauty.

Variety can be an end in itself, as in the case of one of Jupiter's animals, the peacock. The god of tempering is known in the image of the peacock's multicolored tail, which, Jung informs us, is an alchemical image of spring, *primavera*, the arrival of new life.[30] This *cauda pavonis* appears after the dark night work of blackening (*nigredo*) and, along with the rainbow, signals the fruitfulness of the earth. Jung also refers to the classic work on zoological mythology by Angelo de Gubernatis where the peacock is joined in imagination to the brilliance of the sky:

> The serene and starry sky and the shining sun are peacocks. The deep-blue firmament shining with a thousand brilliant eyes, and the sun rich with the colors of the rainbow, present the appearance of a peacock in all the splendour of its eye-bespangled feathers.[31]

The eyes of the sky, so important in Ficino's natural magic, show up here in the tail of Jupiter's bird. Jung ties it all together by reminding us that in alchemy the colors of the peacock's tail correspond to the seven planetary spheres.

Once an individual begins to think polytheistically, words once used in the context of integration and wholeness take on a new diaphanous vitality. So it is with tempering. Rather than a term for a process of narrowing and rigidly ordering, tempering becomes the spreading of the peacock's tail, a revelation of the beauty of multiplicity. Life, otherwise drab, opaque, and unimagined, is given color and tone. If psychology as a discipline were to value finally the variety in psychological life the peacock represents, then maybe that long-sought elixir of the "liberated life" might be found.

A similar challenge must be made with reference to this book, for there is little doubt that the rays pouring into its pages have descended from Saturn and Mercury, leaving at least five other ways to imagine Ficino's apothecary, and at least five other spirits to acquire through his words. Some of these other deities are not easily encountered on the printed page, but they have their proper spheres of life, their planetary houses, where their rays may be absorbed. In the end it takes a wide variety of travels, experiments, and quests to temper the gods so that their high overtones scintillate in tune and their low fundamentals quiver at an honest pitch and at solid depth.

Notes

Foreword

1. James Hillman, *Revisioning Psychology* (Harper & Row, New York, 1975), 201.
2. Ibid, 202.
3. See James Hillman, "Cosmology for Soul—From Universe to Cosmos" in *SPHINX 2* (The London Convivium for Archetypal Studies. London, 1989).
4. Cf. Hillman, "Anima Mundi—The Return of Soul to the World" in *SPRING 1982* (Spring Publications, Dallas).
5. I have tried to develop this inkling in the paper "Who Is Behind Archetypal Psychology?" in *SPRING 1988* (Spring Publications, Dallas).
6. Hillman, *Revisioning*, 202.

Introduction

1. James Hillman compares the content of Ficino's philosophy with psychoanalysis and suggests a psychological reading of his works in the following: "Plotino, Ficino, and Vico as Precursors of Archetypal Psychology," in *Loose Ends: Primary Papers in Archetypal Psychology* (Zurich: Spring Publications, 1975), pp. 146-69; and *Re-Visioning Psychology* (New York: Harper and Row, 1975), pp. 197-202.

Chapter 1: Marsilio Ficino

1. Paul Oskar Kristeller, *The Philosophy of Marsilio Ficino*, trans. Virginia Conant (Gloucester, Mass.: Peter Smith, 1964), p. 21.
2. Christopher Hibbert, *The House of Medici: Its Rise and Fall* (New York: William Morrow and Co., 1975), p. 97.
3. Ibid., p. 77.
4. Marcel Brion, *The Medici: A Great Florentine Family*, trans. Gilles and Heather Cremonegi (London: Elek Books, 1969), p. 62.
5. Ibid.
6. Kristeller, *Philosophy*, p. 314. See C. G. Jung, *Psychological Types*. Revision by R. F. C. Hull of H. G. Baynes's translation. CW, vol. 6, Bollingen Series 20. (Princeton, N.J.: Princeton University Press, 1971), pp. 126-27. Jung claims that the "aim of exorcistic rites is to bring back the soul and release it from enchantment."
7. See Brion, *Medici*, p. 106; and Hillman, *Re-visioning Psychology*, pp. 204ff.
8. On this widespread misconception, see: Frances Yates, *Giordano Bruno and the Hermetic Tradition* (New York: Vintage Books, 1969), chap. 1.; D. P. Walker, *The Ancient Theology* (Ithaca, N.Y.: Cornell University Press, 1972); and Kristeller, *Philosophy*, pp. 25-26.
9. As translated in Kristeller, ibid.
10. Ibid., p. 14.
11. The following summaries are further contractions of Yates's summaries, *Giordano Bruno*, chap. 2.

Chapter 2: A World with Soul

1. Such a distinction between "soul" and "psyche" and a corresponding distinction between "sacrament" and "symbol" is made in Ann Ulanov and Barry Ulanov, *Religion and the Unconscious*.
2. For a thorough study of the Greek underworld as an image for the containing space of psyche, see James Hillman, "The Dream and the Underworld," *Eranos Jahrbuch* 42 (1973) [Leiden: Brill, 1975].

3. Patricia Berry, "The Rape of Demeter/Persephone and Neurosis," *Spring 1975* (New York: Spring Publications, 1975), pp. 186–98. Berry interprets the rape of Persephone as a pull toward depth imagined as the death-world over which Persephone rules. The cosmology pictured is thus a two-tiered universe, but obviously not an ontological one. The invisible world of psyche exists in tandem with the visible world of nature and what we consider natural. See also Carl Kerenyi and C. G. Jung, *Essays on a Science of Mythology* (Princeton, N.J.: Princeton University Press, 1969).

4. An idea presented in a lecture by Patricia Berry entitled "What's the Matter with Mother?"

5. Hillman, *Re-Visioning Psychology*, chap. 2, "Pathologizing."

6. On the dream as a transformation of the natural to the imaginal, see Hillman, "The Dream and the Underworld," and Patricia Berry, "An Approach to the Dream," *Spring 1974* (New York: Spring Publications, 1974), pp. 58–79.

7. James Hillman, "Anima," *Spring 1973* (New York: Spring Publications, 1973), p. 122. As I am using the terms here, "fantasy" is the subjective aspect of the world experienced imaginally, while "image" connotes the specific imaginal world in which I may find myself, in the past, present, or future.

8. June, *Psychological Types*, p. 287.

9. Marsilio Ficino, *Opera Omnia*, 2 vols. (Basel, 1576; reprinted, Torino: Bottega d'Erasmo, 1959), p. 196. Quoted in D. P. Walker, "Ficino's *Spiritus* and Music," *Annales Musicologiques* 1 (1953): 133.

10. C. G. Jung, *Memories, Dreams, Reflections*, ed. Aniela Jaffe; trans. Richard Winston and Clara Winston (New York: Vintage Books, 1963), p. 82.

11. Kristeller, *Philosophy*, p. 236. In this imaginal epistemology, the external world when perceived takes its form from fantasy, not vice versa.

12. Quoted in ibid., p. 372. The comet's tail is an exceptionally suitable image for various psychological phenomena related to Ficino's theory of *idolum*. Dreams, for example, seem to pass through the soul in the wake of some central movement in the psyche; or various conscious activities may take place, all part of the tail of some stirring in psyche. People often report several life experiences all of which seem to enact the seed fantasy glimpsed in a dream.

13. See Kristeller, *Philosophy*, p. 373.

14. Frances Yates, *The Art of Memory* (London: Routledge and Kegan Paul, 1966).

15. Quoted in Kristeller, *Philosophy*, p. 237.

16. Rollo May, *Love and Will* (New York: W. W. Norton and Co., 1969), p. 135. The daimon, like any figure in psyche, may be experienced as if external, though it is internal insofar as it is in pscyhe. The notions of internal and external are not clear in May's placement of the Heraclitean daimon.

17. In Paul Friedländer, *Plato: An Introduction*, trans. Hans Meyerhoff, Bollingen Series 59 (Princeton, N.J.: Princeton University Press, 1973), p. 37. Friedländer and May offer useful overviews of the notion of "daimon." Both, however, stress an existentialist viewpoint that loses the *image* of daimon.

18. On the classical imagery surrounding "genius," see Richard Broxton Onians, *The Origins of European Thought* (Cambridge: Cambridge University Press, 1951), passim.

19. The problem of psychological monotheism will be discussed further in chapter 14 below. See also James Hillman, "Psychology: Monotheistic or Polytheistic?" *Spring 1971* (New York: Spring Publications, 1971).

20. In a letter to Cavalcanti, Ficino provides some details about his horoscope and the dominant influence of Saturn: "This melancholy temperament seems to have been imposed on me from the beginning by Saturn, set almost in the center of my ascendant sign, Aquarius (the Water-Bearer) and being met by Mars in the same sign, and by the Moon in Capricorn—while looking toward the Sun and Mercury in the Scorpion, occupying the ninth zone of Heaven." Quoted in Jean Seznec, *The Survival of the Pagan Gods*, trans. Barbara F. Sessions, Bollingen Series 38 (Princeton, N.J.: Princeton University Press, 1972), p. 61.

21. Ficino, *Opera*, p. 534, *The Planets*, chap. 2.

22. Ernst Cassirer, *The Individual and the Cosmos in Renaissance Philosophy*, trans. Mario Domandi (Philadelphia: University of Pennsylvania Press, 1963), p. 133.

Chapter 3: "Dissolve and Congeal"

1. C. G. Jung, ed., *Man and His Symbols* (New York: Dell Publishing Co., 1968), p. 40.
2. C. G. Jung, *Psychology and Alchemy; CW*, vol. 12, 2nd ed. (Princeton, N.J.: Princeton University Press, 1968), p. 34.
3. Helena M. E. De Jong, *Michael Maier's "Atalanta Fugiens": Sources of an Alchemical Book of Emblems* (Leiden: Brill, 1969), p. 168.
4. On these analogies and the theory of the affections of the soul, see Kristeller, *Philosophy*, pp. 388–99.
5. C. G. Jung, *Mysterium Coniunctionis; CW*, vol. 14, 2nd ed. (Princeton: Princeton University Press, 1970), p. 472.
6. Quoted in Charles Lemmi, *The Classical Deities in Bacon: A Study in Mythological Symbolism* (Baltimore, Md.: Johns Hopkins Press, 1933), p. 83.
7. Jung, *Mysterium Coniunctionis*, p. 236, n. 606.
8. See David L. Miller, "Orestes: Myth and Dream as Catharsis," in *Myth, Dreams, and Religion*, ed. Joseph Campbell (New York: E. P. Dutton, 1970) pp. 26–47; Leon Golden, "Mimesis and Catharsis," *Classical Philology* 64 (1969): 145–53; and Leon Golden, "Katharsis as Clarification: An Objection Answered," *Classical Quarterly*, 23, no. 1 (May 1973): 45–46.
9. C. G. Jung, *Civilization in Transition; CW*, vol. 10, 2nd ed. (Princeton, N.J.: Princeton University Press, 1970), p. 90.
10. Ficino, *Opera*, p. 843.

Chapter 4: The Elements of Psyche

1. On the alchemical notion of psychological water, see Jung, *Mysterium Coniunctionis*, passim, e.g., Mercurial water, p. 503. On the phenomenology of the elements, also consult the works of Gaston Bachelard.
2. See James Hillman, "Dionysos in Jung's Writings," *Spring 1972* (New York: Spring Publications, 1972); James Hillman, *The Myth of Analysis* (New York: Harper Colophon, 1978), Part Three, "On Psychological Creativity"; Carl Kerenyi, *Dionysos: Archetypal Image of Indestructible Life*, trans. Ralph Manheim, Bollingen Series 65 (Princeton, N.J.: Princeton University Press, 1976); Norman O. Brown, *Life against Death* (New York: Vintage Books, 1959); Walter Otto, *Dionysus: Myth and Cult*, trans. Robert B. Palmer (Bloomington, 2nd.: Indiana University Press, 1965).
3. Onians, *Origins.*, p. 216; Petronius, *Satyricon* 34.7.
4. Onians, *Origins*, p. 228; Ovid, *Metamorphoses* 13. 929.
5. Juan Eduardo Cirlot, *A Dictionary of Symbols*, trans. Jack Sage (New York: Philosophical Library, 1962), pp. 6 and 240.
6. W. B. Yeats, "All Souls Night," in *A Vision* (New York: Collier Books, 1966), p. 303.
7. Ficino, *Opera*, p. 651; quoted in Kristeller, *Philosophy*, p. 308.
8. Susanne K. Langer, *Feeling and Form* (New York: Charles Scribner's Sons, 1953), p. 117.
9. Ficino, *Opera*, p. 651; quoted in Kristeller, *Philosophy*, p. 308.
10. This idea was suggested in conversation by Dr. Robert Sardello.
11. Ficino, *Opera*, p. 639.
12. Ibid., p. 977, ch. 5.
13. Ibid., p. 978, ch. 7.
14. Hillman, "Plotino, Ficino, and Vico," *Loose Ends*, p. 155. "His position that mind has its home *in the soul*, is like Jung's—an *esse in anima*."
15. Ficino, *Opera*, p. 983.
16. Ibid., p. 984.

Chapter 5: Necessary Madness

1. Sears Jayne, "Marsilio Ficino's Commentary on Plato's *Symposium*," *University of Missouri Studies* 19, no. 1 (Columbia, Mo.: University of Missouri Press, 1944), p. 231. (A commentary and translation.)

2. See Hillman, "Pothos: The Nostalgia of the Puer Aeternus," *Loose Ends*, pp. 49–62.

3. See below, chapter 11, "Saturn."

4. Charles Edward Trinkaus, *In Our Image and Likeness: Humanity and Divinity in Italian Humanist Thought*, 2 vols. (Chicago: University of Chicago Press, 1970), p. 480.

5. Jayne, "Ficino's Commentary," p. 231.

6. E. R. Dodds, *The Greeks and the Irrational* (Berkeley, Calif.: University of California Press, 1951), p. 82.

7. On the general issue of personifying our complexes, see Hillman, *Re-Visioning Psychology*, chap. 1, "Personifying or Imagining Things." "Rather than a field of forces, we are each a field of internal personal relationships, an interior commune, a body politic" (p. 22).

8. Sigmund Freud, *The Interpretation of Dreams*, trans. James Strachey (New York: Avon Books, 1965), p. 530.

9. Jayne, "Ficino's Commentary," p. 231.

10. Ficino, *Opera*, p. 634.

11. Norman O. Brown, *Love's Body* (New York: Vintage Books, 1966), p. 259.

12. John G. Neihardt, *Black Elk Speaks* (Lincoln, Neb.: University of Nebraska Press, 1961).

13. Jayne, "Ficino's Commentary," p. 232.

14. C. G. Jung, *Psychology and Religion: West and East*; CW, vol. 11, 2nd ed. (Princeton, N.J.: Princeton University Press, 1969), p. 8.

15. Ficino, *Opera*, p. 319; in Kristeller, *Philosophy*, p. 318.

16. André Chastel gives the following table indicating various names Ficino gave to the four furors—*Marsile Ficin et l'art* (Geneva: Droz, 1954), p. 130.

De divino furore (1457)	*Convivium (1475)*
vaticinium/conjectio	Venus: furor amatorius-mens angelica
mysteria/superstitio	Apollo: vaticinium-ratio animae
poesis/levior musica	Bacchus: sacerdotium-opinio
amor/amor vulgaris	Musae: furor poeticus-natura

Ep. a Pietro Divitio (1491)	*Commen. in Phaedrum (1492)*
mysterium: Bacchus	vaticinium
vaticinium: Apollo	sacerdotium
poesis: Musae	furor poeticus
amor: Venus	furor eroticus

17. Ficino, *Opera*, p. 927.

18. Edgar Wind, *Pagan Mysteries in the Renaissance*, rev. and enl. ed. (New York: W. W. Norton and Co., 1968), p. 17.

19. Ficino, *Opera*, p. 562.

20. Carl Kerenyi, "The Mysteries of the Kabeiroi," in Joseph Campbell, ed., *The Mysteries, Papers from the Eranos Yearbooks, II* (New York: Pantheon Books, 1955), p. 37. Not only nature, but the images of psyche themselves contain such "sacred open secrets."

21. Ibid.

22. Jayne, "Ficino's Commentary," p. 232.

23. Ficino, *Opera*, p. 625.

24. See Kristeller, *Philosophy*, p. 309, for these examples and documentation.

25. Jayne, "Ficino's Commentary," p. 231.

26. Ficino, *Opera*, p. 288, and Kristeller, *Philosophy*, p. 312.

26. For a critique of the fantasy of "growth," see James Hillman, "Abandoning the Child," *Loose Ends*, pp. 5–48. The widely used phrase "personal growth" may make sense with regard to certain ego achievements, but even then more precise words would be appropriate, perhaps "maturing" or "ripening."

28. Martin Heidegger, "The Ode on Man in Sophocles' *Antigone*," in *Sophocles: A Collection of Critical Essays*, ed. Thomas M. Woodard (Englewood Cliffs, N.J.: Prentice-Hall, 1966), p. 93.

29. Quoted in Kristeller, *Philosophy*, p. 313.

30. Wind, *Pagan Mysteries*, pp. 63–64.

31. Jayne, "Ficino's Commentary," p. 232.
32. Ficino, *Opera*, p. 1323; in Kristeller, *Philosophy*, p. 264.
33. Ibid., p. 306; in Kristeller, *Philosophy*, p. 267.
34. James Hillman, "Anima," *Spring 1973*, pp. 106–9.
35. Plato, *Symposium*, 193.
36. Jayne, "Ficino's Commentary," p. 140.
37. We find this in Ficino's essays on love and also in courtly love poets, for example.
38. Emma Jung, for example, speaks of the integration of the anima as part of the individuation process in *Animus and Anima* (Zurich: Spring Publications, 1974), p. 86; and June Singer argues with the fantasy of "serial monogamy" in *Boundaries of the Soul* (New York: Doubleday, 1973), p. 253. To be vigilant in maintaining the psychological perspective is one thing, to support a social norm and pattern with pychology is another — moralism in disguise.

Chapter 6: Zodiacal Reflections

1. James Hillman, "Peaks and Vales," in *On the Way to Self-Knowledge*, ed. Jacob Needleman and Dennis Lewis (New York: Alfred A. Knopf, 1976), p. 121. Hillman points out the tendency toward literalism in matters of the spirit.
2. See Kristeller, *Philosophy*, pp. 310 ff.
3. Ficino, *Opera*, p. 771.
4. David Miller points out this tendency in the study of religion in a review — the tendency toward "pre-Barthian romanticism, a mythologized and psychologized 'faith' whose idolatry is located interiorly." *Journal of the American Academy of Religion* 46, no. 1 (March 1978): 94.
5. See, for example, Singer, *Boundaries*, chap. 10. "The primary, all-encompassing archetype is the archetype of the self" (p. 276).
6. Ficino, *Opera*, p. 533.
7. Ficino, *Opera*, p. 553.
8. Quoted in Lemmi, *Classical Deities*, p. 77.
9. In Ibid., p. 75.
10. See Berry, "Demeter/Persephone."

Chapter 7: Sol

1. Ficino, *Opera*, p. 534.
2. Quoted in Georges Poulet, *The Metamorphoses of the Circle*, trans. Carley Dawson and Elliott Coleman (Baltimore, Md.: The Johns Hopkins Press, 1966), p. 5.
3. Jung, *Mysterium*, p. 106.
4. Ibid., p. 96.
5. Ficino, *Opera*, p. 533.
6. Roberto Assagioli, *Psychosynthesis* (New York: Viking Press, 1965), p. 17.
7. Johanm Jakob Bachofen, *Myth, Religion, and Mother Right (Selected Writings)*, trans. Ralph Manheim (Princeton, N.J.: Princeton University Press, 1967), pp. 144– 45.
8. Ficino, *Opera*, p. 574.
9. Ibid., p. 530.
10. Ibid., p. 532.
11. Ibid., p. 536.
12. Joan Evans and Mary S. Serjeantson, *English Medieval Lapidaries* (London: Oxford University Press, 1933), p. 124.
13. L. Oscar Kuhns, ed., "Bestiaries and Lapidaries," *Medieval Song and Story*, Columbia University Course in Literature, IV (Freeport, N.Y.: Books for Libraries Press, 1928–29), pp. 515–16.
14. Ficino, *Opera*, p. 968.
15. Kuhns, *Bestiaries and Lapidaries*, p. 512.
16. Jung, *Mysterium Coniunctionis*, p. 100.

Chapter 8: Venus

1. Yates, *Bruno*, pp. 76–77.
2. See Seznec,*Survival*, pp. 76–77.
3. Yates, *Bruno*, p. 77.
4. Wind, *Pagan Mysteries*, chap. 7. Disputes over whether this painting is a calendar image, specifically an astrological allegory, or a Neoplatonic metaphor miss the point that all three intentions may be affirmed at once. Here we are following Yates by adding the function of "natural magic" to the painting, as well as the psychological interpretation.
5. Yates, *Giordano Bruno*, p. 77.
6. Jayne, "Ficino's Commentary," p. 133.
7. Erwin Panofsky, *Renaissance and Renascences in Western Art*, 2nd ed. (Stockholm: Almqvist and Wiksell, 1965), p. 200.
8. Friedländer, *Plato*, p. 56.
9. Wind, *Pagan Mysteries*, p. 36.
10. Ficino, *Opera*, p. 546.
11. Ibid., p. 536.
12. Sandor Ferenczi, *Thalassa: A Theory of Genitality*, trans. Henry Alden Bunker (New York: W.W. Norton and Co., 1968), p. 49.
13. Ficino, *Opera*, p. 837.
14. An idea suggested by Hillman in "Anima," p. 108. An archetypal study of the humanistic movement in psychology, viewed through the prism of Venus, might help us to better discriminate the spirits in this movement.

Chapter 9: Mercury

1. André Chastel, *The Myth of the Renaissance*, trans. Stuart Gilbert (Geneva: Albert Skira, 1969), p. 179.
2. Ficino, *Opera*, p. 542.
3. Chastel, *Myth*, p. 108; see also Seznec, *Survival*, pp. 159 and 165.
4. Ficino, *Opera*, p. 912.
5. Ibid., p. 875.
6. We may also see a regressive movement in Daphne's swift movement and her transformation into a tree — a flight of the nymph from Apollo's heat and light. The demands of Apollonian intensity seem to chase the soul toward vegetative concerns.
7. Norman O. Brown, "Daphne or Metamorphosis," in *Myths, Dreams, and Religion*, ed. Joseph Campbell (New York: E.P. Dutton, 1970), p. 106.
8. Ficino, *Opera*, p. 546.
9. Ibid., p, 557.
10. See Berry, "Dream."
11. Brown, "Daphne," p. 108.
12. Chastel, *Marsile Ficin et l'art*, p. 141. Surprise is another important emotion, often taken for granted, but, like longing and nostalgia, significant in establishing and maintaining a psychological vulnerability.
13. The significance of this phrase from Stevens for the development of an imaginative hermeneutic comes out of the lectures of Stanley R. Hopper.
14. Paul Radin, *The Trickster: A study in American Indian Mythology*, with commentaries by Karl Kerenyi and C. G. Jung (New York: Philosophical Library, 1956), pp. 174 and 190.
15. Rafael Lopez-Pedraza, *Hermes and His Children* (Zurich: Spring Publications, 1977), p. 32.

Chapter 10: Luna

1. Ficino, *Opera*, p. 546.
2. Ibid., p. 537.
3. Kristeller, *Philosophy*, pp. 136–37.

4. Ficino, *Opera*, p. 917.
5. Bachofen, *Mother Right*, p. 115.
6. Ficino, *Opera*, p. 805.
7. Ibid., p. 538.
8. Ibid., p. 537.
9. Ibid., p. 540.
10. Ibid., p. 557.
11. Ibid., p. 537.
12. De Jong, *Atalanta*, p. 381.
13. See Hillman, "Abandoning."
14. Michael R. Best and Frank H. Brightman, eds., *The Book of Secrets of Albertus Magus* (Oxford: The Clarendon Press, 1973), p. 72.

Chapter 11: Saturn

1. Raymond Klibansky, Erwin Panofsky, and Fritz Saxl, *Saturn and Melancholy* (New York: Basic Books, 1964).
2. James Hillman, "*Senex* and *Puer*: An Aspect of the Historical and Psychological Present," in *Eranos Jahrbuch* 36 (Zurich: Rhein, 1969); "On *Senex* Consciousness," *Spring 1970* (New York: Spring Publications, 1970); and "*Senex* Destruction and a Renaissance Solution," *Spring 1975* (New York: Spring Publications, 1975), pp. 77–109. We may consider Saturn as one specific mythological figure representing aspects of the *senex*.
3. See A. Vitale, "The Archetype of Saturn or Transformation of the Father," in *Fathers and Mothers*, ed. Patricia Berry (New York: Spring Pubications, 1973), pp. 5–39.
4. Ficino, *Opera*, p. 533.
5. Sigmund Freud, "Mourning and Melancholia," trans. under supervision of Joan Riviere, *Collected Papers*, vol. 4 (New York: Basic Books, 1959), pp. 152–170. Contained within Freud's personalistic analysis are archetypal images of death, loss, grief, and absence. Losses of many kinds generate the feelings and fantasies of melancholy, even so subtle a loss as a change in perspective or attitude.
6. Ficino, *Opera*, p. 496.
7. See Murray Stein, "The Devouring Father," in *Fathers and Mothers*, pp. 64–74.
8. See note 5 above.
9. Ficino, *Opera*, p. 536.
10. Onians, *Origins*, p. 133, n. 1.
11. Ficino, *Opera*, p. 565.
12. Ibid.
13. Hillman, "*Senex* Destruction and a Renaissance Solution." Kristeller supports Hillman's point, referring to Ficino's comments in the first book of *De Vita* (*Opera*, p. 294): "The melancholic temperament facilitates a liberation of the soul from external events and so constitutes one of the favorable conditons for prophecy" (p. 212).
14. Klibansky *et al.*, *Saturn and Melancholy*, p. 273.
15. Ibid., p. 271.
16. Ficino, *Opera*, p. 496.
17. Ibid., p. 565.
18. Ibid., p. 522.
19. Ibid., p. 534.
20. See, for example, Jung's "Psychotherapists or the Clergy," *Psychology and Religion*, CW, vol. 11, pp. 327–47.

Chapter 12: Jupiter

1. Ficino, *Opera*, p. 935.
2. Ibid., p. 531; see also Kristeller, *Philosophy*, p. 386; and Wayne Shumaker, *The Occult Sciences in the Renaissance* (Berkeley, Calif.: University of California Press, 1972), pp. 122–27.

3. Ficino, *Opera*, p. 935.
4. Ibid., p. 944.
5. Ibid., p. 846.
6. Ibid., p. 536.
7. Ibid.
8. Ibid., p. 538.
9. Ibid., p. 537.
10. My occasional references to architecture are quite Ficinian. He considered architecture second only to mathematics among the arts, and he called it a "Mercurial" art. See *Opera*, p. 1267; and G.L. Hersey, *Pythagorean Palaces: Magic and Architecture in the Italian Renaissance* (Ithaca, N.Y., and London: Cornell University Press, 1976), pp. 34–37.
11. Ficino, *Opera*, p. 56ʋ.
12. See Seznec, *Survival*, pp. 137–43. For the image, see p. 138.

Chapter 13: Mars

1. Yates, *Giordano Bruno*, p. 63.
2. Ficino, *Opera*, p. 843.
3. Jung, *Archetypes and the Collective Unconscious*, CW, vol. 9, pt. 1, 2nd ed. (Princeton, N.J.: Princeton University Press, 1968), pp. 286 and 288: The archetypal personalities "form a species of singular beings whom one would like to endow with ego-consciousness; indeed, they almost seem capable of it. . . . Conscious and unconscious do not make a whole when one of them is suppressed and injured by the other. If they must contend, let it at least be a fair fight with equal rights on both sides. Both are aspects of life."
4. See Hillman, *Re-Visioning Psychology*, chap. 1, "Personifying."
5. Ficino, *Opera*, p. 545.
6. Ibid., p. 539.
7. Ibid., p. 534.
8. Ibid., p. 557.
9. Ibid., p. 542.
10. Ibid., p. 819.
11. Ibid., p. 1348.
12. Wind, *Pagan Mysteries*, p. 90.
13. Ficino, *Opera*, p. 1339.
14. Michael J. B. Allen, *Marsilio Ficino, The Philebus Commentary: A Critical Edition and Translation* (Berkeley, Los Angeles, London: University of California Press, 1975), p. 244.

Chapter 14: The Well-Tempered Life

1. Aristotle, *Politics* 8.6., trans. H. Rackham, Loeb Classical Library (Cambridge, Mass.: Harvard University Press, 1959), p. 657.
2. *Institutiones* 5.2. ed. by R. A. B. Mynors (Oxford: The Clarendon Press, 1937), p. 143.
3. For a thorough study of this relationship, without, however, a psychological analysis, see D. P. Walker, "Ficino's *Spiritus*."
4. See also Tom Moore, "Musical Therapy," *Spring 1978* (New York: Spring Publications, 1978).
5. Ficino, *Opera*, p. 546.
6. Curt Sachs, *The Commonwealth of Art* (New York: W. W. Norton and Co., 1946), p. 105.
7. Paul Henry Lang, *Music in Western Civilization* (New York: W. W. Norton and Co., 1941), p. 193.
8. The famous "serial" composer Anton Webern made some interesting and relevant observations on these matters. He defined music as "natural law as related to the sense of hearing." He also noted that "the diatonic scale was not invented, it was discovered." *The Path to the New Music* (Bryn Mawr, Penna.: Theodore Presser Co., 1963), pp. 11 and 14.

9. See Leo Spitzer, "Classical and Christian Ideas of World Harmony," *Traditio* 2 (1944): 414.

10. On the first two applications mentioned, see Hersey, *Palaces,* and for a modern theory of Pythagorean proportion, see Hans Kayser, *Akroasis: The Theory of World Harmonics* (Boston: Plowshare Press, 1970). For a technical analysis of Pythagorean proportions, see Richard L. Crocker, "Pythagorean Mathematics and Music," *Journal of Aesthetics and Art Criticism* 22, no. 2 (1963): 189–98; 22, no. 3 (1964): 325–36.

11. Albert Seay, *Music in the Medieval World* (Englewood Cliffs, N.J.: Prentice-Hall, 1965), p. 20.

12. On Fludd's musical philosophy, see: Frances Yates, *Theatre of the World* (Chicago: University of Chicago Press, 1969); John Hollander, *The Untuning of the Sky* (Princeton, N.J.: Princeton University Press, 1961); and Peter J. Amman, "The Musical Theory and Philosophy of Robert Fludd," *Journal of the Warburg and Courtauld Institutes* 30 (1967): 198–227.

13. Ficino, *Opera,* p. 651.

14. Ibid.

15. Ibid., p. 566.

16. Ibid., pp. 537 and 562.

17. Ibid., pp. 559–60.

18. See Hillman, "Polytheistic?"

19. See Hillman, *Re-Visioning Psychology,* chap. 2, "Pathologizing or Falling Apart."

20. Quoted in Klibansky, "Saturn," p. 5. Diels frag. Alcmaeon, B4.

21. A young American composer, Charles Wuorinen, makes the point from a musician's point of view: "the whole point of functional harmony and modes of musical thought derived from it is that it gets somewhere (usually to a 'home' key) in a certain specified period of time. Now this, it seems to me, is absolutely contrary to the marvelously improvisatory spirit of real 'spontaneously' created music." Elliott Schwarz and Barney Childs, eds., *Comtemporary Composers on Contemporary Music* (New York: Holt, Rinehart and Winston, 1967), p. 374.

22. Ficino, *Opera,* p. 560.

23. Hillman, "Psychology: Monotheistic or Polytheistic?" p. 198. The italics are mine. Notice the use of the image "circulate," particularly relevant to a zodiac of Gods.

24. See, for example, June Singer, *Androgyny: Toward a New Theory of Sexuality* (New York: Doubleday, 1976), pp. 86–89. Singer inexplicably identifies polytheistic consciousness with "desacralization" and suggests "androgynous monotheism" as an alternative.

25. See Hillman, *Re-Visioning Psychology,* p. 36 and passim; and Henry Corbin, "*Mundus Imaginalis,* or the Imaginary and the Imaginal," *Spring 1972* (New York: Spring Publications, 1972), pp. 1–19.

26. Ficino, *Opera,* p. 920; see Kristeller, *Philosophy,* p. 358.

27. See D. P. Walker, "Ficino's *Spiritus,*" pp. 143–44.

28. Ficino, *Opera,* p. 563.

29. See Amman, "Musical Theory."

30. C. G. Jung, *The Psychology of the Transference,* in *The Practice of Psychotherapy,* CW, vol. 16, 2nd ed. (Princeton, N.J.: Princeton University Press, 1966), p. 271.

31. Angelo de Gubernatis, *Zoological Mythology; or, The Legends of Animals,* 2 vols. (London: Truebner and Co., 1872), 1:323. See also Jung, *Mysterium* p. 291.

Bibliography

Allen, Michael J. B. *Marsilio Ficino, The Philebus Commentary: A Critical Edition and Translation.* Berkeley, Calif.: University of California Press, 1975.

Amman, Peter J. "The Musical Theory and Philosophy of Robert Fludd." *Journal of the Warburg and Courtauld Institutes* 30 (1967): 198–227.

Bachofen, Johann Jakob. *Myth, Religion, and Mother Right (Selected Writings).* Translated by Ralph Manheim. Princeton, N.J.: Princeton University Press, 1967.

Berry, Patricia. "An Approach to the Dream." In *Spring 1974.* New York: Spring Publications, 1974.

_____. "The Rape of Demeter/Persephone and Neurosis." In *Spring 1975.* New York: Spring Publications, 1975.

Best, Michael, and Brightman, Frank H., eds. *The Book of Secrets of Albertus Magnus.* Oxford: Clarendon Press, 1973.

Brion, Marcel. *The Medici: A Great Florentine Family.* Translated by Gilles and Heather Cremonegi. London: Elek Books, 1969.

Brown, Norman O. "Daphne or Metamorphosis." In *Myths, Dreams, and Religion.* Edited by Joseph Campbell. New York: E. P. Dutton, 1970.

_____. *Life against Death.* New York: Vintage Books, 1959.

_____. *Love's Body.* New York: Vintage Books, 1966.

Cassirer, Ernst. *The Individual and the Cosmos in Renaissance Philosophy.* Translated by Mario Domandi. Philadelphia: University of Pennsylvania Press, 1963.

Chastel, André. *Marsile Ficin et l'art.* Geneva: Droz, 1954.

_____. *The Myth of the Renaissance.* Translated by Stuart Gilbert. Geneva: Albert Skira, 1969.

Cirlot, Juan Eduardo. *A Dictionary of Symbols.* Translated by Jack Sage. New York: Philosophical Library, 1962.

Corbin, Henry. "Mundus Imaginalis." In *Spring 1972.* New York: Spring Publications, 1972.

Crocker, Richard L. "Pythagorean Mathematics and Music." *Journal of Aesthetics and Art Criticism* 22 (1963): 189–98; 22 (1964):325–36.

Dodds, E. R. *The Greeks and the Irrational.* Berkeley, Calif.: University of California Press, 1951.

Evans, Joan, and Serjeantson, Mary S. *English Medieval Lapidaries.* London: Oxford University Press, 1933.

Ferenczi, Sandor. *Thalassa: A Theory of Genitality.* Translated by Henry Alden Bunker. New York: W. W. Norton and Co., 1968.

Ficino, Marsilio. *Opera Omnia.* 2 vols. Basel, 1576; reprint edition, Torino: Bottega d'Erasmo, 1959.

Freud, Sigmund. *The Interpretation of Dreams.* Translated by James Strachey. New York: Avon Books, 1965.

————. "Mourning and Melancholia." Translated under the supervision of Joan Riviere. *Collected Papers,* vol. 4. New York: Basic Books, 1959.

Friedländer, Paul. *Plato: An Introduction.* Translated by Hans Meyerhoff. Bollingen Series 59. Princeton, N.J.: Princeton University Press, 1973.

Golden, Leon. "Katharsis as Clarification: An Objection Answered." *Classical Quarterly* 23 (May 1973):45–46.

————. "Mimesis and Catharsis." *Classical Philology* 64 (1969):145–53.

Gubernatis, Angelo de. *Zoological Mythology; or, The Legends of Animals.* 2 vols. London: Treubner and Co., 1872.

Heidegger, Martin. "The Ode on Man in Sophocles' *Antigone.*" In *Sophocles: A Collection of Critical Essays.* Edited by Thomas M. Woodard. Englewood Cliffs, N.J.: Prentice-Hall, 1966.

Hersey, G. L. *Pythagorean Palaces: Magic and Architecture in the Italian Renaissance.* Ithaca, N.Y., and London: Cornell University Press, 1976.

Hibbert, Christopher. *The House of Medici: Its Rise and Fall.* New York: William Morrow, 1975.

Hillman, James. "Abandoning the Child." In *Loose Ends: Primary Papers in Archetypal Psychology.* Zurich: Spring Publications, 1975.

————. "Anima." In *Spring 1973.* New York: Spring Publications, 1973.

————. "Dionysos in Jung's Writings." In *Spring 1972.* New York: Spring Publications, 1972.

————. *The Dream and the Underworld.* New York: Harper and Row, 1979.

————. *The Myth of Analysis.* New York: Harper Colophon Books, 1978.

————. "On *Senex* Consciousness." In *Spring 1970.* New York: Spring Publications, 1970.

————. "Peaks and Vales." In *On the Way to Self-Knowledge.* Edited by Jacob Needleman and Dennis Lewis. New York: Alfred A. Knopf, 1976.

————. "Plotino, Ficino, and Vico as Precursors of Archetypal Psychology." In *Loose Ends: Primary Papers in Archetypal Psychology.* Zurich: Spring Publications, 1975.

_____. "Pothos: The Nostalgia of the Puer Aeternus." In *Loose Ends: Primary Papers in Archetypal Psychology.* Zurich: Spring Publications, 1975.

_____. "Psychology: Monotheistic or Polytheistic?" In *Spring 1971.* New York: Spring Publications, 1971.

_____. *Re-Visioning Psychology.* New York: Harper and Row, 1975.

_____. "*Senex* and *Puer*: An Aspect of the Historical and Psychological Present." In *Eranos Jahrbuch,* vol. 36. Zurich: Rhein, 1969.

_____. "*Senex* Destruction and a Renaissance Solution." In *Spring 1975.* New York: Spring Publications, 1975.

Hollander, John. *The Untuning of the Sky.* Princeton, N.J.: Princeton University Press, 1961.

Jayne, Sears. "Marsilio Ficino's Commentary on Plato's *Symposium.*" *University of Missouri Studies* 19 (1944).

Jong, Helena M. E. De. *Michael Maier's Atalanta Fugiens: Sources of an Alchemical Book of Emblems.* Leiden: Brill, 1969.

Jung, C. G. *The Archetypes and the Collective Unconscious.* CW, vol. 9, Translated by R. F. C. Hull. 2nd ed. Princeton, N.J.: Princeton University Press, 1968.

_____. *Civilization in Transition.* C.W, vol. 10. Translated by R. F. C. Hull. 2nd ed. Princeton, N.J.: Princeton University Press, 1970.

_____. *Man and His Symbols.* New York: Dell Publishing Co., 1968.

_____. *Memories, Dreams, Reflections.* Edited by Aniela Jaffe. Translated by Richard Winston and Clara Winston. New York: Vintage Books, 1963.

_____. *Mysterium Coniunctionis.* CW, vol. 14. Translated by R. F. C. Hull. 2nd ed. Princeton, N.J.: Princeton University Press, 1970.

_____. *The Practice of Psychotherapy.* CW, vol. 16. Translated by R. F. C. Hull. 2nd rev. ed. Princeton, N.J.: Princeton University Press, 1966.

_____. *Psychology and Alchemy.* CW, vol. 12. Translated by R. F. C. Hull. 2nd rev. ed. Princeton, N.J.: Princeton University Press, 1968.

_____. *Psychology and Religion: West and East.* CW, vol. 11. Translated by R. F. C. Hull. 2nd ed. Princeton, N.J.: Princeton University Press, 1969.

Jung, C. G., and Kerenyi, C. *Essays on a Science of Mythology.* Translated by R. F. C. Hull. Princeton, N.J.: Princeton University Press, 1969.

Jung, Emma. *Animus and Anima.* Zurich: Spring Publications, 1974.

Kayser, Hans. *Akroasis: The Theory of World Harmonics.* Boston: Plowshare Press, 1970.

Kerenyi, C. *Dionysos: Archetypal Image of Indestructible Life.* Translated by Ralph Manheim. Bollingen Series 65. Princeton, N.J.: Princeton University Press, 1976.

_____. "The Mysteries of the Kabeiroi." In *The Mysteries: Papers from the Eranos Yearbooks.* Edited by Joseph Campbell. New York: Pantheon Books, 1955.

Klibansky, Raymond; Panofsky, Erwin; and Saxl, Fritz. *Saturn and Melancholy.* New York: Basic Books, 1964.

Kristeller, Paul Oskar. *The Philosophy of Marsilio Ficino.* Translated by Virginia Conant. Gloucester, Mass.: Peter Smith, 1964.

Kuhns, L. Oscar., ed. "Bestiaries and Lapidaries." In *Medieval Song and Story.* Columbia University Course in Literature 4. Freeport, N.Y.: Books for Libraries Press, 1928–29.

Langer, Susanne K. *Feeling and Form.* New York: Charles Scribner's Sons, 1953.

Lemmi, Charles. *The Classical Deities in Bacon: A Study in Mythological Symbolism.* Baltimore, Md.: Johns Hopkins Press, 1933.

Lopez-Pedraza, Rafael. *Hermes and His Children.* Zurich: Spring Publications, 1977.

May, Rollo. *Love and Will.* New York: W. W. Norton and Co., 1969.

Miller, David L. "Orestes: Myth and Dream as Catharsis." In *Myth, Dreams, and Religion.* Edited by Joseph Campbell. New York: E. P. Dutton, 1970.

Moore, Tom. "Musical Therapy." In *Spring 1978.* New York: Spring Publications, 1978.

Onians, Richard Broxton. *The Origins of European Thought.* Cambridge: Cambridge University Press, 1951.

Otto, Walter. *Dionysus: Myth and Cult.* Translated by Tobert B. Palmer. Bloomington, Ind.: Indiana University Press, 1965.

Panofsky, Erwin. *The Life and Art of Albrecht Dürer.* Rev. 4th ed. Princeton, N.J.: Princeton University Press, 1955.

Panofsky, Erwin. *Renaissance and Renascences in Western Art.* 2nd ed. Stockholm: Almqvist and Wiksell, 1965.

Radin, Paul. *The Trickster: A Study in American Indian Mythology.* New York: Philosophical Library, 1956.

Seznec, Jean. *The Survivial of the Pagan Gods.* Translated by Barbara F. Sessions. Bollingen Series 38. Princeton, N.J.: Princeton University Press, 1972.

Shumaker, Wayne. *The Occult Sciences in the Renaissance.* Berkeley, Calif.: University of California Press, 1972.

Spitzer, Leo. "Classical and Christian Ideas of World Harmony." *Traditio* 2 (1944):409–64; 3 (1945):307–64.

Stein, Murray. "The Devouring Father." In *Fathers and Mothers.* Edited by Patricia Berry. New York: Spring Publications, 1973.

Trinkaus, Charles Edward. *In Our Image and Likeness: Humanity and Divinity in Italian Humanist Thought.* 2 vols. Chicago: University of Chicago Press, 1970.

Vitale, A. "The Archetype of Saturn or Transformation of the Father." in *Fathers and Mothers.* Edited by Patricia Berry. New York: Spring Publications, 1973.

Walker, D. P. *The Ancient Theology.* Ithaca, N.Y.: Cornell University Press, 1972.

_____. "Ficino's *Spiritus* and Music." *Annales Musicologiques* 1 (1953): 131–50.

Webern, Anton. *The Path to the New Music.* Bryn Mawr, Pa.: Theodore Presser Co., 1963.

Wind, Edgar. *Pagan Mysteries in the Renaissance.* Rev. and enl. ed. New York: W. W. Norton and Co., 1968.

Yates, Frances. *Art of Memory.* London: Routledge and Kegan Paul, 1966.

_____. *Giordano Bruno and the Hermetic Tradition.* New York: Vintage Books, 1969.

_____. *Theatre of the World.* Chicago: University of Chicago Press, 1969.

Index